ROUTLEDGE LIBRARY EDITIONS:
ACCOUNTING HISTORY

Volume 15

CONTRIBUTIONS OF FOUR ACCOUNTING PIONEERS

CONTRIBUTIONS OF FOUR ACCOUNTING PIONEERS

Kohler, Littleton, May, Paton: Digests of Periodical Writings

JAMES DON EDWARDS AND
ROLAND F. SALMONSON

Routledge
Taylor & Francis Group
LONDON AND NEW YORK

First published in 1988 by Garland Publishing, Inc.

This edition first published in 2021
by Routledge
2 Park Square, Milton Park, Abingdon, Oxon OX14 4RN

and by Routledge
52 Vanderbilt Avenue, New York, NY 10017

Routledge is an imprint of the Taylor & Francis Group, an informa business

British Library Cataloguing in Publication Data
A catalogue record for this book is available from the British Library

ISBN: 978-0-367-33564-9 (Set)
ISBN: 978-1-00-304636-3 (Set) (ebk)
ISBN: 978-0-367-53512-4 (Volume 15) (hbk)
ISBN: 978-0-367-53516-2 (Volume 15) (pbk)
ISBN: 978-1-00-308229-3 (Volume 15) (ebk)

Contributions of Four Accounting Pioneers Kohler, Littleton, May, Paton

Digests of Periodical Writings

JAMES DON EDWARDS
ROLAND F. SALMONSON

GARLAND PUBLISHING, INC.
NEW YORK & LONDON 1988

For a list of Garland's publications in accounting,
see the final pages of this volume.

Peprinted by permission of the author and Michigan State University Press, and reproduced from a copy in the American Institute of Certified Public Accountants.

Library of Congress Cataloging in Publication Data

Edwards, James Don.
Contributions of four accounting pioneers : Kohler, Littleton, May, Paton : digests of periodical writings / James Don Edwards, Roland F. Salmonson.
p. cm. — (Foundations of accounting) (Classics series / Academy of Accounting Historians)
Reprint. Originally published : East Lansing : Bureau of Business and Economic Research, Graduate School of Business Administration, Michigan State University, 1961. (MSU business studies)
Includes index.
ISBN 0-8240-6137-3 (alk. paper)
1. Accounting—Abstracts. 2. Accountants—United States. I. Salmonson, R. F. (Roland Frank), 1922- . II. Title. III. Series. IV. Series: Classics series (New York, N.Y.)
HF5629.E4 1988
657'.0973—dc 19 88-16038

Design by Renata Gomes

The volumes in this series are printed on acid-free, 250-year-life paper.

Printed in the United States of America

CONTRIBUTIONS OF FOUR ACCOUNTING PIONEERS

MSU Business Studies

CONTRIBUTIONS OF FOUR ACCOUNTING PIONEERS

Kohler Littleton May Paton

Digests of Periodical Writings

James Don Edwards

and

Roland F. Salmonson

MSU BUSINESS STUDIES, 1961

Bureau of Business and Economic Research
Graduate School of Business Administration
Michigan State University, East Lansing

Library of Congress Catalog Number: 60-64043

PREFACE

Accounting has traveled a long way on the road to securing recognition of its professional status. Since the turn of the century, many events, both economic and legislative, have profoundly influenced its development. In the course of these sixty years, the accounting profession has fought and won the struggle for recognition as a subject worthy of being taught in the colleges and universities of our nation. The success of the fight was largely due to the growth of the professional accounting organizations.

Coupled with the ever-increasing leadership of these professional societies has been the growth in volume of accounting literature. From a mere trickle, this material has increased to a flow of such flood-like proportions that even an avid reader is in danger of being inundated. The quantity of currently available accounting literature is so great that worthwhile articles are oftentimes overlooked by those who could benefit from reading them. Since, by the same token, much valuable time might be spent reading numerous articles which are of no particular value to a specific project, this book was designed to serve as a handy reference and time saver as well as a digest of the contributions to periodical literature in accountancy by four major contributors of the twentieth century.

The four authors — Eric L. Kohler, A. C. Littleton, George O. May and William A. Paton — represent a total of over two hundred years of experience and leadership in the accounting profession. The arrangement of each author's writings is chronological, and the detailed index should compensate for the absence of a topical sequence listing which would not, due to the large number of different topics, have been possible without excessive cross-referencing. Under each entry a synopsis is presented in sufficient detail and in such a manner that the author's major points and arguments can be quickly noted, thus enabling the reader to determine quickly whether he wishes to read the entire article. Since there are included summaries of articles dealing with almost every major event of significance to accounting since the turn of the century, in many respects this book can be described as a brief history of accounting thought since 1900. The particular manner in which each author has contributed to the development of the profession is detailed in the biographical sketch preceding each section.

Contrasting the views of two leading teachers with those of two leading practitioners should, it is hoped, be of interest to all students of accounting.

The two practitioners do not always take the same position in opposing the views presented by the two teachers. To cite one example, the four authors split into two groups of two, a teacher and a practitioner, in their views as to how accounting should proceed under conditions of changing price levels.

With regard to the selection of the articles, a list of his periodical writings was prepared and submitted to each author, who checked it for accuracy. Not all the writings of the four authors are included. We have omitted almost all correspondence, editorial comments, chapters of books, articles which are essentially reprints of other articles, those which deal with topics rather far removed from accounting, and those which, by their nature, were of significance only at the time of their publication. The responsibility for the exclusions, as well as for the accuracy of the annotations and for whatever defects or misinterpretations may exist, lies solely with the compilers of this volume. At the same time, thanks must be expressed to a number of graduate students at Michigan State University, in particular Darwin Casler and Salvatore Costella, who assisted in bringing together the summaries included herein, Roger Hermanson for his work on the index, as well as to Esther B. Waite and Christiane Kerner, of the Bureau of Business and Economic Research, who assisted with the editing, and to Beatrice Tabata of the Bureau's clerical staff.

The period covered by the writings included here has been the most interesting and dynamic in the history of accounting. It is sincerely hoped that those using this book will gain as much benefit and pleasure from it as have we who prepared it. If this book serves to make more widespread use of the writings of Eric L. Kohler, A. C. Littleton, George O. May, and William A. Paton, it will, indeed, have rendered a service, for their contributions are far too valuable to lie little noticed in the pages of history.

James Don Edwards
Roland F. Salmonson
East Lansing, Michigan

CONTENTS

I. ERIC L. KOHLER

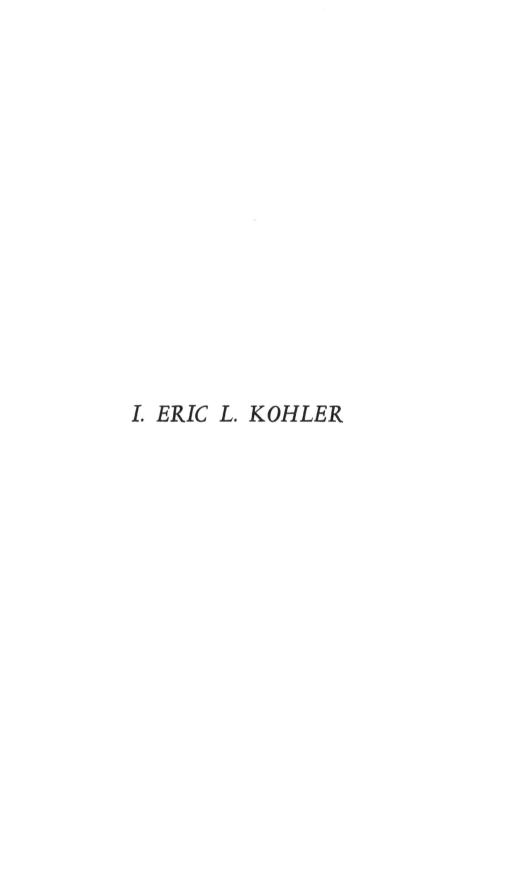

Fabian Bachrach

ERIC L. KOHLER

Eric L. Kohler was born in Owosso, Michigan in 1892. He received the A.B. degree from the University of Michigan in 1914 and the M.A. degree from Northwestern University in 1915.

He was a member of the firm of Arthur Andersen & Co. during the years 1915-17, 1919-22 and 1933-37; he was associated with Kohler, Pettengill & Co. from 1922 to 1928 and with the firm of E. L. Kohler & Co. from 1928 to 1933. He was professor of accounting at Northwestern University from 1922 to 1928 and has served as a visiting professor at The Ohio State University and at the University of Minnesota. Since 1938 he has practiced as a consulting accountant, taking time from his personal practice to serve as Controller of the Tennessee Valley Authority from 1938 to 1941 and as Controller of the Economic Cooperation Administration from 1948 to 1949.

Through his work in the practice of public accounting, as an author and educator, and as a holder of important posts in governmental agencies, Mr. Kohler is known and respected by many accountants, businessmen and government officials.

Mr. Kohler is the author of a number of books in accounting as well as many articles for professional journals. Among his books are *Principles of Accounting,* with Paul W. Pettengill (1924), *Accounting Principles Underlying Federal Income Taxes* (1925), *Principles of Accounting,* with Paul L. Morrison (1926), *Accounting for Business Executives* (1927), *Auditing: An Introduction to the Work of the Public Accountant* (1954), *Accounting in the Federal Government,* with Howard W. Wright (1956), *A Dictionary for Accountants* (1957), and *Advanced Accounting Problems* (1959). Special note should be made of the praise accorded Mr. Kohler for his dictionary.

Mr. Kohler has held positions as management consultant for the Office of Emergency Mobilization and the War Production Board, executive officer of the Petroleum Administration for War, financial adviser to the Secretary of Agriculture, member of the Excess Profits Council of the United States Treasury, Chairman of the Advisory Board to the Illinois Auditor General and member of the Illinois State Board of CPA Examiners. He was also President of the City Club of Chicago.

He is a member of the American Accounting Association and has served two terms as its president. In addition, he was editor of *The Accounting Review* from 1928 to 1944. He is a member of the American Institute of Certified Public Accountants, the Illinois Society of Certified Public Accountants and the National Association of Accountants.

His honoraries include Beta Gamma Sigma and Beta Alpha Psi. He served the latter as president of its Grand Council. He was awarded the Alpha Kappa Psi 1958 award for contributions to accounting.

At the present time Mr. Kohler is a member of the Board of Trustees of Roosevelt University while continuing his practice as a consulting accountant in Chicago.

I. ERIC L. KOHLER

SUMMARIES OF PERIODICAL WRITINGS

ACCOUNTING THEORY AS AFFECTED BY FEDERAL INCOME TAXATION, *Papers and Proceedings of the Seventh Annual Meeting* (1922), The American Association of University Instructors in Accounting, VII (1923), 73-83. [1]

One of the reasons for the many pages of tax regulations is that accountants have left so much unsaid. For example, accountants have said very little about "the subject of income except that there are a great many ifs and ands in connection with the preparation of a *statement* thereof." Accounting texts mention the fact that there are the cash and accrual bases of accounting and that single-entry and double-entry methods may be employed, but do little to elaborate upon these topics as regards distinguishing between them. Treasury regulations require the taking of inventories and the reporting of them, while at the same time accounts receivable may be omitted. Such a manner of accounting cannot yield a logical method of determining income.

The Treasury Department recognizes ordinary depreciation but has lagged behind accounting in recognizing obsolescence. When extraordinary repairs are charged to the reserve for depreciation, Treasury's use of old accepted rates of depreciation will not write the asset off over its useful life. Obsolescence occurring prior to 1918 must be carried forward and recognized in the year of disposal of the asset. The Department has commented favorably upon the straight-line and production methods of recognizing depreciation.

Almost all of our present knowledge of depletion has its origin in the Department's findings. The Department requires that if depletion is to be based on March 1, 1913 values, such values must be recorded in the accounts. Since accounting texts say nothing on the subject, the Treasury Department and the courts have had to develop theories of accounting for investment costs, such as the *Eisner* v. *Macomber* decision that stock dividends are not income and that the cost of shares sold shall, if identification is not possible, be determined on a first-in, first-out basis. The Department also did the pioneering work in the installment sales method of recognizing gross profits according to collection. Congress has also shown a tendency to postpone recognition of income in "*un*-completed" transactions, such as securities exchanges in corporate reorganization, voluntary securities exchanges and involuntary conversions.

INVESTMENT STOCK COSTS UNDER THE 1921 REVENUE ACT, *Administration,* V (January, 1923), 86-94. [2]

Federal income tax regulations have clarified the concept of income as it relates to stock investments. This clarification has not been secured without opposition and the federal courts have been called upon to act as arbiters between the government and the taxpayer.

In circumstances in which an individual sells a part of his holdings, acquired at different times and different prices, the average cost of the securities sold should be used to determine gain or loss. Average cost is preferable to the specific allocated cost which must be used, according to a Treasury rule. It is logical to assign a third of the cost of an individual's holdings to the securities sold, if he sells a third of his interest in the corporation.

The first-in, first-out method of determining the cost of securities sold in merged lots of stock as required under present law is wrong, since average cost should be used.

The Revenue Act of 1921 requires the proration of the cost of the securities surrendered among the several types of securities received in reorganization according to the relative market values of the securities received.

The treatment to be accorded stock dividends is well settled. The cost of the original shares must be prorated over the old and the new shares upon receipt of a stock dividend.

Property dividends are taxable to the extent of the fair market value of the property received. Such dividends, as well as cash dividends, do not affect stock costs unless such dividends are liquidating dividends or are dividends paid from surplus accumulated before March 1, 1913.

If stock rights are received and sold, a portion of the cost of the securities held must be allocated to the rights sold.

Provisions in the existing tax laws are such as to make it desirable that the cost of individual purchases of a stock be kept separate and not merged. The 1921 act also provides for the use of a substitute value rather than cost under certain circumstances.

NEW ACCOUNTING CONCEPTIONS IN THE REVENUE ACT OF 1924, *National Income Tax Magazine,* III (January, 1925), 17-21. [3]

Certain relatively well-defined principles relating to the income tax levy have become apparent in recent federal revenue acts. These relate to the different times at which it has seemed desirable to limit taxation of certain forms of profit, namely:

(1) Profits realized in one year which have been accumulating over several years.

(2) Profits from uncompleted transactions.

(3) Profits from transactions over which the taxpayer has no control.

(4) Profits, resulting from exchanges, which cannot be accurately measured.

(5) Profits invested in property acquired in an exchange, which is similar in form or use to the property given in exchange.

While these principles have been given expression and have been applied with varying degrees of emphasis, it should not be "inferred that Congress and the Treasury Department have at all times been remiss in the imperfect and often badly confused expressions of principles appearing in the law and in the regulations governing its administration." There has been almost a complete lack of appropriate knowledge upon which to base a definition of income. The "Department's dicta concerning income . . . is a more complete exposition of individual income" than an accountant can find anywhere else.

Of particular interest to the accountant is a comparison of the Revenue Act of 1924 with prior revenue acts. Specific attention and study should be directed toward computations of cost in tax-free and partially tax-free exchanges; exchanges of similar property; exchanges in reorganization; involuntary conversions of property; mergers and consolidations; losses from partially tax-free exchanges; transfers in trust; "wash-sale" transactions; the March 1, 1913 value rule; corporate distributions; earned income.

REORGANIZATIONS AND THE FEDERAL INCOME TAX LAW, *National Income Tax Magazine,* IV (May, 1926), 161-63, 178-80. [4]

The term *reorganization* is defined as any important financial readjustment of a business enterprise whether caused by success or failure, including revisions of financial structure in proprietorships, partnerships, and corporations, as well as the formation of new enterprises from old with or without change in ownership.

The present income tax laws reflect the policy of Congress to promote sound mergers and consolidations, with the result that most reorganizations may be classified as continuing transactions and any resulting profit will be reported as income in the future when finally realized in the form of assets other than those involved in the merger. This treatment is closely analogous to the treatment of installment sales, involuntary conversions and stock dividends. Also, double taxation is avoided where a vendor corporation immediately distributes the proceeds of the sale of its assets to its stockholders. There are, however, some restrictions. Actual sales of property where substantial control is not retained, or where cash or other property passes rather than merely corporate securities, are not non-taxable reorganizations.

Attention is then directed toward a situation wherein a single proprietor contributes his assets to a partnership and becomes a partner, and to whether a profit, if arising, is taxable income. Similarly, the current tax law provisions are examined to determine under what conditions taxable income may emerge as a result of a partnership contributing its assets to a corporation, either new or existing. Generally, no taxable gain emerges if, after transfer, the transferrers possess at least 80 percent of the voting stock and 80 percent of all other classes of stock, if the sole consideration consists of stocks and bonds, and if the securities are distributed in the same proportion as the interests in the assets before transfer.

TENDENCIES IN BALANCE SHEET CONSTRUCTION, *Accounting Review*, I (December, 1926), 1-11. [5]

Present day balance sheets are grossly inadequate and unreliable for interpretive and analytical purposes. Defects include those of failure to show the basis of valuation of assets and the inclusion of large reserves among the liabilities, with no further explanation. Accounting terminology is equivocal and some accountants apparently believe that balance sheets are not intended for laymen, since they cannot be expected to understand the complex financial facts of a business.

Present day balance sheet terminology is inadequate because there is no commonly accepted basis of valuation attaching to each of the terms. Suggestions are then presented as to what each of the more commonly used terms in the balance sheet should mean. For example, *cash in bank* may include bona fide deposits in transit but should exclude restricted cash. *Accounts receivable* means short-term customer debt from uncontrolled sales and should not include officers' borrowings. *Unearned gross profit* should be shown in a valuation account deducted from *installment accounts receivable* and not shown as a liability. The basis of inventory valuation should be shown and the term *market price* may be more meaningful than "market" if the "cost or market, whichever is lower" method of valuation is employed.

Prepaid expenses are current assets and should be distinguished from deferred charges, which frequently includes *unamortized bond discount* which should be shown as a deduction from the bond liability. The basis of valuation of investments should be shown, whether short-term or long-term and, with respect to the latter, the purpose of the investment, the degree of control exercised and a notation of earning power should be shown. The basis of valuation of fixed assets should be shown, and, if necessary, the inadequacy of the *reserve for depreciation* must also be noted.

Similar suggestions are made with respect to liabilities and stockholders' equity. A person with little business experience should be able to interpret a balance sheet. "Until the constructors of balance sheets realize this, they will continue to permit the issue of unintelligent financial statements which are the despair of the analyst and the cause of repeated apologies for the profession."

ACCOUNTANT SUGGESTS IMPROVEMENT IN INCOME-TAX LAW, *American Accountant,* XII (August, 1927), 13-17. [6]

The problem of determining gain subject to federal income taxation is one of defining income. The work of the Board of Tax Appeals would be reduced tremendously if a definition of income could be devised which would be as widely accepted as is the definition of negotiable instrument.

The problem of determining taxable income is essentially fourfold: the amount of the gross income, and the deductions therefrom, must be determined and distinguished from realizations and expenditures of capital; and a decision must be made as to when the deduction is incurred or the income realized.

A number of the existing rules are illogical, inconsistent and administratively difficult to apply. Following are ten specific suggestions which should be incorporated in the future law:

(1) "Mercantile organizations extending sales credits, say, of not more than ninety days, should be required to follow the accrual method of accounting."

(2) "Non-mercantile organizations should be permitted to elect the cash or accrual basis of accounting."

(3) "If changes are made from one method of accounting to another, the accrued items relating to prior periods should be permitted to affect current income as though the previous method of accounting were still in effect."

(4) The instalment sales basis of computing realized profits should be continued. The present 25 percent limitation should be eliminated since it discriminates against sellers of real property and against those engaging in casual sales of personal property. This 25 percent limitation is also the source of tremendous administrative difficulties.

(5) "Future-expense liabilities, including estimated taxes and interest, should be allowed as an addition to cost in sales of real estate, without the restrictions now in force, whether or not the cash or accrual basis is followed."

(6) "When the accounts receivable of any dealer, real estate or otherwise, are of the long-term variety (more than ninety days) and have no market value within, say, 80 percent of their face value, the dealer should be permitted to choose the installment method or the cost-recovery method, whether or not he follows, in computing other income and expenses, the cash or accrual basis of accounting."

(7) An adequate definition of fair market value should be presented to be applied in the above-mentioned circumstances and to other exchanges falling outside the exempt group.

(8) Present rules governing income realization in reorganizations and involuntary conversions should be continued and extended so as to apply to situations involving the change from a corporate to a partnership form of business organization. "Withdrawals other than fair salary allowances should be taxed as dividends until the earned surplus at the date of reorganization is exhausted."

(9) Deductions from gross income should be allowed for estimated future expenses to be incurred in fulfilling guarantees issued at the time of sale.

(10) Present rules governing discount and premium should be continued with the addition that amortization be allowed, but not required of, bondholders who are on the accrual basis.

EXAMINATION OF THE AMERICAN INSTITUTE OF ACCOUNTANTS, *Accounting Review,* II (December, 1927), 354-61. [7]

One provision of the constitution of the American Institute of Accountants provides that the Institute should "develop and improve accountancy education." The establishment of an endowment fund and the work of the Committee on Education are major steps toward the fulfillment of this objective.

While not being exploited to their full extent, the Institute's examination questions and problems are being subjected to careful academic study. A number of reasons exist for this careful study, including the lack of adequate text and problem material for advanced courses in accounting theory and practice, the nearly universal adoption of the problem method of accounting instruction, and, because these examinations can serve as a standard of preparation for certification, they are excellent for review purposes in preparation for the examination.

Unfortunately, the examinations are not as free from error as they should be. Of the twelve problems in the May, 1927, examination, only three were free from error of some type. The Institute should not be condemned as a result, since, in some cases, it takes many years to perfect an advanced accounting problem. The severest criticism that can be leveled is that the examinations frequently contain ambiguities which waste valuable testing time, and test an examinee's ability to make assumptions rather than his accounting ability.

ACCOUNTANTS' REPORTS AND CERTIFICATES, *Robert Morris Associates Bulletin*, XII (July, 1929), 50-56. [8]

The progress made along the lines of the professional development of accounting arising as a result of constructive criticism from those who use and interpret financial data is most encouraging.

Of the four principal types of reports issued by professional accountants on which bankers rely, the audit report is the most common. Of the various types of audit reports, the balance sheet audit report, without the auditor's formal certificate, is perhaps the most valuable because of the interpretive details and comments made with respect to items in the financial statements.

A second type of audit report, the so-called certified balance sheet, accompanied by a statement of profit and loss, usually includes the balance sheet contained in the more elaborate audit report. The certificate accompanying the report may vary in length from a few lines to a few pages. The language frequently employed in these certificates is open to criticism. Especially desirable would be the substitution of "we believe that" for "certify."

Qualifications appearing in the certificate arise primarily from the voluntary restriction by the accountant of the scope of his work or from involuntary limitations due to a lack of time or an inability to resolve differences of opinion with the client. Qualifications arising from the latter source are most apt to bring questions from the banker. In this respect, it should be noted that bankers frequently overestimate the abilities of the average accountant. ". . . an accountant of integrity will not permit any but minor qualifications to appear in his certificate." Bankers could do a better job of reading that which the accountant has presented.

Bankers can do much to understand and improve accounting service. They should insist that accountants adhere to the minimum standards, at least as outlined in "Verification of Financial Statements." Certain bank employees should also be trained in accounting and auditing. Bankers should also strongly urge adoption of the natural business year by their clients.

THE CONCEPT OF EARNED SURPLUS, *Accounting Review,* VI (September, 1931), 206-17. [9]

The Committee on the Definition of Earned Surplus faced many obstacles. The first of these was the fact that many terms used in financial statements have no fixed meaning. Secondly, there was apathy, if not actual resistance, toward greater exactness in usage. Also encountered were the many state laws and court decisions relating to dividends and the maintenance of capital.

Although the term *capital surplus* should not be used as a balance sheet title, it does serve as a generic term substituting for *surplus* other than *earned*. Capital surplus includes revaluation surplus and paid-in surplus. Paid-in surplus includes the excess of values received over par or stated value of stocks issued; excess of par or stated value over cost of stock retired; gains, less losses, from sale of treasury stock; stockholder assessments and donations.

In defining *earned surplus* the term *profits* had to be defined and the Committee restricted its definition of the latter term by excluding profits on capital asset exchanges and those resulting from the sale of any asset for "unmarketable paper." The definition finally presented was: "Earned surplus is the balance of net profits, net income, and gains of a corporation after deducting losses and after deducting distributions to stockholders and transfers to capital stock accounts."

With respect to appreciation, "the Committee finally yielded to . . . widespread practice of recognizing an annual realization of appreciation, but only in the instances where the practice had already been established."

Dividends are presumed to come from earned surplus; if not, the balance sheet should be qualified. Also, earned surplus dates from the formation of the enterprise. Changes in all net worth items should be revealed, capital stock should be segregated from all forms of surplus, and appropriated surplus items should be grouped under a heading of earned surplus.

BALANCE SHEET STANDARDS, *Certified Public Accountant,* XI (December, 1931), 373-76. [10]

Several prominent men have recently pleaded for adoption of uniform financial statements as an aid to stockholder understanding. The several reasons for these pleas are that the depression forced management to take stockholders into their confidence, resulting in more expansive annual reports, and that these reports have frequently been filled with technical language not readily understood by skilled business executives.

Accountants should condemn and refuse to certify condensed balance sheets. The descriptive balance sheet should also be condemned in that such balance sheets frequently contain detailed descriptions of cash and pass entirely over fixed assets.

Six standards detailing the minimum requirements for a so-called all purpose balance sheet are set forth. Included are the assumption of an intelligent reader, presentation of maximum information for interpretive purposes, intelligent grouping under descriptive headings of items in the balance sheet, statement of the valuation basis, full description of secured liabilities and the assets securing them, and detailed presentation of changes in funded debt and net worth. The balance sheet should never be longer than one page and the accountant's certificate might well appear on the page.

Many other recommendations with respect to balance sheet presentation are made. For example, accounts and notes receivable past due should be noted; valuation reserves should be deducted from the assets to which they relate; liability reserves should not be mingled with net worth reserves; inventories should be subdivided and the basis of valuation expressed; prepaid expenses should be current assets; contingent liabilities must be noted; the amount of underwriter's commission, although deducted from proceeds as reported in the balance sheet, might well be stated in a footnote.

Accountants have tried to avoid the problem of valuation of assets, especially in cases of reorganization or recapitalization. Accountants in the future will have to assume greater responsibility for such valuations.

NEEDED: A RESEARCH PLAN FOR ACCOUNTANCY, *Accounting Review*, VII (March, 1932), 1-10. [11]

Ten illustrations are presented to show that "standards of accounting instruction and accounting practice are all too often feeble affairs." Educators and practitioners have been somewhat liberal in their criticisms of each other. The professional societies have not stated the qualifications necessary for an accountant, and training in accounting is dependent upon the "existence of adequately defined and reasonably developed professional standards."

There are "implications of a profession . . . in the field of accountancy . . . [but] many steps must be taken to prove that accountancy can reach and maintain a true professional level."

The accountant of the future will rank above all others as a business adviser; will be "an exponent of good financial practices [and] bring about the dissemination of full facts and figures . . ., will be depended upon as the fiscal agent of the stockholders . . . responsible for keeping them informed . . ."; will act as an adjuster and fact-finder in labor disputes and as an arbitrator in commercial disputes; will eventually eliminate the differences between financial and tax theories; will serve as an arbiter of rates in public utilities; and will take an active part in the administration of governmental bodies. To fulfill these responsibilities, professional standards will have to be developed, and a "wide field of research preceding the adoption of standards" lies before us.

". . . a ten year, perhaps a permanent program of research [should] be initiated and guided by . . . this association. . . ." The cooperation of other societies should be secured and research projects undertaken with the result that from time to time bulletins announcing the results of the research would be issued.

SOME PRINCIPLES FOR TERMINOLOGISTS, *Accounting Review,* X (March, 1935), 31-33. [12]

Adherence to the following suggested rules will produce a good definition: "(1) It must set forth the fundamental and unique attribute or attributes of all members of the class but of no other class. (2) It may be stated in terms of the next larger class, thus avoiding a more elaborate differentia. (3) If the class and differences of a term cannot be readily recounted, a *genetic* definition may be resorted to; that is, the sense of a thing may be gained from a knowledge of how it is produced. (4) There must be no *circulus in definiendo,* or repetition of the term to be defined. (5) Where the same meaning attaches to more than one word or term, preference should be given to one of them. (6) Where a word has more than one meaning, the separate uses must be appropriately distinguished. (7) Plain, direct language is highly desirable. (8) A negative statement must not be used except where the positive has a clear disadvantage."

STANDARDS: A DIALOGUE, *Accounting Review,* X (December, 1935), 370-79. [13]

The article is written in the form of a dialogue with an assumed cast of characters.

"A standard is merely an accepted rule." Standards, in order to have authority, must be accepted and used by a significant majority of accountants.

National accounting organizations could take action to emphasize the need for standards and hasten the development of a body of standards. A difficult problem faced in developing standards is that of allowing for flexibility. Many accountants feel that the individual who has but one solution fails to distinguish between theory and practice. "Actually the difference lies between a conclusion traceable to well conceived postulates or universals and conclusions which vary because the selection of premises leading to them has been allowed to remain in the hands of others."

The lack of acceptable standards is evidenced by the treatment of prepaid expenses as deferred charges and the many definitions of current asset. The banker's point of view should not be allowed to mold accounting standards, since his point of view is that of liquidation rather than that of the going concern. The intent of management must play a prominent role in the classification of assets and liabilities, and the accountant should not substitute his judgment for that of management.

". . . regulation of the profession can best come through the self-imposition of standards or accepted rules." Three major benefits will result: "first, the profession from such standards can more easily define its rules of ethics by the enforcement of which a profession exists; second, the public has a vehicle through which it can expect from the profession performances of a high order and can examine critically the foundations on which the profession rests; third, and most important, those practicing and otherwise vitally interested in accounting will have a basis upon which to grow."

REPORT OF THE PRESIDENT OF THE AMERICAN ACCOUNTING ASSOCIATION, *Accounting Review,* XII (March, 1937), 70-71. [14]

"I conceive it to be the function of this Association to promote the development of accounting theory." Accounting and law are similar in that both are dominated by practitioners who are assumed to have reached the pinnacle of success. Accountants differ from lawyers in that through their certified statements they are in effect addressing and responsible to the world. Also, schools teaching accounting are not unduly influenced by practitioners' demands for only practical courses.

The development of accounting theory by accounting instructors should be encouraged. The public practice of accountancy should be thoroughly examined in all its aspects by accounting instructors. The Federal Securities Acts have been of great help to instructors, since these acts "forced . . . the adoption of standards of practice and of statement presentation which years of committee work within the profession were wholly unable to do."

The difference between accounting theory and practice lies in the expedients practitioners adopt for prompt disposal of cases. Good judgment based on experience does not necessarily offer "the most effective safeguard to the profession, especially where that experience is born of daily compromises with good theory. . . . The need for the promotion of good theory has never been greater. . . ."

The accountant will play an important role in the solving of the "socio-economic problems" of the future. ". . . we shall have a stabilized economic structure created through a uniform application of a controlled cost: a structure built and maintained by accounting and accountants."

SOME TENTATIVE PROPOSITIONS UNDERLYING CONSOLIDATED REPORTS, *Accounting Review,* XIII (March, 1938), 63-73. [15]

Ten tentative propositions, with interpretations and applications, are presented with regard to the preparation of consolidated financial statements. Summarized, the ten propositions are:

(1) Combined financial statements are the summation of the statements of two or more units with common control; if control lies in one unit the statement is called a consolidated statement. Combined statements show the operating results or joint position of two or more units as though one existed, and are secondary rather than primary statements.

(2) "Consolidated financial statements have more significance where the subsidiaries are homogeneous with the controlling company or with each other, and where the display of the financial or operating characteristics of any one subsidiary is not material to an understanding of the group as a whole."

(3) Group statements may be substituted for consolidated statements where financial or operating characteristics of the controlling company differ from those of the subsidiaries, or where subsidiaries' activities differ.

(4) A combining statement (a summary worksheet) is a helpful supplement to consolidated statements where individual subsidiaries' activities differ and where material intercompany eliminations are not readily determinable from other data.

(5) ". . . the complete elimination of intercompany accounts, gains, losses, and transactions is necessary," regardless of the percentage of control.

(6) "Elimination . . . of intercompany investments in capital stock against the equities shown by the records of the issuing company may give rise to differences which should be distinctively labeled on the balance sheet."

(7) Consolidated surplus should be adjusted in the elimination of inter-

company investments in obligations. Circumstances may also require current profit and loss to be adjusted.

(8) The consolidated balance sheet should show the outside stockholders' interest in capital stock and surplus.

(9) "Complete books of account are necessary for each subsidiary."

(10) "No practical benefits are derived from accruing profit and loss from subsidiaries on the books of the controlling company; reserves for losses on investments in subsidiaries are preferably based on estimates of ultimate realization rather than on amounts of operating losses."

SOME DEBATED ISSUES ON CONSOLIDATED FINANCIAL STATEMENTS, *Accounting Principles and Procedures,* Papers Presented at the Fifty-first Annual Meeting, 1938 (New York: American Institute of Accountants, 1939), pp. 42-46. [16]

A number of communications have been received since the publication of the ten tentative propositions underlying consolidated reports in the *Accounting Review* for March, 1938 (see §15). Attention is here directed to some of the adverse criticisms.

Earned surplus existing prior to acquisition of control should be eliminated entirely, even if the subsidiary stock is acquired in successive blocks, and designated, where appropriate, as surplus from consolidation. Intercompany profits must be completely eliminated from inventory in consolidation, regardless of the existence of a minority stock interest. "If we are to adopt the theory of the economic unit, we cannot present a picture that treats minority stockholders' profits as a cost."

In determining whether or not control of one company is exercised by another, factors other than the percentage of stock owned must be considered. Control may be exercised with less than 50 percent stock ownership through officer and employee ownership of subsidiary company stock, through the solicitation of proxies, and for other reasons. At the same time, a strong minority may make control by a parent company somewhat ineffective even with over 50 percent stock ownership.

Premiums and discounts on intercompany obligations should be treated as balance sheet items upon acquisition prior to acquiring control; after control is established they should be treated as income statement items. Before acquisition of control they are a part of the investment cost calculation. After control is acquired, these premiums or discounts should be treated in the same fashion as a single economic unit would treat them when it reacquired some of its own obligations, that is, as a financial gain or loss.

THE AIA BULLETINS ON AUDITING PROCEDURE, *Addresses Delivered at Accounting Clinic and Central States Accounting Conference,* Stevens Hotel, Chicago, May 28-29, 1941. Sponsored by American Institute of Accountants, Loyola University, and various state CPA societies, pp. 123-29. [17]

The seven bulletins issued by the Committee on Auditing Procedure of the Institute deal primarily with problems arising out of the McKesson & Robbins case and "substantially confirm practices already well established in some quarters, with, perhaps, a number of shifts in emphasis."

The Committee does not state clearly the nature of the evidence relied upon by the auditor. Such evidence consists of the "written records . . . the effectiveness of the system of internal control . . . the statements and recorded acts of officers and employees . . . the representations by outsiders . . . contacts with physical property . . . the processes of test-check . . . the degree of independence given to the controller, [and] the auditor's intuition. . . ."

The first bulletin deals with the audit of inventories and receivables, the form of the audit certificate and the appointment of the auditor. Physical tests should be made of inventories and receivables circularized when material in amounts. The Committee also recommended that the phrases "obtained information and explanations from officers and employees" and "based upon such examination" be omitted from the certificate. The certificate is also clearly recognized as containing two paragraphs, one pertaining to the scope of the audit and the second to the auditor's opinion.

Bulletin No. 2 discusses a case involving a head office and branches, and the question of whether an audit can be limited to the head office.

Bulletin No. 3 raises the question of whether the inventory and receivable auditing procedures can be applied to department stores, installment houses, chain stores and other retailers. The Committee answered that such procedures must be reasonable and practicable.

Bulletin No. 4 points out the lack of uniformity relative to clients' representations to auditors and details items which such representations might cover.

Bulletins No. 5 and 6 further modify the certificate following revision by the SEC of its Rule 2-02. The Committee recommended the inclusion of the phrase now found in certificates relating to the making of an examination in accordance with generally accepted auditing standards.

The subject matter of Bulletin 7 is of little interest here.

ADMINISTRATIVE DEVELOPMENT OF FINANCIAL CONTROLS IN GOVERNMENT, *Municipal Finance,* XIII (May, 1941), 4-10. [18]

Many municipal administrators are not taking advantage of the benefits which the proper use of accounting information could supply. Accounting provides the language by which governmental affairs can be pictured for those who control it and who must judge its performance.

The increased responsibilities of government have expanded the duties of municipal administrators. Although the specific requirements of these administrators vary widely, a number are universal in nature. These are: (1) appropriate and functioning budgetary procedure; (2) a classification of accounts adhering to a national standard so that some operations and unit costs can be compared with similar activities elsewhere; (3) adequate stores and property records; (4) a successful system of revenue collection; (5) pre-audits and post-audits; (6) informative reports.

The growing demand for improved financial practices at all levels of government will have to be met by either legal or voluntary controls. While either one may not be superior to the other, the most effective controls will probably include a combination of both types. Legal controls should be broad so as to allow for maximum use of local talent and initiative and so as not to abolish home or local rule. Municipal administrators must increase their efficiency through voluntary and broad legal controls or be subjected to detailed legal controls with the resulting restriction of functioning at maximum capability.

Three tools of budgetary reporting that can be used to control operations are (1) a moving budget, (2) continuous surveys, and (3) a separation of capital and operating budgets.

Annual reports should be made available to the public. The content and appearance of these reports would be determined by local needs and conditions, but they should meet the minimum standards as described in the many textbooks on government.

ACCOUNTING FOR THE T. V. A., *Accounting Forum,* XIII (June, 1941), 48-51, 61-62. [19]

Accounting requirements of the TVA do not differ in a material way from those of a private corporation. In the balance sheet appropriations are shown instead of capital stock, and a number of operating statements are shown covering the four broad programs of the TVA rather than one income statement.

All general ledger accounts, other than balance sheet accounts, are activity accounts. An *activity* is an organizational unit's contribution to some division of a project, a major construction program, or a program, a major operation. Thus, the general ledger accounts may be grouped so as to classify expenditures by organizations or by functions. Postings to the ledger are keyed by object of expenditure and the total monthly expenditure is broken down by functions (for financial reporting purposes), organizations (for reporting to organizational heads), and objects (for reporting to general management, the Bureau of the Budget and Congress).

The flexibility and speed of the bookkeeping procedures make possible the presentation of financial statements before the twelfth of the month. The accounts are consistently kept as simple as possible and recordings are confined primarily to original transactions.

"Pre-audit of all transactions is elaborate, much more so than would be necessary in a private enterprise." Post-audits are conducted by the Comptroller-General, but the comprehensive reviews are made by independent public accountants.

"Subsidies have often been mentioned in connection with TVA operations. The answer is that there aren't any." Power revenues are sufficient to cover all costs, including true joint-costs, interest on borrowed money and tax equivalents paid to local governments. Much credit for the cheap power rates of the TVA must be given to the carefully selected staff which operates the power portion of the TVA's activities.

THE GOAL OF ACCOUNTING EDUCATION, *Experiences with Extensions of Auditing Procedure,* Papers Presented at the Fifty-third Annual Meeting (New York: American Institute of Accountants, 1941), pp. 84-88. [20]

". . . uncorrelated techniques indicate that the philosophy on which accountants have rested their case may need an overhauling; because if that philosophy shows up badly when accounting practices are dissected, and no orderly body of theory can be presented, it may be true that only the procedures exemplified in practice sets, and not abstract principles, can be taught." Accounting research has been dominated by practitioners with the results that the subjects for researchers have been chosen, the "orderly development of lay controls over professional activities" postponed, and "acquired inhibitions" have prevented "anything like a scientific growth of accounting thought by practitioners."

Accountants have been unable to free themselves from the notion that their services are for business management purposes only. There is tremendous room for the developing of accounting in other areas, such as governmental accounting.

Accounting, as a language, should be spoken by the greatest number of people possible. Accounting principles can be developed by patient, scholarly research. The Institute's research should be transferred to a non-practitioner group, since in the past there has been no attempt to correlate the findings of the committee on given subject matter with "any coherent concept of accounting." A knowledge of business practice should be taught before commencing accounting instruction. Accounting principles can be taught without practice sets. Under such conditions, accounting and non-accounting students could be given the same one or two beginning courses. Attention should be directed toward extending accounting and auditing to other fields. ". . . the goal of accounting education should be to make of accounting something more than a well ordered collection of procedures, and to extend its usefulness far beyond its present confines."

FOREWORD: ACCOUNTING PRINCIPLES UNDERLYING CORPORATE FINANCIAL STATEMENTS: A SYMPOSIUM, *Accounting Review*, XVII January, 1942), 1-3. [21]

For nearly ten years various members of the American Accounting Association had proposed a restatement of its aims and purposes, suggesting a broadening of scope and a more direct participation in practical affairs. A statement of professional principles and policies was highly desirable, since the ability of practitioner organizations to produce such a statement was questioned.

"...a set of principles or standards becomes a definition of the profession itself . . . serves as a discipline for those inside the boundaries, and as a guide to outsiders who have relations with those within the delimited area." When the Association's name was changed, the passive interest in accounting instruction was changed to that of active participation in virtually all areas of accounting. The experimental statement of principles by the executive committee was welcomed by many accountants. There were also criticisms — the most curious of which was "that the ethical precepts of accountants stood at various levels of compulsion and deserved to be considered, in their applications to particular situations, on such levels," for which the Institute gave a substantial prize.

The present statement is the product of the work of many persons and represents a step in a task that "conceivably never can be completed."

WHAT IS AHEAD FOR THE ACCOUNTING PROFESSION? *Proceedings of the Fifth Annual Institute on Accounting,* Ohio State University Publications, College of Commerce Series, No. C-20, 1942, pp. 20-30. [22]

The war caused accounting staffs to dwindle and at the same time placed tremendous responsibilities upon accountants. Accountants need to look for ways to overcome the reduction in staff. In this respect, working papers should be reduced to an absolute minimum and certain non-essential analyses eliminated. Great possibilities for saving time can come from using routine reports and analyses prepared by the client's staff and by having this staff prepare special reports and analyses.

A permanent file should be developed and working papers, especially those with narrative rather than tabular information, should be accumulated in this file. A notation as to the client's practices, especially operating peculiarities and deviations from standard practices, should also be filed here. Much future work can be saved if the auditor insists upon the adoption of stricter methods of internal control.

A procedural audit, consisting of a complete examination of almost all phases of the client's operations, organization, policies and enforcement thereof, should be substituted for the ordinary interim audit. The procedural audit could be made in the slack summer months by a senior accountant; over the course of a year a surprisingly precise amount of information relative to the client could be acquired. Many extensive reviews at the time of the annual audit would be made unnecessary by this procedural audit.

The accountant's habit of shying away from matters of government must be changed. The average individual has difficulty understanding the nature of government's activities. Accountants have found that as a corporation's affairs are exposed to the public, the corporate officials develop a greater sense of social obligation. The same may very well be true of government. An adequate system of accounting does not exist in government, or if it does exist, it does not produce results which can be interpreted by enough people. The federal government is the worst offender in this respect. Accountants, especially, should demand clearer statements of governmental operations.

EXPENDITURE CONTROLS IN THE UNITED STATES GOVERNMENT, *Accounting Review,* XX (January, 1945), 31-44. [23]

The procedures and the accounting processes involved in the spending of money by the federal government can be classified into six steps.

First, estimates of future expenditures are prepared annually within the various spending agencies. For many reasons "the budget ultimately concocted from the estimates appears never to have been more than a device for setting a top limit on expenditures."

Second, the budgets are reviewed and frequently reduced by the Bureau of the Budget and the President. The Bureau obtains the annual budget by combining the estimates of the various agencies after approval by the Estimates Division which, on the whole, has done a "good job."

Third, the President's recommendations are reviewed by congressional committees and an appropriation measure is enacted. "Nowhere is there more evidence of the conflict among the three branches of the federal government . . . than in the proceedings of the House Committee on Appropriations. . . . Most of the conflict arises from uncertainty as to the degree of supervision that the Congress should exercise over the activities of individual agencies."

Fourth, the expenditure is made by the spending agency. Precedent is the chief automatic factor involved in making an expenditure. "Conscientious administrators are aware of this stagnating effect on their organizations. . . ."

Fifth, the goods or services are received, followed by preaudit and payment of the bill. "Preaudit within agencies is largely routine, and in the hands of audit clerks."

Sixth, a postaudit is conducted by the General Accounting Office. The usefulness of the GAO could be increased many times by the substitution of test audits for legal examinations, by the making of prompt audits and the rendering of intelligible reports.

Expenditure control in the federal government could be improved by (1) strengthening the position of the budget officer of the agency; (2) requiring periodic reviews of an agency's activities via the internal audit function; (3) requiring cost studies and the classification of federal expenditures along functional lines; (4) using organizations, such as the American Accounting Association, the American Institute and the Chamber of Commerce, to stimulate government officials' interest in accounting and auditing; (5) overhauling the government's reporting system, which would follow if the four preceding objectives could be attained.

With W. W. Cooper, COSTS, PRICES AND PROFITS: ACCOUNTING IN THE WAR PROGRAM, *Accounting Review,* XX (July, 1945), 267-308. [24]

The central planning and control of materials for war purposes depended heavily upon accounting data. The OPA price freeze of October, 1941 created hardships in a number of instances and brought requests for price adjustments. Price increases considered justifiable were those required by law and those needed to maintain production of essential materials. Profitability was recognized as depending upon cost, price and volume. Average cost was used by OPA. Field surveys were relied upon almost exclusively in determining costs. Financial data obtainable from other governmental agencies were unsatisfactory or too slow in processing, and a central reporting system was established. Companies and their auditors could thus be informed of OPA requirements. The initial forms employed were revised and simplified in 1944. Attempts to obtain uniformity encountered many obstacles. Even the determination of net sales was difficult, due to differing accounting treatments of discounts, freight and other items. OPA avoided establishing detailed accounting requirements, and it is a tribute to accounting that so much of the price-control program could be based on existing practices.

Contract renegotiation, with its objectives of preventing excessive profits on government contracts and reduction of cost, has an extended history. Earlier renegotiation methods adopted the contract approach, while the Price Adjustment Boards adopted the "total company approach." "The cross-delegation of authority to settle for all agencies concerned and the tremendous number of contracts made the total company approach advisable." Legislation granted the right to renegotiate to eliminate excess profits on the total of all contracts without renegotiating the price of any one contract. It was not considered desirable to have renegotiation discussions conducted by those who negotiated the original contract, so new staff and organizations had to be secured and established. Difficult problems were encountered relative to costs to be included or excluded as part of the costs of the contract, such as the "reasonableness" of reserves, costs, salaries and the proration of joint and common costs. Many of these problems were settled by the adoption of the total company approach. Heavy emphasis was placed upon the profit and loss, rather than the balance sheet, approach. In the case of OPA, the commodity approach was used, while in renegotiation, the Price Adjustment Boards emphasized risk and production factors in the individual organization.

Renegotiation tended, and later by law was confined, to recapture of excess profits. In this respect it functioned ineffectively because of emphasis on return on sales rather than return on net worth. Production and delivery were of paramount importance and the older methods normally employed were too slow. The renegotiation law, which was passed in recognition of the disregard for careful pricing, "actually accentuated the tendency toward loose pricing." Renegotiation was looked upon as a corrective for errors in pricing. Many contractural devices were adopted which were "merely variants of cost-plus-a-fee arrangements." The unhappy experiences with these devices have given impetus to fixed price contracts. Unfortunately, the skilled negotiators needed in the making of such contracts are not available. In some cases benchmark type information may be secured on costs from governmentally owned and operated plants.

Accountants also serve on war contract termination teams along with lawyers and engineers. Contract settlements have been reached with a degree of professionalism, and "sharp practices" and "fraud" have been reduced. The Joint Termination Accounting Manual emphasizes "recognized commercial accounting practices" and "reasonable" termination profit and costs.

Accounting has played an important role in the war effort although some may say that accounting practices have suffered and degenerated. Experience has shown that "accountants might well explore the possibility of obtaining some agreement on the problems of cost spreads" and the development of accounting-statistical techniques. The future seems to hold many added responsibilities for the accountant, and "if a national crisis is again faced, the existence of an articulate, coordinated, self-imposed body of standards would add immensely to the worth of the profession to the nation."

ACCOUNTING PROGRESS IN THE FEDERAL GOVERNMENT, *Illinois Society of Certified Public Accountants Bulletin,* VIII (September, 1945), 10-13. [25]

Accounting, in the administration of the federal government, "has played less than a minor part . . . has remained static during its great advances in commercial fields." Costs, as "measuring sticks," have been accumulated in a few instances in the past, and are now being looked upon as the medium of reporting on the increasing complexities of government.

Little attention is paid to accounting in federal departments or agencies, and the devices employed are "necessarily weak and practically always ineffective." Appropriation, allotment and expenditure ledgers are maintained, the first two of these being wholly unnecessary and usually out of agreement. "Postings and reports, such as there are, lag far behind." No functional analysis of expenditures is made, as expenditures are classified by object of expenditure only.

Agencies do not have controllers, and the budget officers are usually not accountants. ". . . the average budget is still a propagandistic device. . . ." The House committee reviewing agency appropriation requests has, on the whole, done a good job, but it "rarely gets down to considered appraisals of work costs. . . ."

Some progress has been made in auditing governmental agencies in that the Comptroller-General recently "espoused the idea of commercial audits . . . for government corporations."

What is needed now is a "chief accounting officer for the Government as a whole . . . a controller for each spending agency . . . budgeting and reporting methods based on analyses of the Government's functions and work programs [and] a scheme of auditing. . . ."

THE DEVELOPMENT OF ACCOUNTING FOR REGULATORY PURPOSES BY THE FEDERAL POWER COMMISSION, *Accounting Review,* XXI (January, 1946), 19-31. Reprinted from *George Washington Law Review,* XIV (December, 1945), 152-73. [26]

". . . accounting as it has been practiced by the Federal Power Commission has inspired a good deal of angry rhetoric . . . not only from those who imagine that their interests have been adversely affected, but from accountants themselves, the validity of whose traditional practices has been put to the test."

The commission's requirements have resulted in (1) the segregation, up to August, 1945, of $870 million of excess of book values over original cost of properties into accounts 100.5 and 107; (2) depreciation reserves being increased by 70 percent from 1937 to 1943; (3) reported net income, showing no observable trend, sufficient to yield 6 percent preferred dividends and 7 percent common dividends and to absorb $1,100 million surplus charges; (4) property additions of $1,300 million, debt and paid-in capital reductions of $320 million and a $330 billion increase in working capital. Output has increased 65 percent, customers 15 percent, gross revenue 38 percent, while net income has remained fairly stable.

A number of trends in accounting are observable in this period. Attempts have been made to define and improve accounting terms and standards, and accounting is being used as a basis for action. The cost principle is being stressed and intangibles are being eliminated. Depreciation rates and reserves have received more attention.

The motives of the commission appear to be: (1) to correct the practices followed by holding companies in the twenties when "accounting followed fantastic standards"; (2) to point out the downward revision which investors and utility companies knew were coming; (3) to reject the engineering and appraisal approach to valuation because of the many intangibles frequently involved; (4) to reject replacement cost as a cost upon which to base rates; (5) to counteract the tendency of the utility to neglect the customer; (6) to reduce investor risk "to the vanishing point"; (7) to do the task of valuation assigned it by the Congress. Furthermore, the original cost rule is not a violation of accounting principles, as this modified principle is applicable where the "natural deterrent" of a competitive market does not exist.

The defects in the uniform system of the commission are: (1) the allowance of interest on the utility's own funds as cost of construction; (2) the showing as assets of items such as losses from disposal or destruction of assets, stock discount and expense, discount and expense on refunded issues and securities reacquired; (3) the large number and dollar amounts of surplus charges; (4) the poor form of the balance sheet, and the showing of valuation reserves on the liability side of the statement.

RESTORATION OF FIXED ASSETS TO THE BALANCE SHEET — FIRST NEGATIVE, *Accounting Review*, XXII (April, 1947), 200-3. [27]

The Association's executive committee in its statement on accounting principles in 1941 stated that " the cost of depreciable property was regarded as allocable over future years in accordance with a specific plan therefor." Since partial cost expirations could not be measured precisely, they must be based on business experience and expert opinion and not on rigid formula. Adherence to the cost principle would bring an end to the practices of revaluing assets, up or down, according to current price levels and business developments. This statement makes it clear that cost allocations, once made, should not be disturbed.

The first of three main reasons why fixed assets, once allocated to cost of operations, should not be restored to the balance sheet centers around the policies to be adopted in view of the tremendous problems involved in the transition from wartime to peacetime operations. Because of the problems to be faced, rapid amortization of wartime plants was "at least a discreet policy, deemed conservative and fully justifiable at the time." Such a policy was followed as a result of considered judgment, not only by management, but also by the public accountants who in effect approved the practice. Is management now to be called in error and the public accountant's certificate improper? If restoration is proper then financial statements will have lost their significance and integrity.

With respect to the matching process, the service for which an asset was acquired was rendered during the war years, and the writing off of the asset during those years results in "a completed transaction requiring no further attention."

Finally, if the earlier estimates regarding an asset are deemed faulty, what assurance is there that the new estimates are any better? Restoration will open the door to "financial jockeying the end of which is difficult to see."

THE TVA AND ITS POWER ACCOUNTING PROBLEMS, *Accounting Review,* XXIII (January, 1948), 44-62. [28]

A recent article, appearing in both the *Journal of Accountancy* and the General Accounting Office report, implies that the "TVA has deliberately omitted important elements of cost from its books and financial statements." A careful reading of the "facts" would show that GAO has made no demands upon the TVA to change or adjust its accounts, and that TVA reports contain more detailed information than that reported by private power companies.

TVA follows a practice of activity accounting and "an activity is the lowest practicable coincident level of function budgeting, and accounting." A well-defined summary of principles and definitions is employed to tie in accounting with management. Although TVA bookkeeping is of the utmost simplicity, a monthly managerial review is required. The system of accounts does not follow the typical pattern of governmental accounting in that both budgetary and commitments items are omitted from the formal records. Elaborate files, maintained for control over properties, are regularly inspected and the depreciation rates and accumulations studied continuously. Effective decentralization was secured by establishing accounting units wherever operating heads desired them. TVA also renders accounting and engineering services to its retail outlets. Joint costs are allocated 40 percent to power and 30 percent each to flood control and navigation.

A comparison of TVA financial statements with those of industry averages for Class A & B utilities shows that (1) prices paid by consumers of private utility power were 2.4 times those paid by TVA customers; (2) on a per kwh basis the yields were 32.9 mills and 16.6 mills respectively for residential customers of private industry versus TVA; (3) TVA costs were less because of the less expensive hydroelectric generation of power; (4) transmission costs were roughly comparable, but TVA distribution costs were markedly less; (5) TVA depreciation expense was 3 percent of gross property cost as compared to 2½ percent for private utilities; (6) income taxes account for 2.7 mills of the 9.5 mills difference in expenses per kwh sold; (7) TVA general overhead expenses are much lower than those of private utilities; (8) comparable figures for acquisition adjustment amortization cannot be obtained; (9) interest expense is nominal for TVA because of the 1 percent rate, while private utilities pay more than 2½ percent. The "omitted" costs alleged by the GAO consist of depreciation on land, mythical or theoretical costs such as federal income taxes, interest on federal government contributions and interest on construction. The fifth "omitted" cost pertains to compensation claims for injuries sustained, which are paid through a separate governmental agency and not charged to the employee's agency. Most of these costs are analogous to that of the salary of the owner of a single proprietorship. There is no objective method of determining the amounts involved.

DEPRECIATION AND THE PRICE LEVEL: A SYMPOSIUM: THIRD NEGATIVE, *Accounting Review*, XXIII (April, 1948), 131-36. [29]

The present period of rising price levels has produced a lot of mumbo-jumbo and misconceptions with respect to depreciation, depreciation reserves and profit levels. A number of devices have been used in attempts to find the "solution" to high prices, such as the immediate absorption of all or a part of the cost of new assets, increasing the depreciation rates, reversing accrued depreciation and various write-up methods, including that of the quasi-reorganization.

Another fallacy encountered is the belief that increasing depreciation charges will increase working capital. Those who persist in the cry of "unreality" with respect to business profits should recognize that "men's minds as well as prices are infected by inflationary movements." There is also the worshipping cult which asserts that accountants should use index numbers in valuing fixed assets, but which fails to recognize that a proper application of index numbers to the conditions attaching to a particular business will probably justify continuation of recording assets at cost and the taking of depreciation on the cost basis.

Recognition of all pertinent factors leads to the conclusions that: (1) original cost should be retained in the records as the basis for depreciation until prices become stable and business as a whole can make an adjustment; (2) straight-line depreciation rates should be employed, adjusted where necessary according to periodic reviews of estimates of useful life; (3) depreciation or amortization entries, once made, should not be subject to reversal, but explanations may be used to inform the reader that current depreciation is less than that which would have been recorded had present circumstances been known sooner; (4) in some cases the inflated prices paid for assets may justify an immediate partial write-down which should be fully explained; (5) earned surplus reserves may be established for the excess of replacement cost over recorded cost of assets, although even more commendable would be a simple statement that surplus and working capital are being retained to finance future fixed assets purchases without resorting to borrowing.

ACCOUNTING AS A MANAGEMENT CONTROL, *Municipal Finance*, XXI (August, 1948), 3-8. [30]

In the federal governmental structure a fairly common management pattern can be found. The top level is the agency head or group — the department secretary or the corporate board of directors — which is usually concerned with Congressional relations. This level of administration frames the operating policies within the limits set by the Congress.

The operating responsibilities are vested in those administrators next in line — the undersecretary, assistant secretaries, division chiefs or general managers. Under this group are those people who perform the everyday work of the agency, and the majority of appropriations are expended at this level.

The goal of management in the federal government, as in business, is that of coordinating the effects of a group of people working in accordance with a preconceived plan toward a predetermined goal. The various groups must be recognized and their functions clearly assigned and differentiated from those of other groups if accounting control is to be employed.

Unfortunately, the accountant in the average federal organization is hardly more than a bookkeeper. Hence the use of accounting as a means of internal control will not be possible until the accountant is elevated to a higher position.

Of special interest is the development of a new concept referred to as the *activity.* Accounting, as a means of internal control, can function more effectively if each government organizational unit is classified by the activities it performs. Acceptance of the concept of activity will result in a better understanding of use of accounting, and a greater amount of useful financial information will be provided the director or head of the agency.

FINANCING EUROPEAN RECOVERY, *Technical Papers of the 23rd Annual Michigan Accounting Conference* (Ann Arbor: University of Michigan, Bureau of Business Research, 1948), pp. 14-18. [31]

A declaration of policy by Congress, incorporated in the Economic Cooperation Administration legislation, was that our aid to Europe is premised on the formation of a "joint organization" of European countries and on the "continuity of cooperation among countries participating in the program."

Briefly discussed are the manner in which grants are given, the guarantees required, the pricing policies employed, the documentation which must be supplied covering ECA financed purchases, and the end use reports which must be presented.

Various European countries have made serious and impressive efforts to lay the ground work for lasting economic recovery. There has been a revitalization of inter-country and intra-country economic planning, and this particular form of development may be one which is destined to have a wholly different effect on the trend of social controls over economic activity.

Accountants will play an important part in this program of aid to foreign countries. A program calling for the preparation of national balance sheets and operating statements is to be launched. Such a program, it is hoped, will be financed by local counterpart funds arising out of ECA grants.

AMENDMENT OF REGULATION S-X, *Illinois Certified Public Accountant,* XIII (March, 1951), 50-55. [32]

Rule 5.03 of the SEC Regulation S-X calls for the presentation of income statements following substantially the "all-inclusive" concept, except for one special section at the bottom of the statement following net income or loss, wherein "special items" may be listed.

In all probability, this special items section will rarely be used and the SEC attitude toward surplus charges and credits will become even more restrictive. Many types of charges to reserves, now recognized as surplus reserves, will be charged to expense, and reserve charges will be limited primarily to those reserves which are valuation accounts. Reserves originally created out of surplus may be returned to surplus, and large amounts of intangibles written off may be charged to surplus. Certain accounting procedure bulletins may be revised. Income statements to stockholders will probably conform to the net income as agreed upon by the Commission and the registrant; investment analysts are apt to quote the after special items income figure, with a qualifying footnote, and the trend toward the all-inclusive type of income statement has been given a "notable, if somewhat restricted, impetus."

The term *material* has been substituted for *significant* in many places in Regulation S-X and a 10 percent test substituted for a 5 percent test of materiality for certain classes of balance sheet items. Other new requirements with respect to the balance sheet relate to classification of fixed assets; disclosure of basis of valuation of fixed and intangible assets and method of amortization of the latter; disclosure of defaults; details on debt issued; pension plans; material commitments and other items. Almost all of the new requirements have long been standard practices in many accounting firms.

Requirements governing consolidated statements have also been changed to include increasing the percentage from five to fifteen in defining a "significant subsidiary"; prohibition of the use of consolidated statements by registrants in the promotional or exploratory stage; disclosure of the effects of foreign exchange restrictions, of the basis and amount of securities consolidated and eliminated, and "the effect on any balance-sheet item of profits or losses resulting from transactions with affiliated companies."

With respect to the accountant's certificate, the rules have been changed to include more severe tests of independence; simplification of the certificate by removing reference to the adequacy of the system of internal control; the requirement that the accountant must now give his opinion on material changes in, or methods of applying, accounting principles or practices.

SOMETHING ABOUT DEFINITIONS, *Illinois Certified Public Accountant,* XIV (September, 1951), 1-9. [33]

Much of the author's spare time in the last fifteen years has been devoted to the definition of accounting terms. This interest was aroused by the Committee on Terminology, following publication of its book, *Accounting Terminology,* in 1931. In 1936 the Committee, under the chairmanship of the author, prepared a second report covering 991 terms which was mimeographed and circulated, but never published.

Soon to be published is the author's new book, *A Dictionary for Accountants,* in which some 2,000 terms are defined. Some terms can be defined in a few words, while others, such as *cost absorption,* require a page or more. Accountants, in general, have been somewhat careless about employing the best term available. "A dictionary for the profession should help in the development of a parsimony of language that has long been needed."

For illustrative purposes, definitions of a number of terms are presented, as they will appear in the forthcoming book. These include: accounting, accountancy, audit, cost absorption, materiality, net income, permanent file, random, renewal, scope, standard, symbolization, validation and verification.

PANEL DISCUSSION ON INTERNAL CONTROL, *Proceedings of Symposium on Internal Control,* Special Issue of the *Federal Accountant* (January 10, 1952), pp. 23-32. [34]

An internal auditor need not necessarily be an accountant, although in the average situation considerable public accounting experience is desirable. To be successful, an internal auditor must view the "essence of what goes on in an organization." Thus the type of experience acquired is of great importance.

The internal auditor should not participate in the installation of procedures. Such work can be very time consuming and as a result the internal auditing function suffers.

No specific answers can be given to the questions of whether recruiting for the internal audit staff should be done from inside or outside an organization, and whether regional or individual bureau audit staffs should be maintained. Regional internal auditors might be employed in situations where local management is quite independent in relation to top level supervision.

The internal auditor should take an evaluative position with respect to the judgment exercised by management. He must, of course, have confidence in his own judgment, but he can be on dangerous ground if he ventures an opinion in areas where he is not qualified. However, his action might bring about a needed review of an area or activity, which would be of value to the organization.

"Cost accounts can take the place of a multiplicity of funds without the various difficulties that attend the setting up of a complete set of books for each particular appropriation." Congressional appropriations for a certain agency might very well be combined, with the result that duplication of records would be avoided and labor saved.

Controls and the responsibility for controls should be placed at the level at which action is taken. Authority, responsibility and accountability should not be divorced.

ACCOUNTING CONCEPTS AND NATIONAL INCOME, *Accounting Review,* XXVII (January, 1952), 50-56. [35]

Numerous problems have been encountered in attempting to present statistics on national income, including those of definition, varying degrees of accuracy in the available information and "many missing links." In countries preparing national income estimates four "sector accounts" are employed — namely, personal, business, government, and the "rest-of-the-world" sectors. The largest and most important is the personal sector, and information published to date permits balancing of only this account. Most of the current problems fall into a number of major areas as outlined below.

(1) Recent refinements in sampling methodology suggest that direct sampling may replace reliance upon the statistical data now obtained from other agencies.

(2) The concept of money flows should be tied in with that of national income and the "distinction between cash and accruals can be derived as a feature of the sampling technique."

(3) Some if not all imputed transactions, such as the adjustment for inventory profit, may very well be omitted.

(4) Certain items that are at present "polished" with a great many assumptions may be omitted or accepted in raw data form.

(5) The determination and disclosure of capital turnover would be most desirable.

(6) A national balance sheet is needed in order to realize fully the importance of the income statement.

(7) The closer "the methodology of compiling national-income detail" is to accepted accounting concepts the greater will be the benefits.

(8) The methods now employed in compiling the data should be disclosed in understandable form and detail.

(9) The uses to which national income data are put should be discovered to determine whether alternative data might not have been employed.

(10) A more orderly account structure, especially a method of coding and matching entries, is needed.

(11) Trade associations and other organizations might very well be asked to assist in securing the sampling data needed from business.

CHANGING CONCEPTS OF BUSINESS INCOME, *Illinois Certified Public Accountant*, XIV (March, 1952), 11-17. [36]

Changing Concepts of Business Income, the final report of the Study Group on Business Income, has many shortcomings, namely:

(1) "The disparagement of current reporting practices because historical costs are matched against revenues: a detraction that may alienate the profession. . . ."

(2) The recommendation is made that the accountant's opinion should also be expressed on non-accounting data, the extent, nature and form of which is not defined in the reports.

(3) The report is almost propagandistic in its espousal of *Lifo* and omitting the arguments against it and the possible long-run effects which may follow from its use.

(4) "The absence of historical perspective in the developmental sections of the report and the exaggerated omniscience and infallibility ascribed to certain quoted AIA pronouncements in the early 30's."

(5) "The want of understanding of the meaning and limitations of general price indexes and their possible application to the affairs of an individual business enterprise." The use of statistics in accounting should be welcomed, but it would not be beneficial to subordinate accounting to statistics.

(6) An appraisal of the writeups of the twenties followed by the write-downs of the thirties should not have been omitted from the report.

(7) The report fails to comprehend the possible inflationary effects resulting from the use of *Lifo* and other writeups of costs.

(8) The report also attempts to relate to both current and fixed assets prices, prices prevailing in markets "differing in time, place, and volume from that in which they were purchased."

(9) The report also fails to recognize that the measurement of business income has always involved the use of different standards of measurement for costs as opposed to revenues, and that use of index numbers or industry averages may produce a greater than expected "retreat from reality"; that "the intent of accounting for business income has been to portray past transactions, not provisions for future transactions"; that widespread use of *Lifo* can produce only higher tax rates and temporary tax benefits; that "improved budgetary practices . . . might provide a more intelligible sector of management's report to stockholders than a dressed-up version of an income account for a past period."

(10) There is no evidence that attempts were made to "convince the economists in the Group of the propriety and usefulness of current methods of accounting." The Institute "owes it to the profession to follow this book with a statement of the meaning, worth, and applications of accounting in its present form."

ESSENTIAL ELEMENTS IN A PROGRAM OF INTERNAL AUDIT, *Accounting Review,* XXVIII (January, 1953), 17-24. [37]

The first of a number of organizational essentials for a workable system of internal audit is a "full-scale recognition of the nature and interdependence of authority, responsibility, and accountability. . . ." Second, activity centers must be established in the organizational structure. Third, each center must be empowered or charged with authority, responsibility and accountability. Fourth, the top administrator must be one who earnestly desires the best solution to operational problems, secures and makes use of competent supervisory skills, delegates authority and depends upon his internal auditor. Fifth, the accounting scheme must fit and aid the administrator's delegation of authority, responsibility and accountability.

"Here are six items which as a minimum I should like to see on the program of the internal auditor of a governmental agency: 1. Adhere to high standards. . . . 2. Know your agency and work for its organizational operational improvement. . . . 3. Develop gradually orderly procedures and an effective internal-audit-reporting technique. . . . 4. Make your organization budget-conscious. . . . 5. Assist in developing your agency's method of reporting. . . . 6. Don't be only a watch-dog. . . . "

RECENT DEVELOPMENTS IN THE FORMULATION OF ACCOUNTING PRINCIPLES, *Accountant,* IV (January, 1953), 30-55. [38]

In this long article the author reviews the twenty principles "ventured by the Committee" in 1936; the four Supplementary Statements of the American

Accounting Association; the fifteen chapters of Bulletin 43 of the Committee on Accounting Procedure of the American Institute of Accountants; the fifteen published recommendations of The Institute of Chartered Accountants in England and Wales.

A number of observations with respect to the significance of the above publications can be stated. ". . . a fruitful source of study lies in the examination of the elements that contribute to the *recognition* (e.g., identification, amount, timing, and allocation) of the various types of transactions. For it is at the point of transaction recognition that management decisions are made and accounting controls are, potentially at least, the strongest."

Numerous efforts have been made to "lift the income statement from its cost environs." The Association's Executive Committee in Supplementary Statement 2 "came close to outright advocacy" of expressing values higher than cost in the income statement. The British Institute's recommendation 15 "stands as the best defense of historical cost as the one supportable basis of accounting valuation." Current values are supported primarily for tax reasons and because of the belief that the "consumption of a commodity or service can be expressed only in terms of its market price." *Lifo* has also been used because of tax reasons.

The British Institute proposes that earnings be retained for possible asset replacement at higher prices, which was the point of view expressed in the Association's Supplementary Statement 1. "All three societies now favor the elimination of reserves as a separate balance sheet classification."

The British Institute does not face the problem of surplus charges. The Association tends to favor an "all-inclusive" type of income statement as contrasted to the Institute's favoring of the "current operating performance" type of statement.

The Institute favored restoration of amortized emergency facilities, a view opposed by the Association's Committee.

The two American societies disagree on income tax allocation as proposed by the Institute. The British Institute recommends tax allocation only in situations where dividends have been declared "gross."

More detail is being placed in income statements. The Association recommends the greatest amount of disclosure while the British Institute "stops short of recommending disclosure of gross revenues."

Yet to be developed is a device which imparts a "forward look" to statements, and it is in this area that budget techniques may have much to offer.

SOMETHING ABOUT ACCOUNTING LANGUAGE, *Massachusetts Society of Certified Public Accountants News Bulletin,* XXVIII (October, 1954), 2-5. [39]

For some time accounting has been developing its own "cant expressions" — words and phrases that form a part of the stock in trade of a specialized group of persons. Cant expressions are common terms from everyday language to which have been given a special technical slant, such that they are not readily understood by the uninitiated.

The terminology employed by British accountants does not contain numerous differences in the sense in which language is used as compared to American terminology. The language in the various bulletins of the Institute of Chartered Accountants is relatively clear and concise although there are some phrases, especially those signifying employment of value judgment, which have a professional cant.

The works of the American Accounting Association are exceptionally free from cant expressions, while the bulletins of the Institute's Committee on Accounting Procedures contain a real abundance of "stop-gap" terms. Such terms as "proper, reasonable, acceptable, appropriate, desirable, significant, adequate, permissible, preferable, useful, practical, practicable and sound" appear numerous times.

Some day an accountant will say "permissible applications of accounting that are sound and proper, appropriate, and significant, and both practicable and useful, seem not only to be acceptable and adequate but also to be reasonable and desirable, even preferable."

THE ACTIVITY: NERVE CENTER OF MANAGEMENT AND ACCOUNTING, *N.A.C.A. Bulletin,* XXXVI, Sec. 1 (August, 1955), 1627-33. [40]

Management has given accounting full recognition as a "tool of communication between those who plan and those whose primary concern is with daily output." The "growing interdependence of management and accounting" has also received attention in the top fiscal agencies of the federal government.

The basic elements of this new development are: (1) use of the budget for "controlling *operations* as well as costs"; (2) extension of the unit cost concept beyond factory operations and output; (3) the use of "current cost standards reflecting efficient but attainable operating conditions"; (4) the "deserved popularity" of direct costing; (5) responsibility costing under which costs, especially variable factory costs, are identified with an individual; (6) activity accounting, which is an extension of responsibility costing; (7) feedback, which presently means reporting promptly to management and in sufficient detail to provide for both review and possible modification of operating performance. Other factors worthy of mention are the insistence upon the adoption of internal controls; the growth of internal auditing; the importance attached to explanations of variances; the "contribution of probability theories to judgments concerning accounts and accounting data"; the "growing conviction that operating leeways established for organizational subdivisions assure smoother production and generate efficiencies not otherwise obtainable."

The future will see further extensions, modifications, applications, and developments of and with respect to the above elements. Top management will participate actively in "the accounting domain." The activity is the "focal point to which recent cost trends appear to be converging. Its future lies in the skill with which the accountant will shape his thinking and adapt his procedures in his effort to maximize his contribution to better management."

BASIC CONCEPTS IN THE REORGANIZATION OF STATE ACCOUNTING AND AUDITING PRACTICES, *Illinois Certified Public Accountant,* XIX (Winter, 1956-57), 7-9. [41]

"Today, in every well-run organization, public or private, the organizational head must account to superior authority for carrying out assigned tasks efficiently and economically. Financial administration is no longer the job of a clerical subordinate."

"Financial administration . . . involves . . . planning, programming, budgeting, controlling, reporting, and postauditing." ". . . *planning* is long-range outlook on what an operation should be. . . . *Programming* is the timing of the plan. . . . *Budgeting* is the application of the agency's programming to a particular bienium. . . . *Controlling* is made up of the many elements that govern day-to-day performance. . . . *Reporting,* both internal and external, is the prompt divulging by the agency of its operating costs and revenues . . . *postauditing* requires the periodic submission of accounts and reports to external examination. . . ."

Included in the administration of financial management are the functions of preaudit, internal audit, procedural audit and postaudit. Preaudit, or voucher audit, is a function of the spending agency. The internal audit, a management device, is normally the responsibility of a qualified auditor who reports to the controller. The procedural audit is conducted by the Department of Finance and involves, among other items, a critical review of the work of the internal auditor. The postaudit is usually the function of the certified public accountant. In the federal government, the postaudit is conducted by members of the staff of the General Accounting Office.

ACCOUNTING PRACTICES IN STATE AGENCIES, *Journal of Accountancy*, CVIII (August, 1959), 52-60. [42]

The modernization of the structure of financial controls recently undertaken by the state of Illinois resulted in the following procedures:

(1) Fiscal control was decentralized; accounting principles and standards were prescribed; periodic financial reports were required; procedural audits were instituted; the agency head was made responsible for maintaining current, accurate professional accounting; agency organizational plans were to be filed with the Department of Finance; each agency was to have a "competent accounting officer" reporting to the agency head; internal-audit procedures were to be instituted; account-keeping was to be separated from other responsibilities; and the accounts were to reflect functional costs. The finance department was to prepare the state's biennial budget, maintain a central purchasing service and administer the state property control law.

(2) A certified public accountant was to be appointed for a term of six years to serve as Auditor General heading a Department of Audits with authority to audit or "cause to be audited" every state agency expending over $100,000 annually.

(3) A Legislative Audit Commission was created to receive and act on the Auditor General's reports.

The first Auditor General's report, based upon audits of 162 agencies, noted a number of defects in accounting, namely: the intermingling of the record-keeping and asset custody function; failure to use and to control prenumbered receipts; delays in depositing receipts; checks mailed or distributed by those authorizing them; lack of adequate inventory control and fixed asset control; partial rather than full employment of the accrual basis, etc.; also the undesirable practice of loading appropriations with encumbrances at year end and loading a given appropriation with deficiencies in other appropriations. Good management of an agency involves an organizational plan, attention to the controllership function, adoption of good budgetary practices, good accounting, periodic review of purchasing operations and timely and useful reporting.

". . . the institution of present-day management and accounting standards would require little change in basic laws." A model policy declaration, which might be employed to bring about such standards, is presented as illustrative of the type of declaration the state's top executive might make.

II. A. C. LITTLETON

Joslin Studios

A. C. LITTLETON

A. C. Littleton was born in Bloomington, Illinois in 1886. He holds three degrees from the University of Illinois: A.B., A.M. and Ph.D., awarded in 1912, 1918 and 1932 respectively.

His professional career in accountancy began in 1912, when he was employed as a public accountant in the firm of Deloitte, Plender, Griffiths & Co. of Chicago. In 1915 he joined the faculty of the College of Commerce of the University of Illinois, where he held the rank of professor of accountancy; he also served as Assistant Dean of the College of Commerce and, for twenty-one years, as Assistant Director of the Bureau of Economic and Business Research.

Mr. Littleton has for many years had a deep interest in the development of graduate training in accounting. He was instrumental in the development of graduate training at the master's degree level at Illinois and later participated there in the development of the first Ph.D. program in accountancy in the United States. Until his retirement in 1952, he served as an adviser on graduate dissertations for a period of thirty years. His sincere interest in accounting education and literature has earned him recognition as a leading accounting educator and author.

Mr. Littleton has written numerous articles which have appeared in various professional and learned periodicals. He is the author of three books: *Accounting Evolution to 1900* (1933), *An Introduction to Corporate Accounting Standards,* with W. A. Paton (1940), and *Structure of Accounting Theory* (1953).

He is a member of the American Institute of Certified Public Accountants and has served on its committees on Accounting Procedure, Selection of Personnel and Accounting History. He is a member of the American Accounting Association, of which he has been President and Research Director; he also was editor of *The Accounting Review* for four years. He is a member of the Illinois Society of Certified Public Accountants.

His honorary memberships include the business honorary Beta Gamma Sigma and the accounting honorary Beta Alpha Psi. He was a charter member of the latter and served a term as president of its Grand Council. Mr. Littleton is an honorary member of the Colorado Society of Certified Public Accountants and was elected a member of The Ohio State University's Accounting Hall of Fame in 1956. In 1955 he received the Alpha Kappa Psi award for significant contributions to accounting.

Since his retirement, Mr. Littleton has served as a visiting professor, conducting seminars and delivering occasional lectures at various universities and colleges.

II. A. C. LITTLETON

SUMMARIES OF PERIODICAL WRITINGS

AN APPRAISAL OF THE BALANCE SHEET APPROACH, *Papers and Proceedings of the Seventh Annual Meeting* (1922), American Association of University Instructors in Accounting, VII (1923), 85-92. [43]

Present bookkeeping texts contain a number of different approaches to the problem of how to teach the beginning student an understanding of accounting. Among these are the account analysis approach, the bookkeeping sequence approach and the "sheer memory" approach, with variations to be found for some of these methods. The first approach involves a detailed study of an account in all of its aspects. The second involves the teaching of accounting essentially as a bookkeeper would complete his normal routine. The third requires the students to make entries without knowing how to journalize, relying upon memory alone.

The balance sheet approach would reverse the usual sequence of presenting topics and would follow the following sequence: "administrative need for facts — balance sheet — changes therein necessitated by the transaction of business — services of the account in recording changes — the ledger — nominal accounts as explained — inventory and simple closing — technique of transaction analysis — journal to record results of transaction analysis — posting and trial balance — and need for subdivision of the journal."

This approach is to be favored because it aims "at the beginner's mind rather than his hands." It is directed toward the "whys" of accounting. The student "feels the arbitrariness of cut and dried rules." In the balance sheet approach he is made to feel that there is some meaning in what he does. This approach also emphasizes the teaching of business which must be done in the beginning course due to lack of knowledge about business on the part of the student. The principle of learning about the "whole" and then proceeding to the parts, as it is employed in other fields of study, is appropriate in the teaching of accounting.

DISCUSSION OF "PRINCIPLES OF VALUATION AS RELATED TO THE BALANCE SHEET," *Papers and Proceedings of the Eighth Annual Meeting* (1923), American Association of University Instructors in Accounting, VII (1924), 14-15. [44]

The fluctuating price level of recent times shows that there are occasions when the customary balance sheet values do not serve as effective guides to policy or action. However, cost should be consistently maintained in all statements and in the accounts and supplemented with interpretive data.

A question may be raised as to how far accountants should go in incorporating interpretive data into the accounts and mixing them with ascertained facts. Preferably the two should be segregated, but the accountant should provide both types of data.

THE RELATION OF ACCOUNTING TO THE BUSINESS CYCLE, *Papers and Proceedings of the Ninth Annual Meeting* (1924), American Association of University Instructors in Accounting, IX (1925), 108-16. [45]

Since business cycles affect business profits and plans, and the accountant is concerned with reporting profits and the conditions antecedent to profits or losses, it follows that accountants should have some knowledge of the reasons for business cycles and the methods of measuring them.

The accountant cannot escape giving consideration to price levels; witness the cost or market, whichever is lower, rule of inventory pricing. However, footnote interpretations should be given rather than recording alterations of recorded costs. Business cycles also affect the accountant in his application of the concepts of "normal" inventory and "normal" burden. Also, some attention is being directed to the idea that income should be reported for a period equal to the length of the business cycle rather than for the year. Many questions can be raised as to how far the accountant should go in recording, or attempting to isolate, the effects of business cycles.

Knowledge on the part of the accountant of business cycles and their effects upon business will strengthen his position as an adviser to the businessman. "Slowly he is gaining the reputation of being a man who is capable of looking at affairs broadly and with a degree of detachment few others in business possess." The accountant also has special aptitudes and knowledge which are of great value in the preparation of the budget — a device which affords an otherwise impossible degree of control over operations. But budgets cannot be built on "thin air." The accountant must add a knowledge of business cycles to his store of information pertaining to the past in order to make the most significant contribution to the building of a budget.

Statistics are available for use by the accountant, and recent experiments in analyzing the volume of a firm's business as a basis for budgeting have been published. The accountant should consider "serious and sustained study of this new material."

DEVELOPMENT OF ACCOUNTING LITERATURE, *Publications*, American Association of University Instructors in Accounting, IX (1925), 7-17. [46]

"Accounting and the literature of accounting have grown only as commerce and industry have grown." The development of trade brought with it "scattered fragments" of efforts at record-keeping in the thirteenth, fourteenth and fifteenth centuries.

Throughout the history of accounting important books have appeared as a result of the demands placed upon accounting. The first of these was written by Pacioli. In response to the demands placed upon accounting by the industrial revolution, Garcke and Fells wrote *Factory Accounts*. The development of professional auditing in England resulted in the publication of Pixley's *Duties of Auditors* and Dicksee's *Auditing*. Shortly thereafter a number of the first American textbooks in accounting were published including those by Sprague, Lisle, Hatfield, Montgomery and Nicholson.

A period then followed in which more attention was directed toward separation of the study of the theory of accounting from its practical applications. The theory books included the writings of Paton, Cole, and Ficker, while books on the practical application of accounting were written by Jackson, Bell, McKinsey and Bliss.

Attention is beginning to be paid in accounting literature to the relationship of accounting to economics and statistics.

RESEARCH WORK AT THE UNIVERSITY OF ILLINOIS, *Accounting Review*, I (March, 1926), 31-38. [47]

A number of possible areas exist for research work in accounting, including: (1) the historical development of accounting, (2) accounting theory and its relationship to other subjects, (3) teaching methods, (4) verification techniques, (5) methods of fraud detection, (6) methods of interpretation, (7) extension of statistical methods to accounting.

At the Bureau of Business Research at the University of Illinois two projects are underway dealing with the application of statistical methods to accounting data. The first project deals with the compilation of data secured from public utility companies, and the elimination of the seasonal and trend factor in an attempt to isolate the effects of the cycle. A routine is being prepared so that other companies may apply the same techniques to their own data. A further goal involves an attempt to find some means whereby current and past data may be projected into the future with some degree of accuracy. The second project entails the formulation of standard ratios for utilities which will be free of the many criticisms directed at those now being employed.

Experience gained in the second project shows that one of the greatest difficulties faced is that of securing homogeneous data. This difficulty can be overcome by governmental fiat or by the cooperation of individuals. The preferred way is the latter. Consequently, the cooperation of accountants is needed to develop the standard ratios. If members of the profession would cooperate, it would be possible to develop ten or a dozen standard ratios, classified according to size of the firm and its geographical location. A suggested standard report form is presented for illustrative purposes.

ITALIAN DOUBLE ENTRY IN EARLY ENGLAND, *Accounting Review,* I (June, 1926), 60-71. [48]

Double-entry bookkeeping apparently first developed about the time of the Renaissance. Although Pacioli's book (1494) helped to spread the Italian system throughout Europe, double-entry bookkeeping was practiced by Italian branch houses in England as early as 1436.

Early Italian ledger entries were in effect complete statements of the business transaction, with reduction of the entry to technical, symbolized form coming later. The entries also contained, as did early English ledger entries, certain "words of accountability" in that debits were represented by terms such as "must give," "shall give" and "ought to give." Likewise credits were represented by terms such as "must have," "shall have" and "ought to have." The point of view taken in these entries was always personal and the bookkeeper did not have a business entity concept. Also the entries were statements of future expected occurrences. Early English entries were along the lines of debiting "what is received [by me]" and crediting "what is given [by me]." Thus, English entries were stated in the present tense, while the final results obtained are the same as those under the Italian concept. The reasons for the difference in outlook found in Italian and English entries lies in the different stages of commerce to which each country had advanced. Italy, with its more highly developed commerce, naturally tended to emphasize ownership and proprietorship, while agency and stewardship were emphasized in the feudalism of England.

Both methods have survived, although it is the Italian method which is used today with, of course, considerable modification. The English method is recognizable in the present "charge and discharge" accounting for estates.

THE 2 TO 1 RATIO ANALYZED, *Certified Public Accountant,* VI (August, 1926), 244-46. [49]

A study of the financial data of 2,176 companies reveals that over 75 percent of these companies had current ratios of two to one or higher. Hence, the two to one rule of thumb may not be completely arbitrary.

A comparison of the above ratios with similar ratios for utility companies reveals that the rule is not universally applicable. A number of reasons exist for the difference found in the utility company study, including the fact that working capital in utilities comprises only 2 percent of the total investment as compared to 40 percent of the total investment in industrial companies.

The flow of funds is a much more important factor than the amount of working capital for both industrial and utility companies. The two to one ratio is only a starting point. It is not a "standard by which credit should be granted or refused."

EVOLUTION OF THE LEDGER ACCOUNT, *Accounting Review,* I (December, 1926), 12-23. [50]

The fundamental concepts of double-entry bookkeeping have not changed through the years although the "manner of thinking of and handling business details has changed from time to time." Several stages of development of bookkeeping practices are found in the period 1400 to 1900.

Essentially, the characteristics of the first period (1396-1600) are: (1) that the only semblance of form is simply the juxtaposition of debits and credits, (2) the formal phraseology, (3) that the record made in the book of original entry was duplicated in both the ledger account debited and the ledger account credited. During the seventeenth century the narrative form tended to be replaced by tabulations; account titles became headings, and each account had two folios — debit and credit. Two minor changes occurring in the eighteenth century were the establishment of the abbreviations *Dr.* and *Cr.* at the head of each folio and the substitution of *per contra* for the account title at the head of the credit folio.

Late in the nineteenth century the "to so and so" and "by so and so" phrases were dropped thus eliminating the last suggestion that each entry expressed a thought which could be expressed grammatically. The twentieth century has brought about a shift from the artificial debt-relationships classification process to a process of "statistically *tabulating the changes* occurring in a great variety of those financial elements which will reveal financial condition and the course of economic progress."

THE ANTECEDENTS OF DOUBLE-ENTRY, *Accounting Review,* II (*June,* 1927), 140-49. [51]

The significant antecedents of double-entry bookkeeping are (1) the art of writing, (2) arithmetic, (3) private property, (4) money, (5) credit, (6) commerce, and (7) capital. Although most of these antecedents existed to a certain extent in Roman and Greek cultures, double-entry bookkeeping needed something more to foster its development. "The ancient world did not produce bookkeeping [because] it did not have the conception of productive business capital." Capital did exist in the sense of wealth, but wealth alone does not create capital in the modern sense of the word.

The growth of commerce in the period 1200 to 1500 brought with it the demand for capital and the need for credit. Wealth came out of its hiding places and became productive, while at the same time real credit transactions appeared for the first time in that loans were made to trading ventures and various governments. At the same time the great merchant houses began engaging in rudimentary commercial banking. The growing use of arabic numerals also aided in the development of systematic record-keeping.

The circumstances surrounding commerce, credit and capital in the Middle Ages were far different from those encountered in the ancient world. These surroundings, which so changed the size and extent of commerce and the need for capital and credit, together with newer and better arithmetic led directly to the development of double-entry bookkeeping.

Bookkeeping has acquired from economics a "body of concept and a language which has been invaluable" in the development of modern accounting. Likewise accounting has drawn from other fields many of its present concepts, such as the distinction between capital and income which is essentially a legal concept.

THOMAS JONES—PIONEER, *Certified Public Accountant,* VII (June, 1927), 183-86. [52]

"Few indeed were the books in the 350 years between Pacioli (1494) and Thomas Jones (1841) which did more than explain in careful detail the *how* of record-keeping by 'Italian method.' . . . Thomas Jones' bookkeeping theory is remarkably clear and satisfying; and for that reason, in the writer's opinion, his book is a landmark in the development of bookkeeping literature."

The orientation of this book, *Principles and Practice of Bookkeeping,* is toward the result of bookkeeping efforts — the statement reflecting the progress made. Jones was the first writer who treated the material as statistical and used statistical classification.

UNIVERSITY EDUCATION FOR ACCOUNTANCY, *Certified Public Accountant,* VII (December, 1927), 361-65, 369. [53]

The purposes of education are "to pass on the experience of those who go before to those who follow," and "to train minds to function smoothly and rationally." These purposes are accomplished via the printed page, problems and the instructor.

The "ideal five-year program of college work" consists of two years of predominantly liberal arts work, two years of work with a major emphasis on business courses, and a fifth year in the how and why of accounting, report writing and other specialized subjects.

Universities can train accountants since the present aim is to lay sound foundations, with a focus on the future for the next ten or twenty years.

TWO FABLES OF BOOKKEEPING, *Accounting Review,* II (December, 1927), 388-96. [54]

How did double-entry bookkeeping develop? Recently a French author, M. Albert Dupont, wrote an article speculating on the development of bookkeeping. The ideas expressed in his article are surprisingly similar to those which this author has expressed in advanced accounting classes to show that double-entry bookkeeping developed out of necessity and is not an invention.

Double-entry apparently developed out of a situation wherein money lenders and borrowers engaged a third party to keep a record of their transactions. The dual nature of a transaction — what one gives, the other receives — must have become clear. Perhaps sometime later, lenders came to the record keeper with funds to lend; funds, however, for which there were no immediate borrowers. At first this must have presented a problem for the record keeper. However, he undoubtedly soon developed a cash account which he could debit upon receipt of such funds, and thus maintain his double-entry system.

The development of double-entry bookkeeping did not emerge in one lifetime, but was a slow process covering many years.

PACIOLO AND MODERN ACCOUNTING, *Accounting Review,* III (June, 1928), 131-40. [55]

A new English translation of Paciolo's (1494) book raises once again the question of how much bookkeeping has changed in the more than 400 years since its publication. There has actually been little basic change, although "modern practices" have not been "completely foreshadowed."

Ever since its development "bookkeeping has possessed a characteristic *theory,* a characteristic *form,* and a characteristic *technology.*" However, the underlying theory must be read between the lines of Paciolo's book, since his purpose was purely practical, i.e., the giving of rules for orderly account-keeping. Beneath the surface of the methodology presented lies recognition of the fact that every transaction has a dual nature. The search for dual methodology, for arithmetical accuracy alone, could not have produced the impersonal and nominal accounts of that day. Paciolo's writing seems to give evidence of an understanding of the importance of the proprietor and of proprietorship and of the relationship of nominal accounts to capital accounts.

The concept of subtraction by opposition is clearly stated in Paciolo's book and the beginning of technical terminology is also to be found in his work. Paciolo's trial balance is still used unchanged today. Also to be found in Paciolo's book are the "most liquid first" ideas of arraying assets, bad debts, petty cash and separate books for branches.

Although accounting has undergone many changes since Paciolo's time, most of these have been induced by the changed conditions in which records were kept. There was no real need for financial statements, periodic closings of the books, accruals, cost allocations between periods, etc., in his time. Many other items or concepts, such as dividends, distinction between capital and income, earnings, fixed asset accounting, exclusion of personal items from business accounts, and detailed expense classifications, are products of modern times with which record keepers of that time did not need to concern themselves.

PIONEERS OF ACCOUNTANCY, *Certified Public Accountant,* VIII (July, 1928), 201-2, 217. [56]

In an earlier article in the June, 1927 *Certified Public Accountant,* the author cited Thomas Jones (N. Y., 1841) as "an accountancy pioneer who was possessed of a penetrating insight into bookkeeping logic far beyond his contemporaries." The earliest German writers were said to have followed Jones by ten years. Further evidence indicates that "these sweeping statements were too broad."

B. F. Foster's book, *A Concise Treatise on Commercial Bookkeeping* (Boston, 1836), indicates a clear understanding of the fundamental nature of double-entry bookkeeping. He divides the ledger accounts into two classes: Parts of Property and Whole Property. The former consists of money, merchandise and personal accounts from which the nature and extent of the assets and liabilities are computed. The second class consists of profit and loss, charges, interest, commissions, etc., from which the amount of capital originally invested and the gain or loss from any period may be ascertained. However, Foster acknowledges Jones' precedence with respect to these ideas. Jones also had a contemporary in Austria, Franz Hautsche, whose writings in 1840 contain ideas very close to those expressed by the German authors Kurzbauer and Augspurg in 1850. English writers such as Malcolm (1718), Stephens (1735), and Cronhelm (1818) also possessed a rather clear insight into the heart of double-entry. However, a study of their writings reveals that they encountered considerable difficulty in expressing themselves clearly. Simon Stevin, writing around 1660, tried to bring into bookkeeping explanations going beyond the mere reciting of practical instructions. However, much must be read into his text. It was not until the time of Cronhelm that the theory of double-entry was stated with any real degree of clarity.

WHAT IS PROFIT? *Accounting Review,* III (September, 1928), 278-88. [57]

The economist is concerned with explaining the reason for the existence and distribution of profit. The courts are interested in profit available for dividends and are apt to view all except the original contribution of the owners' equity as being available for dividends. In tax cases, legislative intent is the deciding criterion in defining profits. Businessmen view profits as a measure of accomplishment, without, of course, being completely disinterested in the legal availability of profits for dividends.

In all three areas are definitions which could be classified into balance sheet and income statement points of view. Which is more important? Businessmen favor the income and expense method of determining profits and, apparently, the majority of legal views concurs.

Although many reasons are advanced for the existence of profit, these must be rejected in favor of the idea that profit is inherent in our economic system and results from management efforts to keep cost and price apart. Profit then is the "outcome of work" and is a "problem of price (market and cost)."

Profit is not unrelated to value since, if the balance sheet point of view is to prevail, it must rest upon value. Value is capitalized earning power. The value of an article depends on its utility to a consumer as compared with other articles; the value of a plant depends on its productivity of useful goods. Consequently, profit cannot be defined as the difference between present and prior value since value itself (as the value of a plant) depends upon the profits flowing from the goods produced there.

"Cost is definite and, once expended, is unchangeable." Cost can serve as a basis for profit determination. Value is indefinite and as changeable as earnings since it rests primarily upon that basis. It can never serve as a starting point for profit determination.

THE EVOLUTION OF THE JOURNAL ENTRY, *Accounting Review*, III (December, 1928), 383-95. [58]

Earliest known journal entries were not what one might expect in view of the fact that ledger entries were complete sentences recorded twice in full. Such journal entries were not full sentences but were, in fact, quite technical not only in form but in phrasing.

Of the journal entries available from the period 1430 to 1549, all exhibit the same technical characteristics and are of the form: "By A......................., to B......................." The prepositions *per* (by) and *a* (to) are given a special significance not found in common usage, and no explanation is given as to how these terms came to be associated with debtor and creditor respectively. Some information is available which shows that the Germans had started with complete sentences, but that by 1516 words were dropped from the journal entry and the entry was becoming merely technical.

Earliest journal entries show the need for a "four-pointed posting." Hypothetically reconstructed, an actual journal entry reads: "For cash deposited this day, Francisco shall have the stated amount, etc., and to Francisco, cash shall give the stated amount at his pleasure." Shortened, the form of this entry might be: "For cash, to Francisco."

Another form of journal entry found in the period 1491 to 1608 has characteristics which may be generalized into the following variations: "First variation: A is Debetor B is Credetor; Second variation: A is debitor to B; Third variation: A owes to B."

The first form of entry presented above appears to bear the imprint of the ledger entries made at that time, while the second form would appear to follow naturally out of the "daybook" record of personal account transactions. Entries of the first type soon dropped out of use, and the second type is a clearer antecedent of modern entries.

English journal entries show clearly the evolution of the journal entry in the period 1684 to 1900. The abbreviation "Dr" replaces "Debitor" or "Debetor"; the credited account is indented, "Dr" and "Cr" are placed in column headings and finally dropped completely. Finally, bookkeeping procedure became such that debits were thought of as items awaiting posting, not as debts or debtors, and the idea of "personified obligations" was dropped in favor of the notion of "accounting units" being transferred or tabulated. "The process under modern usage becomes a wholly impersonal sorting of facts so arranged as to increase the accuracy of the sorting (posting)."

VALUE AND PRICE IN ACCOUNTING, *Accounting Review,* IV (September, 1929), 147-54. [59]

Since value is subjective, the product of one's mind, an article may have more than one value at one time. Value must be differentiated from price in that the former is an estimate of what the latter ought to be, while the latter is an established fact. Value can exist in one mind, while price is the product of two minds.

The term *value* is used in many ways in accounting, such as market value, going value, cost value, liquidation value, reproduction value, replacement value, etc. Many of these latter values differ from price. Although the businessman may be forced to estimate value, accounting must remain anchored to price, since it is beyond the power of accounting to express all of these "psychological estimates."

"Much of the loose usage of 'value' in accountancy may perhaps be due to the generally held view that value in business has a cost base." But "cost is not the basis of value." An article may or may not be worth what it costs. "The real nature of cost, in relation to price, is to furnish on the supply side the *limiting factor* to price — the point beyond which production cannot be maintained." Cost, when added to profit, is not the basis of price, but the *warning point* in the process of successive deductions from the original offering price in attempting to estimate what people might pay for a product or service. In the long run, cost is the ultimate controlling factor.

Cost prices are recorded in accounting not because they represent value, but because they are ascertained facts and determinants of profit. What goods or productive equipment are worth is dependent upon future events. Fluctuations in repurchase price may affect pricing policy but this does not mean that such fluctuations should affect recorded prices.

Value is based on supply and demand. The accountant has little to offer on the demand side and much to offer on the supply side. He can deal effectively with questions of cost or price, but not with questions of value. If the accountant wishes to provide the type of information desired by all who are interested in financial data, he would have to clothe value with figures and "venture outside of the realm of known facts."

SYMPOSIUM ON APPRECIATION — GENERAL COMMENTS, *Accounting Review,* V (March, 1930), 57-59. [60]

The question whether depreciation is to be recorded on appreciation rests upon what constitutes profit and what is the function of the balance sheet. If the balance sheet is viewed as the residual accounts remaining after the nominal accounts are closed, the double-entry bookkeeping concept, unrealized appreciation constitutes no problem, since all items are expressed in terms of cost outlays. There is no appreciation increment until costs are compared with returns.

If the balance sheet is viewed as a statement of resources and liabilities, a single-entry concept, and a statement primarily for credit purposes, unrealized appreciation may enter in because present values may be recorded. Profit is then viewed not as the excess of returns over cost, but as the difference in net worth, which is composed of two elements — "transaction profits" and "price fluctuation profits."

If the first view prevails, unrealized appreciation is unavailable for dividends. If the second view prevails, "it is difficult to see how appreciation could logically be made unavailable." Thus, the accountant faces a dilemma. He turns to the law for help and finds an even greater dilemma in determining what profits are. If the accountant follows his double-entry approach, the balance sheet is unacceptable for credit purposes. If he follows a single-entry approach, the balance sheet may be adequate for credit purposes, but the concept of profit "is against his interpretation of the nature of business and of accounting."

ACCOUNTING FOR APPRECIATION IN TWO TYPICAL CASES DESCRIBED, *American Accountant,* XV (July, 1930), 302-3. [61]

Accountants typically encounter the problem of appreciation in situations involving either merger (sale) or reorganization. The existence and measurement of appreciation is best determined when it has met the test of the market place. In the event of a merger (sale), the test of the market is met in the bargaining between the seller and the buyer. Such a situation presents little difficulty for the accountant.

A much more difficult problem is encountered when no actual sale has taken place, and the assets are to be revalued in a reorganization. Here the judgment of the board of directors, or an engineering appraisal, serves as a basis for measuring the amount of appreciation.

A difficult problem faced is that of recording the surplus arising from appreciation and interpreting this surplus insofar as its availability for dividends is concerned. American and English courts have presented differing opinions in this respect. However, the accountant should show appreciation surplus in a separate account and not include it in the earned surplus account.

A Cost Approach to Elementary Bookkeeping, *Accounting Review*, VI (March, 1931), 33-37. [62]

Early accounting texts followed the "journal approach" and the student very soon began to journalize transactions based upon certain rules of thumb or examples provided by the author. The "ledger approach," which appeared in the mid-nineteenth century, was based on knowledge of the purpose of the usual account and its debit and credit characteristics. With this foundation, the student could classify transactions into the appropriate debit and credit elements. The "balance sheet approach," in which the student was first taught the purpose and usefulness of accounting and the significance of financial statements to management, probably came into use in the 1920's.

While "earlier bookkeeping was called upon principally to record exchanges, present day bookkeeping is required to trace out the conversions which take place between the original investment of property in a business and its final disappearance in one form or another from the enterprise." In keeping with this function of bookkeeping, a cost approach may be developed. Such an approach would (1) view bookkeeping as a record making device employing an entity point of view; (2) recognize the significance of the separation of the increase and decrease side of each account; (3) involve study of the various accounts and the transactions affecting them; (4) result in statements being prepared from the summary ledger accounts; (5) require introduction of separate journals for cash, sales, and purchases; (6) consider the problems of mercantile business by stressing certain features such as inventory.

"The task is not one of teaching *procedure,* but of teaching *a way of thinking* about business transactions."

Early Transaction Analysis, *Accounting Review,* VI (September, 1931), 179-83. [63]

Since early writers on bookkeeping only concerned themselves with telling the reader how to perform the acts of record-keeping, it is necessary to hypothesize or read between the lines in order to learn something about the reasoning involved in early transaction analysis.

Three characteristics can be deduced from three examples of fifteenth and sixteenth century bookkeeping records:

(1) "The entries are complete sentences expressing complete ideas.

(2) The entries are written from the point of view of the proprietor or agent in question, i.e., his accounts with others.

(3) The entries were definitely stated as memoranda of expected future occurrences, not of present happenings."

Although early writers did not express general rules, it would seem that there are at least two principles followed: "(a) X shall later give what he now receives — (i.e., Dr. X). (b) Y shall later receive what he now gives — (i.e., Cr. Y)."

Early reasoning produced four elements in a given transaction while today the transaction is analyzed in terms of two. The additional two elements in early practice may be explained as proprietorship elements which in effect cancelled each other.

CAPITAL AND SURPLUS, *Accounting Review*, VII (December, 1932), 290-93. [64]

The accountant's concept of net worth includes capital, which is composed of capital stock and capital surplus, and surplus. The lawyer's concept of net worth includes capital stock and surplus which is subdivided into the classes of paid-in, revaluation and profits. To the accountant, surplus is realized and undivided profits, while to the lawyer, surplus represents the excess of assets over debts and stock.

Before the introduction of no-par stock and the recognition of appreciation, these two concepts were identical. Now, however, it is not adequate merely to attach a prefix adjective to the term *surplus*. Better terminology for the legal concept would be Dedicated Capital, Returnable Capital, Revaluation Capital and Retained Earnings. Use of the term "surplus" should be discontinued since it implies profits and availability for dividends, while the Uniform Business Code prohibits dividends from revaluation surplus and requires notification of dividends out of paid-in surplus.

The terms *assets* and *capital* have legal origins, and the latter has numerous meanings in addition to the legal concept of capital being the non-debt portion of the right side of the balance sheet. In economics, capital refers to property and is found on the left side of the balance sheet. Since a business enterprise "is an economic entity before it is a legal entity," the balance sheet should be expressed as Properties (Capital forms) = Investments (Capital sources). A capital statement could be presented showing the kinds of capital, properly classified, on the left and the origins of capital, also properly classified, on the right.

Since suppliers of capital provide a loss-absorbing margin for "outside" suppliers of credit, the word *margin* could logically be substituted for capital, i.e., Creditors Margin (Dedicated Capital), Fluctuation Margin (Returnable and Revaluation Capital), Dividend Margin (Retained Earnings) and Reserved Margin (Surplus Reserves).

CREDITORS' INTEREST IN SURPLUS, *Certified Public Accountant,* XIII (April, 1933), 199-202. [65]

Greater interest is being paid to surplus as a result of the emergence of paid-in surplus and revaluation surplus. The increased use of security issues as a means of financing produced larger amounts of paid-in surplus. The use of the no-par stock device, which at first seemed promising, did not develop satisfactorily and the doctrine of stated value resulted. Stated value was a "pernicious expedient" which enabled directors to designate any part of the capital contributed as a margin of protection for creditors with the balance carried in surplus and held at the discretion of the directors.

Revaluation surplus resulted from the belief that higher earnings justified increased asset valuations. Assets were also written up because of belief in the necessity of recording higher depreciation charges to recover mounting replacement costs. The credit accompanying the recording of appreciation was dumped "in that catch-all, Surplus, and there was no prohibition against" disposal.

The creditors' lines of defense are (1) surplus, (2) capital, and (3) pledged assets. The first of these is under the control of the directors. The second is subject to manipulation over wide ranges. Even the third will not prevent possible loss. Consequently, additional safeguards must be provided if creditors are to be truly protected.

CAPITAL FLEXIBILITY, *Journal of Accountancy,* LVI (August, 1933), 102-8. [66]

Part of this article expresses views similar to those expressed in "Capital and Surplus" (see §64).

The practice of arbitrarily stating the amount of the creditors' margin is a result of the increased use of the corporate form of business enterprise, an increased demand for investment securities, and the introduction of no-par stock.

The flexibility provided by no-par stock in its original issue is ample reason for retaining the device, although restrictions are needed. Acceptance of the whole-contribution concept of capital requires rejection of stated value capital stock. And further, since no direct relationship exists between number of no-par shares issued and the value of the property received, there can be no statutory minimum price.

Under the older practice of creating new corporations to take over old, the problem was one of aggregating capital and issuing ownership evidence. Under the current practice of merging corporations, the problem is one of values, i.e., assets and shares. A problem exists in trying to maintain some agreement between the value of the assets, which fluctuates, and limited liability capital obligations, which are rigid.

The following legal restrictions, relative to corporate capital, may be desirable:

(1) total indebtedness may not exceed a specified percentage of the total assets;

(2) preferred shares should have par value, be preferred as to assets and income, and be cumulative, callable and non-participating;

(3) common shares are to be of no-par value and may be issued for any consideration satisfactory to directors and stockholders;

(4) creditors, including preferred shareholders, should elect a minority (majority in case of default on No. 1 above) of board of directors;

(5) failure to pay interest or principal on debt when due will indicate insolvency and pledged assets may be legally seized.

Such restrictions would give consideration to the interests of all concerned; result in better recognition of the legal distinction between capital suppliers; give creditors a voice in the management of the business and thus a substitute for the fixed sum margin of capital protection while at the same time retaining the flexibility of the capital stock account.

SOCIAL ORIGINS OF MODERN ACCOUNTANCY, *Journal of Accountancy*, LVI (October, 1933), 261-70. [67]

The first part of this article consists of a rather detailed analysis of factors contributing to the development of double-entry bookkeeping and is similar to that found in "The Antecedents of Double-Entry" (see §51).

The nineteenth century development of professional auditing is analogous to the development of double-entry bookkeeping in the sense that both are the results of prevailing conditions. The growth of commerce resulted in a demand for greater freedom to incorporate. The unpleasant experience of earlier fraudulent stock promotions produced a desire for some sort of protective device. The feudal system of earlier times necessitated some sort of control by the master over his servants' and officers' activities — an audit. Combined, these factors resulted in the advent of professional auditing.

A similar analogy can be drawn in relation to the development of accounting theory. Although some of the development of accounting theory can be attributed to curious teachers of bookkeeping, the "many problems raised by corporations have created more discussion — and hence more theory." The limited liability feature of corporations made it necessary to keep intact the capital contribution, and thus capital had to be distinguished from income. As a result, greater attention had to be paid to distinguishing between asset and expense. The "definite continuity of life" and interchangeable membership features of the corporation produced an "economic obligation to maintain the productive power of the enterprise." Here again profit determination was of vital importance. Finally, the delegated management aspect of corporations produced the need for financial information as a substitute for "personal acquaintance" with a business by investors.

Cost accounting also developed from the conditions encountered in business by those charged with the record-keeping function. "The soil in which cost accounting grew was the factory system of production. But it needed the sun of the industrial revolution to help it grow toward its destiny." With the industrial revolution's production of power machinery came problems of accounting for depreciation, fixed assets, overhead, etc. "Costing therefore, like double-entry bookkeeping, auditing and accounting theory, was a product of surrounding conditions."

SOCIALIZED ACCOUNTS, *Accounting Review,* VIII (December, 1933), 267-71; IX (March, 1934), 67-74. [68]

The development of accounting may be divided into three phases. The initial, and longest, phase consisted of two "distinct movements." The first of these movements was the development of bookkeeping — the methodology and mechanics of recording data. The later movement covered the period in which double-entry bookkeeping was expanded to meet changing conditions. The exact origin of double-entry bookkeeping is lost in history, although credit for one of the distinctive elements of double-entry — cancellation by contra entry — can be given to medieval money brokers or can be said to have resulted from early Roman cash book practices. Proprietorship, especially in the sense of productive wealth, generated the need for double-entry bookkeeping.

The second movement of the first phase consisted of the development of what is now called theory. A few teachers recognized the limitations of teaching solely by a process of memorizing rules and sought to bring out the reasonableness and logic of bookkeeping. The development and use of the corporate form of organization may be cited as the second source of theory. Cost accounting was also a part of the second movement of the first phase. The center of attention shifted from the recording of exchanges to the recording of conversions. Budgeting is also a part of the first phase and is "a sign that business is beginning to believe that it may be, in some measure, master of its own destiny, and that planning is not impossible."

The second phase of the development of accounting had its beginning in the use of accounts to control "unsocial individualism." The British Companies Acts sought to control private business by making their accounts semi-public. Despite the "blue sky" laws in many states and the recent passage of the Federal Securities Act, American attempts to secure this control have not been as thoroughgoing as those of the British. Business must recognize the social aspects of its actions and engage in enlightened self-control, or further controls will be imposed upon it by government.

Thus, the third phase of accounting's development appears. Accounting will certainly play a larger part in the self-government of business than it has played in the partial sharing of accounting data as found in the second phase. Already various authors are outlining plans whereby business would be controlled by representatives of capital, labor and the public. Under some of these plans accountants will play a major role, not only in the supplying of data, but also in the auditing of business data. This third phase in the development of accounting may result in "the socialization of accounting through universal accounts and the statistical tabulation of extensive accounting data . . . [and] it may also include the ultimate elevation of auditing to the judicial place for which its nature so well designs it. . . . The period ahead then should be one in which auditing is consciously striving to achieve a real maturity."

THE DIVIDEND BASE, *Accounting Review,* IX (June, 1934), 140-48. [69]

The profits test and the excess-assets test are the two common bases for determination of the availability of a distributable dividend. If the cost principle is followed, thereby excluding the possibility of revaluation surplus, the two bases are identical. Recent statutes, or changes therein, tend to follow the assets test, although the profits test is to be preferred.

The assets test provisions usually do not resolve the problem of the basis of asset valuation. Furthermore, this test is basically a maintenance of capital test rather than a specific directive regarding dividends, and the control aspect is therefore negative rather than positive.

One of the major arguments advanced in support of the assets test is that it affords protection for the creditor. However, "there seems to be a failure to recognize the fact that other parties may be even more concerned in the results of operations of a business than the creditors and that interests of the former may not be satisfactorily met by describing divisible funds in terms of aggregate assets and aggregate of debts and capital."

A correct statement of profits is most significant to management, bondholders, stockholders and government. Since a profits test would protect creditors (by making directors personally liable for dividends not meeting this test) as well as they are now protected, it is logical to retain only the profits test which serves equally well all parties at interest. The problem of definition of profits distributable as dividends is of lesser magnitude than the problem of definition of maintenance of capital.

DIVIDENDS PRESUPPOSE PROFITS, *Accounting Review,* IX (December, 1934) 304-11. [70]

The assets (or capital maintenance) test pertaining to the legality of dividends has not yielded satisfactory results because of the failure of the statutes to define the capital which must be maintained. The profits test has a far greater potential for success because the nature of profits is more widely understood and the accountant is better able to measure profits than capital.

A complete understanding of the differences between realized and unrealized profits as well as earned versus unearned profits is needed. Corporate statutes might well include these distinctions. Operating gains and losses must also be distinguished from realized value increments and decrements (capital gains and losses). There is no logical reason for including the latter in taxable income. Capital gains or losses could be carried to a capital valuation account or to paid-in surplus. With minor modification, the earned surplus account would show only earned profits.

Legal recognition should be granted to the distinction between earned income and income financially available for dividends. Under present corporation law, both realized and unrealized income may be carried to earned surplus. Present understanding of earned surplus as income available for dividends ignores many real restrictions upon dividends, such as contracts with security holders and ability to pay.

In keeping with a concept of surplus as earned and available for distribution, a reserve created out of earned surplus should be closed to a non-distributable capital surplus account when the saved current assets are converted to fixed assets. Similar reasoning and treatment are applicable to sinking fund reserves for debt retirement. Surplus is also unavailable for dividends to the extent that a certain minimum of working capital is necessary; for this reason a reservation of surplus should be made.

AUDITOR INDEPENDENCE, *Journal of Accountancy,* LIX (April, 1935), 283-91. [71]

Many reasons exist for believing that it would not be desirable to adopt, in the United States, the British plan of having a company's auditors elected by its stockholders. Included in the array of reasons are: (1) the fact that the British are not completely satisfied with their system; (2) the difficulty of securing stockholder attendance at meetings; (3) the use in the United States of a wide variety of securities contracts with widely varying provisions, with the result that there is no longer a simple pooling of capital by individuals having the same interests.

The possibilities for investor protection by the use of experienced public accountants have not been fully explored. Unfortunately, public accountants who may be qualified to serve are not free to do so with any real degree of independence because the manner in which they are engaged precludes any real power to enforce their recommendations; they may be dismissed and their reports suppressed.

To remedy these defects, Federal Securities legislation should be amended to require that statements submitted to the SEC be prepared and certified by auditors licensed by the SEC. The requirements for obtaining a license should be enumerated by the commission, which should also set forth the auditor's duties. Because disputes could arise between licensed auditors and their clients, a "board of financial review" should be established to serve as a court of arbitration. Members of the board would be appointed by the president from a list of nominees prepared by leading accounting organizations. Derelict auditors should be subject to clearly defined civil and criminal penalties.

The above plan would bring corporate transactions and proposals under a quasi-judicial scrutiny, thus ending unsound practices and providing a method of review for disputed issues. It would also place the public accountant in a position to make a real contribution toward providing investors with protection against deceit.

EDUCATIONAL BROWSING, *Journal of Accountancy,* LIX (May, 1935), 330-38. [72]

In the education of prospective accountants, certainly the ability to write is of great importance. However, it is not necessary to restrict the practice of writing to report writing. The important objective is the ability to express ideas.

The study of economics and business law must not be neglected by persons whose professional work is very intimately associated with these fields of knowledge.

Rather than attempting to lead the student to broad literary browsing in his college days, we should "give him the technique of browsing, so to speak, lead him to taste its delights."

Not all aspects of culture such as generosity, tolerance and kindness, can be derived from literary browsing. However, "intellectual interests can be stimulated and directed in college courses and in college browsing, and the faculty of appreciation can be uncovered and nurtured a little." The productive time for cultural development is available after college.

A number of books in the fields of education, geography, history, economics, philosophy, science, drama, etc., in which accountants might browse are suggested.

VALUE OR COST, *Accounting Review,* X (September, 1935), 269-73. [73]

Accountants have used the term *valuation* so frequently that they have misled others to believe that valuation is an important part of the accounting process. In reality, much of what is referred to as valuation is actually nothing more than cost apportionment among periods. Historically, cost has been the basis of accounting.

Two reasons for the use of the term valuation are the lack of an acceptable substitute and the failure to distinguish between *value-in-use* and *value-in-exchange.* Value-in-use is "an expression of the direct utility present; value-in-exchange comes to be an expression of marginal utility."

The task of the accountant is to record and trace value-in-use (cost price) from the time it enters a firm until it leaves. Value-in-exchange is too fleeting and subjective to be used as a basis for accounting.

Although original cost has historically been the basis of accounting, considerable pressures have been exerted by various interests at different times for manipulation of this cost basis. Tax laws, the higher price levels of the twenties, regulatory commission use of replacement cost, dividend statutes, bankers' conservatism, the writedowns of the depression, authority vested in boards of directors relative to asset valuation, etc., have all, at one time or other, caused accountants to move from the original cost basis of accounting.

Accountants need training in debate and the unity of professional opinion; they also "should be (1) thoroughly educated in economics, corporation finance, and corporation law in addition to accountancy as such, (2) given authority to criticize valuations and financial adjustments, and (3) afforded protection in that criticism." Such prerequisites "would add immeasurably to sane finance." If professional opinion could be solidified behind "the most important accounting standards, then clinging to costs would be not only desirable but possible."

AN INEVITABLY MEDIOCRE BUREAUCRACY, *Journal of Accountancy,* LX (October, 1935), 264-69. [74]

The suggestion that the SEC be empowered to license auditors and that a "board of financial review" be created to arbitrate disputes between independent public accountants and their clients, as advocated in "Auditor Independence" (see §71), has been attacked as leading to "an inevitably mediocre bureaucracy."

This attack is indicative of the lack of trust in the integrity and qualifications of the accountants who would presumably serve on the "board of financial review." Top professional men could be attracted to such a court by means of long appointments, generous salaries and substantial retirement pensions. Such men of professional skill and integrity would be independent and just in their decisions.

The court's decisions would establish a body of precedent, as in law, which "would dispense with the necessity for any regulations by the S.E.C. regarding the technical duties of an auditor." These decisions, coupled with a broad outline of the auditor's duties, would insure a sound basis for accounting development without binding auditors to detailed regulations and directives.

CONTRASTING THEORIES OF PROFIT, *Accounting Review,* XI (March, 1936), 10-15. [75]

In primitive barter, the basic concept of profit is: "*Profit is an individual's opinion of the increase of total utility, usefulness, or value-in-use that is his as the result of an exchange.*" Certain characteristics of profit appear in the barter situation. The first is that profit is an illusive element, and the second is that the "clue to its existence is *relative utility.*" The former is the basis for the so-called realization principle.

In an economy using money as a medium of exchange the concept of profit can be restated: "*Profit, quantitatively expressed, is the excess of the prices received in bargaining exchanges over the prices previously given.*" The assumptions here are that bargained prices do reflect relative utilities, and that quantified judgments are more useful than imagined advantages in a series of exchanges. Money can be used to quantify and render homogeneous diverse elements, and bookkeeping is an instrument of "quantification." However, the illusive nature of profit remains unchanged and profit figures must still be accepted only with caution.

With the advent of accrual accounting, which has as its purpose the contrasting of inflowing and outflowing services, the concept of profit may be stated: "*Profit (net income) is the result of providing an out-put of economic services (thereby causing an in-flow of gross revenue) which is valued by the purchaser above the amount of in-put of economic services (brought about by an out-flow of expense) required to produce the services put out.*" This refinement of the analysis of things given and things received makes possible a closer comparison of services rendered to others with disservices experienced in rendering the service. The existence of profit or loss indicates to the producer whether he has been successful in providing a service at a price which was acceptable in the market.

The latter concept of profit has been challenged with the suggestion that profit is the excess of revenues over replacement cost. The source of this challenge has come from utility rate discussions and from European situations where deliberate money inflations have been experienced. However, there are too many fallacious assumptions underlying this concept of profit to accept the idea that unusual, temporary conditions should be allowed to dictate the formulation of a concept of profit.

THE PROFESSIONAL COLLEGE, *Accounting Review,* XI (June, 1936), 109-16. [76]

The time has come, perhaps, to drop the experience requirement as a prerequisite to the CPA examination and to substitute education for such experience. Statistics indicate that those with experience have no greater success in taking the examination than those without it. The experience requirement is a carry-over from the old apprenticeship programs instituted when adequate training was not available in colleges, universities and schools.

If the experience requirement is to be dropped, a question then arises as to what sort of education is to be required. A number of suggestions have been offered which for the most part overlook the contributions of the present four-year programs offered by colleges and universities.

The time has not yet arrived for the establishment of professional schools of accountancy. The products of the four-year programs have not been thoroughly tested for adequacy. Sufficient literature and teaching materials are not available for a specialized three-year program in accountancy based upon two years of general education. A problem also exists in staffing such a school with professional teachers and professional practitioners. Also, the "layer-system" of piling three years of specialized education on top of two years of general education is not the only way to gain the desired intellectual and physical maturity.

Drawing an analogy to the professional schools of law or medicine is unwise since accountancy's situation is not really analogous. Medical schools require considerable training in science in the basic years because of the tremendous importance of science to medicine. Law programs are based upon any field of study. Both, however, because of the amount and complexity of knowledge and material, are highly specialized in their professional schools. This is not now true of accountancy.

The profession can exert a steady pressure for improved educational preparation by: (1) giving university graduates of commerce schools a thorough trial; (2) seeking amendments to state laws requiring college education in business as a prerequisite to taking the CPA exam; (3) having the examination given in two parts, one immediately after graduation, the other after one or two years of experience; (4) establishing a joint committee to assist colleges and universities in improving the quality of their offerings.

CONCEPTS OF INCOME UNDERLYING ACCOUNTING, *Accounting Review*, XIII, (March, 1937), 13-22. [77]

Factors such as attention to debt-paying ability and the legality of dividends have led to preoccupation with the balance sheet and seem to give observers the idea that accounting is more interested in capital than income. In reality, "capital is only a means to an end; income is that end."

"The emphasis given by the American Institute of Accountants to the importance of correct income determination and to the isolation of earned surplus, thus join with the new form of audit certificate to indicate a return to basic first principles. Profit, being the focal center of business enterprise, is likewise the focal center of account-keeping."

Accountants must adopt the businessman's point of view of income which is "that *output* is the result of definitely planned work — the consequence of a prior *service-input* made with intent to create output; *money-income* is the earning flowing from the planned work — the consequence of a prior *money-outlay* made with intent to generate income." Income is the money expression of the enterpriser's efforts. Income is the result of revenue, a passive element, being in excess of cost, an active element.

"Costs . . . are quantitative measures of policies translated into action." Cost data are more useful to management than revenue data since costs are more directly under the control of management. Costs are causal factors as is clearly seen in the cost accountant's refusal to add the overhead on idle equipment to the product produced by other equipment, and by his refusal to carry overhead to subsequent periods when it cannot possibly contribute to the production of that period.

A further refinement of accrual accounting which accountants might now undertake is "to distinguish earned income produced and derived profit received." Earned income is the result of revenues generated by costs incurred, while derived profits result from "alienation of property, adjustment of debts or capital structure, or other activities unrelated to the direct performance of the enterprise's particular economic function." At the same time, the principles for distinguishing between asset and expense can be expanded to allow drawing a line of distinction between expense and loss. Drawing such a line could result in allocation to time periods becoming incidental rather than controlling.

BUSINESS PROFITS AS A LEGAL BASIS FOR DIVIDENDS, *Harvard Business Review,* XVI (Autumn, 1937), 51-61. [78]

The two principal influences upon accounting of the Uniform Business Corporation Act have been the isolation and denial of appraisal surplus as a basis for the declaration of cash dividends.

Unfortunately, with regard to the determination of the legality of dividends, "the act also seems to have encouraged a drift toward the further use of the capital impairment test." The use of this test fails "to follow either the spirit of the common law doctrine of a profit base or the general understanding that men have of the nature of dividends. Instead the emphasis upon the impairment test marks an apparent tendency to stress a technicality of protecting creditors of corporations endowed with limited liability."

The many inherent dangers and problems encountered in applying the capital impairment test make the profits test far superior as a measure of determining the legality of dividends. Various concepts of profits and the source of profits can be found in business, economics and law. However, "the Federal Government has recognized the capabilities of public accountants by laying important responsibilities upon them through the income tax laws and the securities acts." Therefore, provisions in statutory law relating to tests for the legality of dividends should be framed so as to place reliance upon the accountant's ability and judgment. Problems of interpretation of a single rule or definition would be avoided and, at the same time, the law would be simplified and brought "into closer harmony with an elemental doctrine of common law . . . dividends presuppose profits."

Accounting now possesses sufficiently mature concepts of profit and techniques for applying the concepts in concrete situations so that "statutory law may confidently rely upon these concepts and techniques."

TESTS FOR PRINCIPLES, *Accounting Review,* XIII (March, 1938), 16-24. [79]

In the conflict over terms such as conventions, generalizations, rules, postulates, principles, standards, practices, etc., a notable advance has recently been made, in that the conflict has been resolved into a question of rules versus principles.

The suggested test of a principle is "that every fundamental principle will be found to be expressive of a coercive or compelling force which carries a penalty for violation of the principle." This coercive force is lodged in economic law, not in accounting. "Accounting principles, then, express fundamental truths about a business enterprise." They may be recognized by way of experimentation and observation, or they may be subject to logical analysis in that the conclusions are tied to acceptable premises. "Fundamental truths in accounting, therefore, may either be generalized out of practical experience or deduced from stated premises which are accepted as true in themselves, or proved to be true by argument." Although logic may lead to a conclusion which will not work well, such an analysis is not useless "for it will have increased our care in weighing the reasons for doing otherwise than logic and consistency might dictate."

The "hypothetical syllogism" form of logic can be used to test accounting principles. For example: "*Major Premise:* (antecedent) If verifiable events like bargained prices constitute the best objective evidence of the reality of new values, (consequent) then revenue from actual sales is a valid realization of profit. *Minor Premise:* (affirming the antecedent) The best objective evidence of the reality of new value (profit) is found in verifiable events. *Conclusion:* (the consequent is true) Therefore revenue from actual sales is a valid realization of profit."

The same form of reasoning may be employed to prove the validity of the following: the matching, historical cost and realization principles, the differentiation of earned surplus from other forms of surplus and from capital, and the basing of dividends upon earned surplus alone.

Thus, through the use of rules of logic, the present body of accepted accounting principles, generalized out of practice, can be subjected to serious study with the development of new principles as a possible result.

HIGH STANDARDS OF ACCOUNTING, *Journal of Accountancy,* LXVI (August, 1938), 99-104. [80]

The concepts of *rules* and *principles* imply rigidity, conformance and a universality which are not realistically applied to accounting. The word *standards,* on the other hand, is more reasonably applied to accounting because "a standard directs a high, but attainable, level of action, without precluding justifiable variations." Accounting standards should be considered normative, and an established standard a guide and not a control. While departures "from standard will always be possible, . . . the burden of proof falls upon the one who advocates a variation."

Illustrative of an accounting standard is the practice of segregating capital from income, which is followed because "transactions in capital equities and transactions in asset utilization are to be sufficiently separated by accounting processes to avoid mixing (a) financial activities concerned with funds and (b) operating activities concerned with assets." This, of course, should be the basic standard for determining whether a particular transaction should be reported via the income statement or the balance sheet. For example, losses should not be carried to surplus because they pertain to fixed assets, are extraordinary and non-recurring, are large relative to current earnings, or because the related assets were related to capital stock. These are invalid criteria.

The concept of standards as points from which departure may be permitted "would emphasize the quasi-judicial nature of the public accountant's consideration of the reasons given him in individual cases in support of departures from the standard."

THE RELATION OF FUNCTION TO PRINCIPLE, *Accounting Review,* XIII (September, 1938), 233-41. [81]

Criticisms of the American Accounting Association's "Tentative Statement of Accounting Principles" fall into two categories. The first of these relates to various details such as the use of vague phrases, elevations of propositions to the status of principles, definitions, unexplained inconsistencies and applications of principles. Much of this criticism is valid, but the second category raises questions of far greater importance.

The position taken by the statement, "the practices that are acceptable at any given time are not thereby made good practices," should be clarified. The statement also rests upon a clear conception of the function of accounting. This single function is "to supply dependable, relevant information about a business enterprise." It embraces three associated functions of accounting: protection of equities, control and records-keeping. For example, protection of equities is but a part of the control function which is based on data supplied by accounting records.

Accounting principles and standards guiding the collection and reporting of information must be unified about the central theme of the economic activities of the enterprise. The enterprise acquires goods and services from others, converts and utilizes them to provide others with new goods and services. Information concerning these activities is of interest to all, especially to management and investors. Therefore a statement of principles must be formulated with the determination of earning power, at least partially, in mind.

The information supplied must be based on the objective, verifiable and factual basis of historical cost, and the matching of cost-prices with revenue-prices within stated periods. The present practice of writing down current assets to market, when it is lower than cost, plays havoc with attempts to weave a consistent body of accounting theory. A question may be raised whether the determination of profit is complete without deducting from revenues "all risks predictable by experience" in addition to expenses. Certainly accounting principles cannot be woven into a single coordinated body of theory if the principles are inconsistent in themselves.

A Substitute for Stated Capital, *Harvard Business Review,* XVII (Autumn, 1938), 75-84. [82]

Early corporation law, concerned mainly with problems encountered in the formation of new organizations, did not allow the payment of dividends except from profits. This provision was a carry-over from the ideas concerning distributions from trusts and estates rather than an attempt to provide creditor protection.

In the next significant stage of development, corporation law recognized the importance of the creditor since stockholder capital was viewed as a capital fund pledged to protect the creditor. Losses incurred, which reduced the capital, had to be replaced with earnings before dividends could be paid.

The third stage in the development of corporation law is characterized by the use of no-par, stated value stock. The use of such stock gave management greater flexibility in the financial direction of a corporation, but placed greater risks upon the creditor.

Corporation law has the dual obligation of providing adequate safeguards for creditors and poorly informed absentee stockholders and of protecting the freedom of management to act as judgment dictates to meet the changing fortunes of the business.

Present laws are often inadequate, because true creditor protection rests more upon the relative proportions of debt and stock rather than on any stated sum of capital. Substitution of an asset-debt ratio for stated capital would necessitate solving a number of problems, such as the manner in which assets are to be valued and whether preferred stocks are to be treated as debt or equity capital. In addition, the problem of determining the size of the ratio to establish the limitation on dividends would have to be faced. Such problems are not incapable of solution.

An asset-debt ratio would serve dually as a creditor and management freedom protecting device, since it does allow management the freedom to reorganize the capital structure if necessary while providing creditors with a prescribed and definite degree of protection.

SUGGESTIONS FOR THE REVISION OF THE TENTATIVE STATEMENT OF ACCOUNTING PRINCIPLES, *Accounting Review,* XIV (March, 1939), 57-64. [83]

The committee should, in the proposed revision, "attempt to state the essentials of a coherent and consistent view of accounting theory resting upon the function and basic concepts of accounting."

"It is an important accounting standard that recognition of revenue for reporting purposes shall rest upon verifiable, objective evidence." Accounting standards should preserve the concept that revenue is to be associated with performance, and the recognition of revenue should neither be anticipated nor delayed beyond performance. Deviation from this standard is acceptable in installment sales and long-term construction contracts. Cost must also be subjected to the test of objectivity and must rest upon exchanges between independent parties. Cash disbursed is not necessarily the objective test to be applied, because the credit system may afford control over services before payment is made. Devaluation of plant, or the writeoff of goodwill or organization cost do not meet the test of objectivity and are departures from standard.

"The central problem of accounting is to bring into association, in the present, the revenues identified with the present and their related costs, and to bring into association, in the future, the revenues identified with the future and their related costs." The balance sheet is the means for carrying forward the "not-yet-deducted costs." In this concept of a balance sheet there is no room for "valuation." Such a concept does not deny the usefulness of other than historical cost data; it merely excludes such other data from the accounts.

If, however, for credit purposes, a more "conservative" balance sheet is desired, showing, for example, inventories at the lower of cost or market, such a writedown of inventories could be shown in the non-operating section of the income statement and the inventory shown reduced by a reserve account.

Arguments are currently raging over the proper statement presentation of unusual items, that is, whether such items should be shown in the income statement or charged directly to surplus. If surplus is properly viewed as being accumulated and withdrawable capital, then direct charges to surplus for unusual items become untenable.

THE USES OF THEORY, *Journal of Accountancy,* LXVII (April, 1939), 227-33. [84]

The evolution of the methods of teaching bookkeeping began with description, followed by the formulation of rules. Simple rules could be memorized, but one still had to use reasoning to select the proper account to receive the entries. With reasoning came theory. Another important step was the recognition of the classification of related accounts as a fundamental characteristic of bookkeeping. This, in turn, led to the recognition of the purpose of bookkeeping and the significance of the content and interrelationship of accounts. "Transaction analysis now rests upon that foundation — the theory of accounts."

Other aspects of accounting theory pertain to the relationship of capital and revenue charges, "maintaining physical property or a money total of investment," and the problems posed by capital gains and losses.

Theory "reached down to such basic elements as honesty and truth, considered in the light of the parties at interest and the purposes to be served by accounting." Theory, having developed from practice, appears to explain that which is done in accounting. However, it also has the duty of "strengthening practice by subjecting customs to analysis and testing their justification by finding the relation of the ideas represented to basic concepts and purposes."

Accounting ideas must be organized into an integrated whole, and this integrated whole, which must be free to grow and develop, we may call accounting theory. While absolute knowledge and truth remain elusive, "accounting theory can still afford a basis for distinguishing necessary or useful variations and unnecessary or deceptive variations."

ACCOUNTING RESEARCH, *Accounting Forum,* XI (November, 1939), 21-22. [85]

"Research is thinking." It involves careful examination of the evidence and the ability to distinguish between the relevant and irrelevant. Training in research is training in exercising judgment and discrimination.

"Research is also hunting" not only for material about a particular problem but to find the problem itself. Reading, especially in current accounting literature, will uncover many problems and a number of ideas or thoughts pertaining thereto.

Research is possible in many areas. For example, histories could be compiled of the accounting profession, professional legislation, auditing, cost accounting and the administrative use of accounting. A study could be made of the relationship of accounting to law and the courts. Research could also be undertaken to determine whether accounting meets the demands placed upon it by corporation financial practice, corporation dividend law, income tax practice and corporation managerial practice.

THE INTEGRATION OF INCOME AND SURPLUS STATEMENTS, *Journal of Accountancy,* LXIX (January, 1940), 30-40. [86]

The trend toward the presentation of a single statement of income and surplus should be continued. The controversy over the nature of surplus has settled into the practice of "separately stating appraisal surplus, paid-in surplus, and earned surplus."

Recent statements by the Institute have been steps in the right direction, in that doubtful charges to capital surplus have been limited. Agreement should be reached on typical items which may be charged to capital surplus, thereby implying that items not mentioned should be associated with current income or earned surplus.

In financial reporting, a balance sheet alone is inadequate, because the assets are the result of "a mixture of equity transactions and economic transactions." A natural emphasis upon the income statement follows, indicating recognition of the role income plays in judging enterprise value and managerial efficiency.

The integrated income and surplus statement emphasizes the lack of preciseness in periodic reports, and all items of income and expense, profit and loss must be included. The combined statement makes it possible to distinguish between capital losses and operating losses as well as to indicate their similarities, which otherwise is not done. Surplus adjustments become more meaningful when associated with current income.

The preferred form of combined statement would show operating net income, recurring non-operating income and expense, corrections of recurring income and expense of prior years, non-recurring losses and gains with the cumulative result obtained thus far being added to the beginning earned surplus balance. This would be followed by showing changes in surplus reserves and dividends and, finally, the earned surplus balance at the end of the year, as per the balance sheet.

Wide differences of opinion exist with respect to the location of certain items in the combined statement, especially with regard to non-operating, non-recurring gains or losses.

A GENEALOGY FOR "COST OR MARKET," *Accounting Review,* XVI (June, 1941), 161-67. [87]

While the real origin of the widely used lower of cost or market rule is unknown, enough evidence is available to indicate that the rule is grounded in expediency and convenience. Herein lies the basis for the notion that "taking inventory is a process of evaluation rather than a process of cost-pricing."

Inventories were priced below purchase cost as early as the beginning of the fifteenth century, perhaps due to the heavy taxes levied upon property. "Valuing" the inventory probably arises from Paciolo's book and his instructions therein. After the development of the practice of maintaining records, "*costing* the inventory [became] the usual case and valuing the inventory the exception."

The cost or market rule was also applied in cases where actual prices were not available, and there is some evidence that the rule was followed in order to ensure a profit on the sale of goods. The provisions in French law from 1673-1807 caused one French writer to caution against estimating merchandise at more than it was worth. The German Commercial Code of 1897 specifically required the use of the cost or market rule for merchandise and securities that had a price quoting market.

Regardless of this support from law, there is no reason why accountants should give a "rule of law the status of a general rule of accounting." The cost or market rule "is a special rule applicable to special circumstances." The primary rule should be "that inventories should generally be priced at cost on a first-in, first-out basis."

INVENTORY VARIATIONS, *Journal of Accountancy,* LXXII (July, 1941), 7-16. [88]

Principles can and should be distinguished from standards. Principles are statements of some importance concerning a particular aspect of accounting. Principles are not laws. The term "accounting standards" is to be preferred, since, unlike principles or rules, variations from standard are implied in the term itself. This idea of variation from standard can be illustrated with an example involving inventory valuation.

The inventory standard is that goods are priced at cash purchase price or the cost of production. Withdrawals are priced at the earliest purchase or production price. The pricing basis is cost.

A necessary variation is found when goods are damaged or destroyed. The cost of the damaged or destroyed goods is transferred to profit or loss when recognized.

An acceptable variation is found when the market value of the inventory has declined below cost and parenthetical notation of this fact is made in the balance sheet.

A questionable variation is that of changing prices in the inventory when current replacement price is less than actual purchase price.

A rejected variation is that of pricing unsold goods at any price higher than cost.

QUESTIONS ON ACCOUNTING STANDARDS, *Accounting Review,* XVI (December, 1941), 330-40. [89]

Principles, standards and rules are not synonymous. Rules dictate action to be taken; principles deal with reasons why rules are what they are; standards are bases against which to compare possible alternative actions. Standards should not be unchanging, but should be stated by authoritative bodies who have considered all the appropriate aspects. Standards cannot be established by each individual for his own use. The term "measured consideration" is used rather than "money value" since accounting statements do not reflect "value."

With respect to the income statement, the position taken in the monograph is that it is the more important single statement, because it covers a period of time. It is not necessary that it be read in conjunction with the balance sheet or vice versa. Each supplements the other, but neither is useless without the other. Data presented by the accountant may be of interest to the creditor. The accountant's primary task, however, is to provide information to the owner-manager group. Accountants should adhere to the cost basis of accounting, but this does not rule out the use of the quasi-reorganization device. The income statement should show both earned income — that resulting from the utilization of an asset, and realized profit — that resulting from nothing more than the giving up of an asset. The accrual idea, with respect to the taking up of interest revenue, should not be extended to operating assets and used as a basis for recognizing accretion due to natural causes. "Profits from present transactions must be measured by accounting methods. Evidence may indicate that these profits may be dissipated by later transactions. But that opinion cannot change the present fact." Hence, the excess of revenue over original cost is "real" although it may be conservative, anticipating future changes (higher purchase prices) before disbursing assets as dividends.

With respect to inventories, original cost should be written off as not recoverable only when the evidence is "irrefutable." The reasoning behind writing off the costs of damaged or obsolete goods is that an irrevocable loss has occurred, which is not true in the case of price declines in merchandise normally purchased. ". . . price changes for others' transactions can hardly constitute conclusive or even persuasive evidence of actual loss in our unsold goods." The first-in, first-out flow of costs expresses that which is usual in business, and standards must be built around the usual rather than the unusual. The cost or market rule is not repudiated because of its relationship to conservatism but because of doubts as to the wisdom of overstating costs of goods sold, of anticipating losses before they have occurred, etc. Accounting measurements can be more precise than those obtained from the arbitrary cost or market rule.

THE MEANING OF ACCOUNTING EDUCATION, *Accounting Review*, XVII (July, 1942), 215-21. [90]

In accounting as in other fields, it is true that no single combination of teaching and experience will yield the best results under all circumstances. Programs for education in accounting may vary according to the degree of emphasis placed upon accounting relative to other subjects.

Some individuals "may need only an appreciation of accountancy as one of a number of social institutions." That is, knowledge of the fact that accounting is used in the social interest as a means to achieve regulation of business may be sufficient for some. College curricula seldom include courses taking this approach.

A second type of program involving education in accounting is that found in business administration, where the student gains an understanding of accounting as an instrument to be used in decision making. In such a program, attention is paid to the meaning and interpretation of items found in the various accounting reports rather than to basic accounting techniques. Stress is placed upon management's need for authoritative facts and upon the theories of accounting which influence the presentation or determination of such facts.

A third type of program is that designed for those who wish to become professional accountants. It embraces far greater amounts of knowledge than the above two programs, but does not by-pass the type of knowledge presented in them. Students in this category "must *know* accountancy." However, "a profession should rest upon a wide knowledge rather than a narrow training." Consequently, training must be secured in all of those areas which relate to business organization and management. Additional questions arise whether a man can be informed about business and its operation without knowing something about the social aspects of business. Does a prospective professional man need to study history, languages, the fine arts, mathematics, science, etc.? If so, how much? The time has come for research and debate on such questions.

AUDITING TECHNIQUES, *Journal of Accountancy,* LXXIV (August, 1942), 106-10. [91]

Mr. Samuel J. Broad, in an article in the *Journal of Accountancy* for November, 1941, implies that the Committee on Auditing Procedure of the Institute will present a statement on auditing standards to replace the pamphlet "Examination of Financial Statements." In his article Mr. Broad compressed the 152 items found in the above pamphlet, which an auditor must do in the examination of a small or moderate sized company, to 27 standards which are "excellent generalizations about the auditor's principal responsibilities." However, these 27 standards still form an inadequate basis for "good professional judgment." They should be expanded "in the direction of theory and technique."

Auditing standards must be established since good judgment does not result from the application of memorized rules. Once standards are established we must be prepared to deal with alternatives and departures from standards.

For each particular area for which standards are to be developed there should be listed (1) auditing standards applicable (a statement of the auditor's duties); (2) the underlying accounting theory (a statement of correct accounting treatment, with perhaps a brief list of references); (3) auditing techniques to be employed (a brief list of methods which auditors have found useful and frequently encountered alternatives).

Such a procedure would result in rather extensive pamphlets covering auditing standards. However, this must not be condemned because "a minimum audit program has apparently done but little to create public confidence in the profession . . . authoritative literature might do so if it plainly showed that the choices made by auditors were not accidental or wilful or biased but deliberate and reasoned."

EXAMINATIONS IN AUDITING, *Accounting Review,* XVIII (October, 1943), 307-16. [92]

A study by Howard F. Stettler of the CPA examinations given during the period 1896 to 1941 shows a clear trend toward the increase of auditing theory and non-auditing questions together with a decrease in questions dealing with auditing procedure.

A further trend to be noted, in addition to a shift in the ranking of the types of questions presented, is that while early examinations dealt with the theory of accounts, in later examinations theory is to be explored from the standpoint of the accounting statements. A decrease is also found in the number of questions dealing with auditing as a "process of checking details and verifying accounts," for which questions dealing with the social significance of the auditor as a professional person have been substituted.

On the whole, changes in the examination content have been few in relation to the changes in auditing as a profession. More questions dealing with the audit report and the auditor's responsibility in situations involving questionable acts by management are needed.

Many questions still remain unanswered, especially the question of whether the examination can truly measure an accountant's ability. Questions dealing with corporation finance, taxation and regulatory accounting should be included. Too much emphasis has been placed upon "memory tests of textbook material." More "essay type" questions should be included, as well as questions dealing with the exercise of judgment.

The examination in accounting theory and practice has been quite successful. What is needed now is an examination in auditing theory and procedure.

OCCUPATIONAL LEVELS IN PUBLIC ACCOUNTING, *Journal of Accountancy,* LXXVIII (December, 1944), 470-76. [93]

An outline of the qualities and responsibilities relative to the various levels of employment in public accounting would be useful as "a means of helping the public to an understanding of the fact that many aspects of a real profession are inherent in the practice of public accounting." Such a study should also prove useful to the growing public accounting firm in handling its staff personnel problems. A third use of such an outline would be to inform staff accountants who aspire to higher positions of what is expected of them in their present position and in the higher positions. Finally, it should be useful to the college student who is contemplating a career in public accounting.

Such an outline should emphasize the need for continuous preparation including the need for experience and formal education, not only in accounting but in other areas such as economics, finance, business administration and business law. Also needed is a statement of the responsibilities to be borne, ranging from those of the junior assistant whose responsibilities may be likened to those of a law clerk, to those of the partner who must face, among other responsibilities, the constant problem of maintaining high professional and ethical standards throughout his entire staff. The qualities necessary at each level, such as the need for stamina and a good attitude, conscientiousness and patience by the junior assistant, and the clear need for leadership ability on the part of the partner, should be enumerated.

GUIDANCE TESTS FOR ACCOUNTING STUDENTS, *Accounting Review*, XXI (October, 1946), 404-9. [94]

Relative to the activities of the Committee on Selection of Personnel established by the Institute in 1943, specialists have begun work in the preparation of testing materials. Questions and subject matter must be devised, tested and validated. Also, a set of statistical norms must be established to be used as a standard of comparison.

Rapid progress was experienced in the development of the vocational interest test since a valid test was already in existence.

The Institute's project is a series of achievement tests designed for use at three levels: (1) at the end of the first year of study of accounting, (2) near graduation, and (3) upon the taking of the CPA examination. For the first two tests national norms will be established. The level three achievement test could become a useful adjunct to the CPA examination as collateral data or as a part of the admission rules of the various state boards.

The development of these tests should naturally bring about closer cooperation between the college and the practicing accountant, and each should benefit as well as the student. More light may be shed upon the type of education or training needed for success in the profession by collecting test data and uniting them with data from curricula and personal transcripts.

There are no plans at the present time to engage in personality testing, but this may reasonably be included at a later time.

THREE AUDIT PRINCIPLES, *Journal of Accountancy,* LXXXIII (April, 1947), 280-82. [95]

Three "principles of auditing" can be developed by combining important ends and means. These principles are:

(1) The balances of accounts and the entries therein should be tested by appropriate audit procedures.

(2) The structure of the accounting system should be examined to check the dependability of account classifications and therefore any interpretations made from the accounts.

(3) Evidence to substantiate management's claims in their financial statements should also be found. Management's accounting policies should also be appraised.

VOCABULARY OF AUDITING TECHNIQUE, *New York Certified Public Accountant,* XVII (October, 1947), 639-44. [96]

The verbs used in auditing literature have some measure of technical significance because they tell what auditors do, and for this reason the verb is the most important part of speech used in a sentence.

A comparison of the verbs found in auditing literature in 1912 and in 1940 showed little change in the number of verbs used. However, one trend can be noted and that is the shift from verbs emphasizing certitude to the use of those merely stressing examination and the completion of certain techniques.

The frequency of the use of a particular verb is not, however, a clue to its significance since frequency does not embrace the qualitative factor. The verbs used can be classified into two categories: those which relate to aims and duties and those which relate to the ways and means of accomplishing the technical work.

The three most important verbs are: ascertain, examine and report. These verbs are important because they in effect mean that the accountant is obligated to satisfy himself as to the accounting truth of that which he examines and reports.

FIXED ASSETS AND ACCOUNTING THEORY, *Illinois Certified Public Accountant,* X (March, 1948), 11-18. [97]

"What do we need to understand about the problem of depreciation under a condition of rising price levels? There are at least three answers."

(1) Accountants must understand that although history repeats itself, seldom is the past duplicated. Accountants must appraise the justifications of the writeups of the twenties and the writedowns of the thirties and those soon to be offered as they seek to advise management.

(2) Accountants must understand the impact of price level change on management, since it is management that actually decides. Shaping policy decision in the light of outside evidence involves the question of value, "and value . . . is not an accounting question."

(3) Accountants must understand why "novel ideas" about depreciation are being advanced. The desire for stability is wholly rational as is the urge to do something about departures from normal.

Accountants should hold fast to cost in the records until the pressure becomes irresistible — when "the time of real full-tide inflation [comes] no accounting record will be useful." Accountants should point out the limitations of accounting, but they should not take over management's responsibilities. Management may make allocations of surplus or additional allotments of "depreciation" out of net income, but accountants should not lay "heavy hands" upon the ledger and submerge the cost data therein.

EXTENSION OF ACCRUAL PRINCIPLES WOULD HELP DEPRECIATION ACCOUNTING, *Journal of Accountancy,* LXXXVI (July, 1948), 21-22. [98]

The problem of what constitutes good accounting treatment is complicated by a contest between two doctrines: that experienced business judgment is the best basis for calculating periodic income since the task is beyond satisfactory treatment by formula, and that freedom to report periodic income according to this judgment will tend to become merely license to manipulate the results willfully and wishfully. Consequently, there is a tendency to place varied restraints on possible treatments and to restrict the freedom to follow the guidance of experience, judgment and the logic of circumstances.

Supplementary charges for depreciation are based upon the same theory as the provision for doubtful accounts. There is no universal formula for the latter and no need for one for the former. The reasonableness of depreciation charges can be tested by hindsight.

Accountants should seek an extension of the principles of accrual accounting, since accounting makes some of its most important contributions by using the accrual method to sharpen periodic income determination.

INVENTORY DISCLOSURES, *New York Certified Public Accountant*, XVIII (November, 1948), 807-10. [99]

The trend of discussion of inventory price may eventually result in the gradual resolution of some of the problems of inventory theory. In time, the traditional "cost or market" rule may be replaced by valuation reserves. Such a change, should it occur, would bring the accounting treatment of inventories up to the same level of informative disclosure that has long been customary for accounts receivable and fixed assets and would replace a rule that has become a traditional habit of thought in inventory pricing.

The use of valuation reserves does not dispense with the question of difference or similarity between (*a*) physical deterioration, (*b*) market deterioration, and (*c*) price level change. If an actual loss exists under (*a*), it should be written off directly. If (*b*) and (*c*) are alike the same treatment should be applied, but if they are different this *unlikeness* should be reflected in the statements. If deterioration or obsolescence is present, the loss is complete and the goods need not assume the status of "doubtful goods." When price level change is involved, the loss is purely hypothetical and the reserve treatment is applicable.

CLASSIFIED OBJECTIVES, *Accounting Review*, XXIV (July, 1949), 281-84. [100]

"Accounting has been developed for the most part inductively out of particulars." The next problem faced was that of organizing the rules and procedures "into a cohesive body of knowledge." A body of knowledge will be recognized as being cohesive if it can be clearly shown that "important relations can be chained downward (deductively) from a top concept."

Accounting thought may be patterned graphically into a pyramid based upon broad accounting action. Thus, basically accounting consists of "(1) *homogenizing* (diverse events), (2) *converting* (events into entries), (3) *classifying* (entries into accounts), (4) *reclassifying* (account data into fiscal periods), (5) *reporting* (summarized periodic data), (6) *reviewing* (accounting data and processes)." The next section of the pyramid would consist of the intermediate objectives of stating objects and events in price data, transforming price data to account data, compressing the mass of account data, assigning such data to time periods, organizing data into reports and examining such reports for adequacy. Antecedent objectives may also be expressed, such as the creation of additional confidence in the reports if they are examined.

At the top of the pyramid rests the top objective of accounting which "is to aid a person to understand a business enterprise by means of data."

INDUCTIVE REASONING IN ACCOUNTING, *New York Certified Public Accountant*, XX (August, 1950), 449-55, 460, XX (November, 1950), 641-51. [101]

In discussions of conventions, rules and principles, differences are usually emphasized when, in reality, the many similarities should be noted. The three concepts were generalized out of satisfactory experience and therefore have a common origin. Also, accountants commonly distinguish between bookkeeping principles and accounting principles although the former are a part of the latter.

Every ledger account has, by convention, two sides, and this convention could be expressed as a rule by adding a justifying reason: "because dynamic balances (those that are modified by either positive or negative changes) are more informative than is a simple total." The chief characteristic of a principle is that it "must express a significant relationship." The above rule can be changed to a principle: "*Dynamic Balances.* By making each account a dual instead of a single category . . . accounting is able to operate its system of classification (bookkeeping) as a scheme of dynamic balances which will be modified by both positive and negative changes."

Similarly, other bookkeeping conventions can be converted to rules by adding justifying reasons. For example, the manner in which the ledger accounts are integrated can be expressed as a rule: "Define the content of the accounts of an enterprise in a way that will make them form an integrated scheme of classification, because it is important that the economic effects (income and expense) and the financial effects (asset and liability) of enterprise activity be coordinated." This rule, in turn, can be restated as a principle: "*Coordinated Effects.* A well designed scheme of interrelating the accounts of an enterprise . . . succeeds in coordinating the records of (*a*) the economic effect on enterprise wealth of enterprise input and output activities, and (*b*) the financial effect on enterprise wealth of enterprise contracts touching the future."

Thus there are, in total, ten "bookkeeping conventions that express basic facts about accounting."

A number of accounting principles are not based upon bookkeeping conventions, but rather upon accounting action, as, for example, communication to parties not having access to the books. Rules can be stated covering the grouping and describing of data, the need for clarity of presentation, recognition of the somewhat provisional nature of financial statements, and for ignoring price level fluctuations. Such rules can be converted into principles if the ends and the means to the ends are included. The resulting principles would be those of interpretative grouping, full disclosure, inconclusiveness of financial statements and the principle of irrelevant effects.

In similar fashion, principles covering assignment to periods, revenue recognition, accrued charges, deferred charges, belated charges, estimated charges, statistical credibility, critical review, and corroborative evidence can be deduced inductively out of accounting rules based upon accounting action.

"Of induction in accountancy this may be said: Rules should be more than directives to action; actions also need justifications. Objectives should be knowable; they should be attainable by existing means. It should be possible always as needed to associate ends and aims with ways and means."

If agreement can be reached on the idea that a pattern exists between accounting ideas and actions, other matters may then be considered. Questions may be raised whether other objectives exist, whether the stated aims and ends are desirable, whether the objectives are clear and convincing, why one possible way or means is preferable to others and whether the means are suited to the attached ends.

EDUCATIONAL VIEWS IN ACCOUNTANCY, *Collegiate News and Views*, IV (May, 1951), 5-9. [102]

Education for business, especially education in accounting, has traveled a long and difficult road on its way to recognition as a university field. Accounting has always been criticized as being narrowly technical and aimed at the CPA examination. However, accounting stresses the power to analyze, and this is useful in other aspects of life. The study of accounting also involves a study of management, finance, law and economics.

At the University of Illinois cost accounting and intermediate accounting are offered in the second year, because many students do not go beyond two years of college. Students of accounting should also be given knowledge of the diversity of accounting early in their formal education. Students in the junior and senior years take the same courses regardless of whether their goal is public or industrial accounting. General and business courses are taken in all four years, in contrast to the layer-type approach to education.

The diverse backgrounds of students in graduate courses cause difficulties, but one should not attempt to bring all students to the same level of accomplishment. "Graduate work is aimed beyond the CPA examination."

Emphasis, at the doctoral level, is placed upon the dissertation, as well as on substantial work in allied fields.

PREPARATION FOR THE CPA, TECHNICAL OR LIBERAL EDUCATION, *Illinois Certified Public Accountant,* XIV (December, 1951), 50-53. [103]

Educational provisions in CPA laws have always met with protest, even those provisions which first required a high school education.

A conflict exists in ideas related to educational requirements. One trend of thought is the belief that technical preparation is important, while the other stresses a four year program of liberal education.

Many educators like to express the purpose of education as being the development of the power to discriminate between degrees of importance, or the development of competent judgment. It cannot be said that the study of political history will do this better than the study of managerial economics, or that college algebra will succeed while elementary accounting will fail in achieving this objective.

It is asserted that liberal education develops in the student a sense of social responsibility. But what constitutes social responsibility? Those who advocate a liberal education should be asked, in effect, to prove that this is the superior type of education.

SIGNIFICANCE OF INVESTED COST, *Accounting Review,* XXVII (April, 1952), 167-73. [104]

Inflation has stimulated a spirited discussion of the possible modification of accounting techniques and ideas. Certainly, questions must be raised whether the proposed modifications would "slow the speed of inflation" or allow an escape from the consequences of extended price increases. Accounting methods have not been responsible for the rising price levels, and accounting should not be "charged with responsibility for mitigating a rising spiral of inflation."

Accounting's primary purpose is to provide management with data about past transactions so that management will have the results of past experience to guide it in making future commitments. The best measure of prior efforts is invested cost. To lose sight of the "risked-cost" nature of investment would mean the loss of a basis for judging the wisdom of having entered into that risk.

Many see unused services in accounting and want to incorporate into accounting methods ideas derived from economic realities and economic theory. However, in the light of centuries of experience with methods acceptable to many users, accounting "has an obligation to record and report historical or invested cost, not as a convention or a tradition, but as a service necessity."

"Collateral interpretations as space permits" may be reported, but should not be used to obscure "management's activities as expressed in the recorded, invested, contractual costs of that particular enterprise."

CHARACTERISTICS OF A PROFESSION, *New York Certified Public Accountant,* XXII (April, 1952), 207-11. [105]

There are certain characteristics of a profession which, broadly speaking, fall into two categories: (1) recognition of professional status, and (2) preparation for professional service. The first category covers informal public recognition, recognition by a demand for service and recognition by membership in a professional organization. The second category covers (1) learning to use a body of knowledge, (2) exercising influence upon the aims of applicable educational processes, (3) acquiring training and competency and (4) learning to live according to high standards of personal conduct.

From these characteristics, it can be clearly shown that the following three elements must be present for a man's activities to be called professional: (1) special knowledge and appropriate skill, (2) public recognition for inherent public interest, and (3) moral and economic independence.

ACCOUNTING THEORY: 1933-1953, *Accounting Forum,* XXIV (May, 1953), 11-15, 21. [106]

Accounting "theory is belief, reasoned and reasonable belief." It is the explanation of actions taken or preferred. It is "strongly influenced by surrounding conditions and problems of the times . . . because accounting beliefs and actions are the preoccupation of accountants, accounting theory and practice are firmly inter-woven."

The two events of major significance in the field of accounting in the period 1933 to 1953 are the shift in emphasis from the balance sheet to the income statement and the problems faced in income determination under changing price levels.

The increased emphasis placed upon the income statement resulted from a shift in corporate financing to equity capital and the rising criticisms of the financial practices followed in the twenties.

Increased emphasis upon the auditor's certificate and upon the phrase therein, "generally accepted accounting principles . . . directed attention as never before to accounting principles."

Accountants must resist efforts being made to induce them to incorporate other types of data in the accounts in periods of inflation. The accounts should continue to show historical cost, since it is accounting's duty to provide management with data about past transactions. Supplemental interpretative data may be reported, but it should not replace historical cost, nor should it be recorded in the accounts.

FORMAL EDUCATION FOR ACCOUNTANTS, *Illinois Certified Public Accountant,* XV (June, 1953), 43-47. [107]

The Wharton School of the University of Pennsylvania and the University of Chicago pioneered in the field of education for business. New York University, Northwestern University and the Universities of Pennsylvania and Illinois were pioneers in the teaching of accounting at the university level.

Some of the early attempts to teach accounting at the university level resulted directly from state CPA laws. The universities, however, moved quickly ahead of the educational provisions of these laws. Today, accounting owes its usefulness and prestige, at least in part, to the high aims of university education in accounting.

University education in accounting paralleled the development of university education in enterprise management and economics, business law and finance, money and credit, statistical methodology and business and technical writing. A danger which must be avoided is overspecialization in accounting education at the expense of general and business education.

A significant phase of the development of formal education in accounting was the initiation of graduate work, especially at the Ph.D. level, which resulted from increasing concern over the education of accountants. Work at the graduate level is far preferable to overspecialization at the undergraduate level.

VARIETY IN THE CONCEPT OF INCOME, *New York Certified Public Accountant,* XXIII (July, 1953), 419-24. [108]

A concept of income has been basic to accounting ever since the integration of real and nominal accounts in the Italian system of double-entry bookkeeping.

Commercial profit calculations were made in the seventeenth century by deducting costs from revenues at the termination of a joint venture rather than by equal periods of time. The results so determined constituted a true profit concept rather than an income concept.

Some of the concepts relative to income, which are accepted today, are relatively new. For example, the principle of realization mentioned in Adam Smith's *Wealth of Nations* was not accepted until the late nineteenth century.

The problem of determining profits available for dividends was not settled until 1930. Up to that time terms such as clear profit, actual profit, surplus profit and surplus were used to describe the profits of a firm. Although dividends were to be paid only from profits, these terms did not specify what was included and what was available for dividends. In 1930, the term "earned surplus" was given to the account from which dividends could be paid.

Different views or concepts of income exist today, due primarily to the devaluation of currency caused by inflation. One view held that income is the difference between historical costs and revenues expressed in current terms. The other view is that both costs and revenues should be expressed in current terms in calculating a net income figure. The first concept is of value to the business enterprise, while the second will be preferred by the individual buyer or consumer. The debate is one of concept rather than of managerial objectives or recording technology. Accounting, because of its flexibility, can incorporate new methodology if the conceptual objectives are acceptable.

PRINCIPLES UNDER CHALLENGE, *New York Certified Public Accountant*, XXIV (January, 1954), 20-22. [109]

Two principles of accounting are currently being challenged. The first requiries that data entered into the accounts be of a homogeneous nature. The second states that such data must be objectively determined via the bargaining process. Together, these principles make up the so-called cost principle.

The main basis for the challenge is that the use of the dollar as a unit of accounting measurement is merely a convention, and that when the appropriateness of the convention is challenged it can be changed by general consent. Basically this argument holds that 1930 dollars are not the same as 1950 dollars and that entering dollars of different dates and of different values into the same accounts produces accounts without significance. It is proposed by some that adjustment through the use of an index number series calculated by governmental departments would produce results which are more purely objective.

However, accountants should continue to record historical cost in the accounts, since such costs are objective and are needed by businessmen to judge the results of past decisions, and because management may be more largely responsible for price rise profits and avoiding price fall losses than many people suspect.

OLD AND NEW IN MANAGEMENT AND ACCOUNTING, *Accounting Review*, XXIX (April, 1954), 196-200. [110]

Efficient management needs to plan future operations and maintain close control over materials and activities. Budgeting is a useful tool in such future planning.

However, the need for controls and for budgeting was recognized many years ago. Sixteenth century records show that a household had employees comparable to our present-day treasurer, comptroller and auditor, and that internal records were kept for various household functions. Internal check on and production standards for the baker, for example, were in effect maintained, in that he was expected to produce a predetermined amount of bread out of a stated amount of materials received. The same records reveal the existence of a form of budgeting in which the prices of supplies were approximated and the times scheduled when stated amounts of money would be transferred to various household officials.

Accountants may take pride in their intricate techniques and in the status of the independent, professional auditor. However, there is no reason to believe that the development of accounting is now complete.

BUT IS IT ACCOUNTING? *New York Certified Public Accountant*, XXIV (November, 1954), 688-92, 695. [111]

A question can be raised whether the so-called social accounting for national income and wealth and the adjustment of historical cost data by the use of index numbers is really accounting.

The objective in compiling national statistics on income and wealth and compressing such data into appropriate classifications and sub-groups "is clearly the same statistical objective that has prevailed in double-entry bookkeeping from its beginning to the present." However, although entries can be made in a double-entry sense and double, equal totals compiled, these totals cannot be informatively described any more than can the totals of the trial balance of a business firm. Such statistics do not portray on a national basis the cost-effort or the cause and effect relationship between costs and revenues found in a business. National "well-being" is not satisfactorily measured by national income, and not all national wealth is used exclusively in the production of national income.

"Since the analogy is so imperfect, the phrase 'double-entry social accounts' is misleading."

Advocates of the use of index numbers to adjust historical cost data imply that such modified data would make businessmen more aware of changing economic conditions and would further extend "accounting in the public interest." However, desirable as a dampening of the upward trend of prices may be, there is no basis for concluding that modification of the accounts would produce such a dampening effect. The use of such modified data will not improve the businessman's ability to preview the future. Since it will not help him to solve his most difficult problem, a question should be raised as to how effectively such a modification would extend accounting to better serve the public interest.

THE LOGIC OF ACCOUNTS, *Accounting Review,* XXX (January, 1955), 45-47. [112]

A number of interesting highlights can be found in the books of E. G. Folsom, published in 1873 and 1881. Folsom attempted to bring about an understanding of the technical features of double-entry bookkeeping by explaining the thought process underlying these features. Like other authors of that time, however, he failed to distinguish between expense and loss. Because of the importance of the proprietor during that period, expense and income were thought of as being, respectively, loss and gain to the proprietor.

Folsom did, however, recognize that costs could attach to a product. He speaks of "the consumptive use of materials, etc.," and states that "these are in the nature of losses unless services of these kinds are treated as embodied in the merchandise and are charged in with it as enhancing its value." Thus, Folsom clearly recognized the concept of cost accounting.

PRESTIGE FOR HISTORICAL COST, *Illinois Certified Public Accountant,* XVII (March, 1955), 23-27. [113]

Historical cost enjoys prestige because it has been a natural cost — a prior figure representing a known fact — and not from an association with double-entry. The integration of real and nominal accounts into a summarized system was the real contribution of double-entry accounting.

If index number adjusted data are entered into the ledger account, the above mentioned integration would be destroyed while an apparent equilibrium, more artificial than natural, would be maintained in the accounts. The balance sheet would then, in effect, become an appraisal statement of property values and known liabilities and the income statement a calculation of "economic" income through application of an index number series.

Index numbers are not as objective as data recorded in the accounts. Data modified by index numbers are not subject to subsequent validation. Accountants can cooperate in attempts to improve the art of statistical analysis but not at the price of giving up the strict historical cost basis of accounting and the integration of the income statement and balance sheet.

TWO PROFESSIONS IN CONTACT, *American Business Law Association Bulletin,* I (March, 1956), 21-26. [114]

Many similarities exist in the positions of the lawyer and the accountant relative to the client. There are also a number of contrasts, the most important being that the CPA stands more in the position of a judge than that of an advocate of the client's position. He must express his own opinion on the client's representations.

There exists today a vital need for cooperation, not struggle, between the professions of law and public accounting. Such cooperation can be effected, and American lawyers and accountants need only to look at the British example wherein cooperation was secured "in a way that reflected a clear vision of the public interest."

Lawyers and accountants often take different views of items which they frequently need to consider. For example, the legal view of a bad debt is quite different from the accountant's concept of bad debts expense. Similar contrasts in views exist relative to assets and the dividend base. These contrasts suggest the need for mutual understanding. Recent changes in certain statutes would seem to indicate an improved understanding of the accountant's view.

With respect to the present problem confronting the professions of the unauthorized practice of law, "the basic question is one of appropriate professional competence, appropriately applied."

CHOICE AMONG ALTERNATIVES, *Accounting Review,* XXXI (July, 1956), 363-70. [115]

There are two basic ways of thinking about accounting theory. First, it may be thought of as the many explanations, reasons and justifications which help us understand the nature of accountancy. The alternative view is aimed at constructing a single, all-embracing theory of accounting built upon tightly reasoned argument.

In thinking about or in trying to develop a theory of accounting, choice must be made among a number of other alternatives:

(1) It can be assumed that the various kinds of enterprise which can use

accounting data are basically alike, or that their differences are significant and controlling.

(2) It can be assumed that intentional action by enterprise management is likely to be significantly rational; or that it is likely, by neglect of reasoning, to be largely intuitive and imaginative, and that therefore, management is in need of rational bases for decision.

(3) It can be assumed that accounting symbols (units of local currency) represent a stable value of money, or that they represent an unstable value of money.

(4) It can be assumed that account data and financial statements are a service function carried on and prepared according to custom and tradition, or that they are prepared and carried on in whatever manner may be appropriate to provide the kind of data the users will need.

ECONOMISTS AND ACCOUNTANTS, *Illinois Certified Public Accountant*, XVIII (Summer, 1956), 18-24. [116]

Early accounting textbooks, dealing only with methodology, included nothing on the theory of accounting. Eighteenth century economists, in their writings on income and capital, supplied the theory framework for double-entry accounting.

This background of relationship would seem to indicate agreement between accountants and economists, which is not the case. Accounting students study economics, but economics students do not study accounting, although a study of statistical methology may embrace a study of quantitative measurement. The recent interest expressed in "social accounting" may tend to bring accounting and economics closer together.

Income, from the economist's point of view, is defined as "wealth which the owner can disburse over a period of time and be as well off at the end as at the beginning." Economists tend to view value as the present value of an expected stream of earnings. The accountant's calculation of net income is not acceptable until adjusted into real terms. Accountants are not willing to surrender the objectivity of costs and accept expected earnings as a basis of accounting. Difficulty would also be encountered in attempting to measure the well-being of an impersonal business enterprise. The objectivity of the accounting concept of income as being the excess of sales price over purchase cost makes it more desirable than the economist's concept. Accountants, however, can supply data desired by many economists.

The criticisms of the economist clearly indicate the need for "clear, logical verbal explanations of and justifications for accounting concepts and terminology."

LEARNING TO WRITE, *New York Certified Public Accountant*, XXVI (October, 1956), 608-12. [117]

The task of learning to write is not easy, as we all have recognized ever since our elementary schools days. Yet writing can become as fluent as speech.

In helping the student to learn to write, the accounting profession can be of assistance. The improved quality of the literature of accounting can serve as an object lesson. As more and more colleges recognize the basic nature of communications, they will succeed in their efforts to impress upon students the need for preparation in communications. However, teachers should not assume sole responsibility for improving a student's communicative ability.

If the ability to write is professionally important, the CPA examination, especially the section on accounting theory, can serve as a means of impressing this fact upon the student's mind by including essay type questions.

Prospective employers could aid in stressing the importance of writing ability by paying higher starting salaries to master's degree holders who have submitted a thesis than to those who have not.

The CPA firm should encourage its members to write articles for publication in periodicals. Teachers can encourage students to adopt a "do-it-yourself" approach to writing, in addition to enrolling in courses in advanced grammar and writing.

THE SEARCH FOR ACCOUNTING PRINCIPLES, *New York Certified Public Accountant*, XXVIII (April, 1958), 247-56. [118]

In the twenty-five years preceding 1958, considerable time and effort have been devoted to a verbal formulation of accounting principles. Much of the material on accounting principles, exclusive of periodical articles, is to be found in compact form in the bulletins and pamphlets of the AICPA or the AAA. Special note must be made of ARB 43 and the subsequent bulletins as well as bulletins issued by other committees of the AICPA. The American Accounting Association's contributions deserving of notice include the 1957 pamphlet of the Committee on Accounting Concepts and Standards, which included reprints of the 1936, 1941, 1948 pamphlets and the eight supplementary statements to the 1948 report. The Association's Monographs Nos. 3 and 5 also deal specifically with accounting principles.

While both organizations have been interested in accounting principles, their points of view have differed. The AICPA's publications "present the considered judgments of experienced practitioners regarding preferred practices in connection with situations met in professional experience." The publications of the AAA attempt to "express the ideological essence beneath the whole of accountancy."

These differences in points of view are evident in the emphasis placed upon various topics. For example, the 1957 AAA statement includes sections on "business entity," "enterprise continuity," "money measurement" and "realization." ARB 43 deals with topics not covered in the AAA publications, such as government contracts and foreign exchange, while also according more extensive discussion to items such as taxes, pensions and lease disclosure. The research activities of the two organizations "admirably supplement each other."

The influence of contemporary conditions upon the formulation of accounting principles is clearly evident throughout the literature dealing with the impact of price level changes upon business. The Association's publications contain the view that historical cost must be maintained in the accounts and in the financial statements. Supplementary data may be supplied by the reporting company. The Institute took the position in ARB 33 that primary responsibility for reporting the effect of price level changes rested upon management. The Institute's study group on business income stated that while an income statement depicting revenue and charges against revenue stated in units of substantially the same purchasing power would be significant and useful, the commonly accepted method should be continued for the present. Larger corporations, however, should be encouraged to provide information that would facilitate measuring income in units of approximately equal purchasing power.

"If an attempt should be made to extract from this part of recent accounting literature a single principle dealing with the central issue, it should probably in some way make the point that these new interpretative data would be adequately communicated by means of schedules supplementary to the usual financial statements."

ACCOUNTING REDISCOVERED, *Accounting Review*, XXXIII (April, 1958), 246-53. [119]

The vitality originally built into early "Italian capital-income accounting" is vividly brought to light by a number of "rediscoveries" of "previously unsuspected potentialities" which have occurred in the last one hundred years.

The first of these rediscoveries involved the use of accounting as a device to protect British investors from a repetition of earlier fraudulent company promotions.

A second rediscovery was the American use of accounting to control mass production operations via the use of standard costs, budgeting, controllership and research in analysis techniques.

A third rediscovery was the development of so-called social accounts, which was a product of the depression and war. Some of the discussion of the desirability of adjusting accounting data for changes in price levels undoubtedly resulted from an interest in social accounting.

A part of this third rediscovery is the growing evidence of an ever-increasing interest in the role played by accounting in "economic science" and a trend toward the study of "pure" accounting theory. More attention is being directed toward accounting education, and "this broadening awareness of the significance of appropriate education in accounting may come to be the hallmark of the latest 'rediscovery' of accounting."

III. GEORGE O. MAY

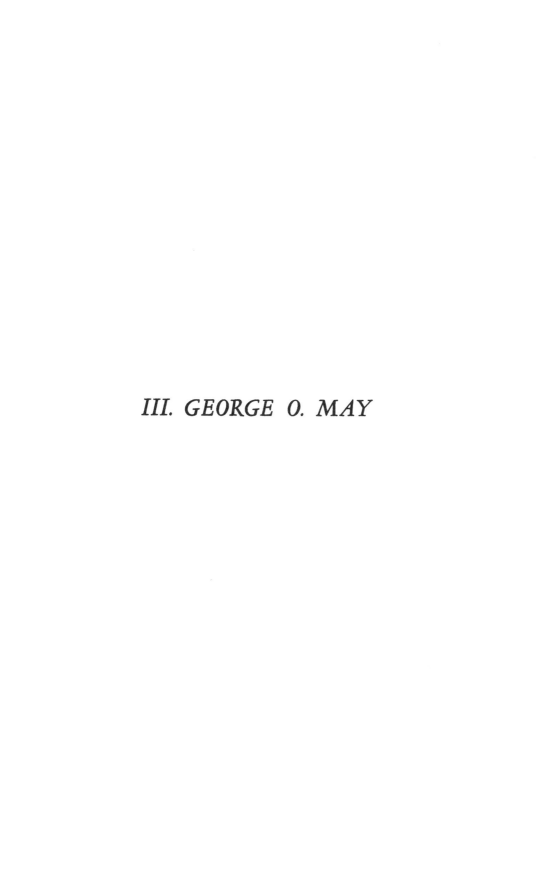

Shelburne Studios

GEORGE O. MAY

George O. May was born in Teignmouth, Devon, England in 1875. He received his basic training in business and accounting as an articled pupil of a chartered accountant in England and in 1897 took his articles with the Institute of Chartered Accountants.

Since 1897, he has been affiliated with the firm of Price, Waterhouse & Co., joining the firm that year in London and coming immediately thereafter to the United States. In 1902 he became a partner of the firm and in 1911 succeeded Sir Arthur Lowes Dickinson as American senior partner. At various other periods he has been a partner of Price, Waterhouse & Co., London, and of other associated firms. He has served as a lecturer at the Harvard University Graduate School of Business Administration, where he was also appointed Dickinson Lecturer, and as a visiting lecturer at many other educational institutions, including Yale, Columbia, Bowdoin, Duke, Indiana, Michigan, North Carolina, Massachusetts Institute of Technology, Northwestern, Stanford, Washington and the London School of Economics. He retired from active practice in 1940.

His long, distinguished and varied career, his many writings on accounting and his service to many different organizations in a number of different capacities have earned Mr. May the unofficial title of dean of accountancy in the United States.

He is the author of two books and over a hundred articles for professional journals. His *Twenty-five Years of Accounting Responsibility,* which was printed privately by his partners in 1936 and taken over immediately by the American Institute, received wide attention. *Financial Accounting* was published in 1943.

Mr. May has held the positions of Director, President and Chairman of the Board of Directors of the National Bureau of Economic Research, Director of the Council of Foreign Relations, Director of the American Statistical Association, Vice-President of the American Economic Association and Chairman of the Committee on Corporate Relations of the Social Science Research Council. He served as a member of the Committee on Double Taxation of the International Chamber of Commerce and as a delegate to the International Conference on

Double Taxation at Geneva. From 1917 to 1932 he made many noteworthy contributions to federal legislation and administrative regulations while serving as an adviser to the United States Treasury and Congress.

Mr. May was primarily responsible for the establishment of the American Institute's Committee on Accounting Procedures and served as its first chairman. He is also a member of the Royal Economic Society of London.

Since his retirement from active practice in 1940, Mr. May has continued to act as a consultant for Price, Waterhouse & Co.

III. GEORGE O. MAY

SUMMARIES OF PERIODICAL WRITINGS

THE PROPER TREATMENT OF PREMIUMS AND DISCOUNTS ON BONDS, *Journal of Accountancy,* II (July, 1906), 174-86. [120]

The premium or discount on a bond is practically a capitalization of an increase or reduction of the rate of interest. On the issuer's books, the discount should be charged to income over the term of the bond, whereas a premium may be carried in a reserve account and charged with extraordinary expenditures or the writeoff of fictitious assets, or gradually credited to income over the life of the bond.

On the bondholder's books, premium should be written off against income each year in such a way that each year's income will be credited with the true yield on the investment, although other methods, if equally conservative, may be adopted. Discount is not usually credited to income, and no great hardship is imposed by this rule. If a credit for discount is deemed equitable, the credit should be limited to the proportion of the discount accrued at the date of realization, or to the proportion actually realized, whichever is lower. From the legal point of view no general rules can be laid down, as each case must be decided on its own facts.

PREMIUMS AND DISCOUNTS, *Journal of Accountancy,* III (November, 1906), 32-33. [121]

This article was written in response to the comments made by Charles E. Sprague concerning premiums and discounts. Accountants are urged to take a more "proper attitude." They should always bear in mind the possibility of the existence of exceptions to even the most firmly established rules. Accountancy is essentially a profession of common sense and good business judgment which should be exercised with constant regard to accounting principles and sound financial and legal theories. Practical difficulties should not be overlooked nor should so much weight be attached to theories that they are enforced at the sacrifice of substantial justice.

THE PROBLEM OF DEPRECIATION, *Journal of Accountancy,* XIX (January, 1914) 1-13. [122]

Measurement of depreciation is necessary in order to determine the value of property and to ascertain what provision is required to be made from earnings before the true operating profit can be determined. In determining the amount of depreciation, exhaustion as well as appraised market value should be considered and kept separate for best disclosure and depreciation provision calculation.

Appraisals are so much a matter of opinion and temperament that resulting benefits are largely illusory. Devaluation is also undesirable since no single year's operation is complete in itself, as benefits or burdens are inherited from transactions of the past. The primary requirement is to ascertain clearly the results of operation under existing conditions, and not upon the basis of imaginary conditions which might exist.

Depreciation must also be viewed in the light of surrounding conditions, that is, in the light of maintenance policy or maintenance and renewal policy. Recognition of depreciation to a large extent rests upon comprehension of the problem of determination of proper depreciation charges.

QUALIFICATIONS IN CERTIFICATES, *Journal of Accountancy,* XX (October, 1915), 248-59. [123]

The impracticability of the suggestion that only unqualified certificates be given is apparent. If disagreement is encountered over the treatment to be accorded an item, such a suggestion would result in either the creation of an exaggerated impression of unreliability of the accounts by refusal to give a certificate, or the auditor would brush aside his convictions and sign an unqualified certificate to avoid the seriousness of a refusal to give a certificate.

Qualifications are of two types — those that merely limit responsibility without either express or implied disapproval of the accounts and those that constitute criticisms of the accounts. In either case, qualifications should be clear, direct and understandable, as should their effect if the auditor's view were adopted. There is a need for better terminology, and the phrase "the balance sheet is in accord with the books and in our opinion shows . . ." might well be substituted for the statement "as shown by the books and accounts" as a limiting phrase. Accountants should understand that the insertion of limiting phrases does not relieve them of responsibility in regard to the assets and liabilities to which such phrases apply.

The accountant, "if he should err in making decisions about qualifications in certificates, should err on the side of the public as not to damage the profession and himself."

REASONS FOR EXCLUDING INTEREST FROM COST, *Journal of Accountancy*, XXI (June, 1916), 401-9. [124]

The suggestion that interest on proprietor's capital should be included as an element of cost at a "rate equal to that at which money can be borrowed for the particular industry" is unsound and unscientific. Money can be borrowed on terms different from those required for capital because of the greater margin of security behind borrowed funds. The inclusion of interest in cost produces results which are financially and economically undesirable and which, in the relations between capital, labor and the public, tend to mislead, thus promoting discord and social injustice.

In determining costs or expenses in total, the accountant must first determine each such item and exclude all others. The exclusion of interest would not impair the value of the other cost determinations. Cost figures should be, as far as possible, actual and should exclude arbitrary or estimated figures. Interest on the proprietor's capital must obviously be an estimate.

Inclusion of interest in cost at a rate which is admittedly less than commensurate with the risk attending investment is commercially and economically unsound. If interest on plant investment is to be included, so should interest on current assets. Inclusion of interest leads to unconservative valuation of inventories and recognizes profits which have not been realized or earned.

The reader of figures in which interest has been included as a cost will assume that the interest included in expense stands to capital in the same relation as the wages included in expense do to labor, and no amount of explanation will be very effective in removing such a misconception. Classifications should not present figures in such a way as to add another misconception to those that already keep capital and labor apart.

TAXATION OF CAPITAL GAINS, *Harvard Business Review*, I (October, 1922), 319-35.* [125]

Present tax treatment of capital gains is not satisfactory, and one of the remedies receiving consideration is the abandonment of the taxation of capital gains and the allowance of capital losses as deductions from taxable income.

Capital gains can result from three sources: (1) natural growth causing change in absolute value, (2) a change in relative value due to external

*Reprinted in *Twenty-five Years of Accounting Responsibility*. Edited by Bishop C. Hunt (New York: American Institute Publishing Co., 1936) II, 180-86.

causes, and (3) a change in money value due to currency depreciation. Gains of the first type are in the investment income category and should be taxed, in principle, as income, while gains of the second type are less entitled to special consideration than recurring investment income, and gains of the third type are more apparent than real. Because of practical difficulties in separating and taxing each class of gain, questions now arise whether all gains should be taxed or excluded from taxation.

Economists would raise the technical point that capital gains should not be taxed under the guise of an income tax. However, wage and salary earners would feel discriminated against if capital gains of the wealthy escaped taxation. If capital gains are taxed, losses should be allowed as deductions, and in a growing country where gains would exceed losses, there is merit in the suggestion that both be treated as income-determining items.

Justice would call for as nearly as possible equal treatment for gains and losses. However, in view of changing rates of taxation, this has not been true in the United States. Discrimination against the taxpaper has resulted in his refraining from taking profits but not losses. The provisions of the Act of 1921 resulted in a change from provisions favoring tax revenue to those favoring the taxpayer.

The complexities and amounts involved concerning capital gains and income and the taxation thereof are illustrated by the Phellis case. The government appealed the verdict of the Court of Claims which stated that no taxable income resulted to stockholders of an old company receiving shares of stock in a new company which had taken over the assets of the old. The Supreme Court reversed this decision, and under the circumstances encountered in later years, the loss of tax revenue to the government was large.

The exclusion of capital gains and capital losses in the determination of taxable income will yield greater revenues, greatly reduce tax avoidance and provide greater equity.

ADMINISTRATION OF THE BRITISH INCOME TAX LAW, *Proceedings, Academy of Political Science,* XI (1924), 143-48.* [126]

Great Britain is collecting surtaxes on the scale at which the United States is attempting to collect them unsuccessfully. There are a number of reasons for this. First, in Great Britain there is executive responsibility for tax legislation as contrasted to the separated executive and legislative functions in the United States. Secondly, having one parliament to deal with tax legislation is a distinct advantage. The same body then controls corporate legislation and levies

*Reprinted in *Twenty-five Years of Accounting Responsibility.*

taxes and is thus in a position to plug loopholes. Also, the British have no constitutional limitation, no basic date such as March 1, 1913, and no tax-free securities.

The main responsibility for the relatively poor collection rate of the United States' surtaxes lies with the Congress which has passed poor tax legislation and imposed collection burdens on the Bureau of Internal Revenue without providing the necessary funds for men and machinery.

" 'High taxes and plenty of holes' is a system that is inefficient, inequitable and demoralizing" and makes taxpaying a "function of the conscience of the taxpayer."

THE TAX MAZE, *Atlantic Monthly*, LXXXV (April, 1925), 538-47.* [127]

The present tax law is filled with "an extraordinary series of contradictions." Congress has gone to great lengths to define its purposes and to prevent granting to administrators discretionary powers in some instances, while in others concerning certain areas of vast importance, only a brief clause in an act is to be found to guide the Commissioner. For example, the simple clause in the 1918 act allowing a reasonable deduction for depreciation based on the value of the property at March 1, 1913, in effect implied that the Commissioner was to make or approve valuation of all depreciable property in existence in the United States at March 1, 1913. Similar situations are found with respect to depletion allowances and inventory valuations.

Many other cases of gross inequality exist, which were perhaps justifiable as wartime measures, but "what is both regrettable and preventable is that six years after the Armistice so many of the important tax-controversies should be still unsettled." A high quality Commission with broad powers is needed to dispose of all of the unsettled tax problems relating to the war years.

Present tax law goes to great length on immaterial items such as officer uniform allowances being taxable income and epaulets and campaign bars being business expenses, while at the same time it shows, through the publication of recent tax returns, "name after name . . . set opposite a tax figure which is ridiculously small in proportion to the obvious income and ability to pay of the taxpayer."

Some of the devices employed to obtain tax avoidance from high surtax rates, apart from the creation of trusts, are: "investments in tax-exempt securities; losses, real or artificial; and the transfer of property to corporations that pay few or no dividends." Some immediately needed remedies are the reduction

*Reprinted in *Twenty-five Years of Accounting Responsibility.*

of the maximum tax rate on individuals to a rate reasonably close to the corporate tax rate, prohibition of future issuances of tax-exempt securities and a clearer conception and agreement on a definition of income and its time of emergence. Also, the issue of politics should be taken out of taxation.

TAXABLE INCOME AND ACCOUNTING BASES FOR DETERMINING IT, *Journal of Accountancy,* XL (October, 1925), 248-66.* [128]

What is income? When does it emerge? "The general test of the existence of income is whether there is gain, but . . . items which ordinarily constitute gain and are commonly regarded as income may be taxed as such even though in exceptional cases they may not result in gain to the recipient."

The above general test of income is subject to few exceptions in the determination of commercial income. In many cases the allocation of income to periods of time, which is of crucial importance in taxation, is an extremely difficult task. This is especially true if a number of years elapse between the purchase of raw materials, the manufacture of goods and the ultimate sale to the customer. Estimates and opinions are necessary. The Act of 1918 which allowed inventories to be valued according to best trade practice, thus recognizing the lower of cost or market method, and the Act of 1921, which permitted the deduction of a reasonable reserve for bad debts, both recognized well established trade practices. At the same time, however, arbitrary limitations were placed upon certain deductions such as depletion and interest.

The removal of these arbitrary limitations means that the acts can now be criticized primarily for "their lack of precision and clarity and their failure to recognize business methods and considerations of practical convenience."

The Act of 1909 spoke of net income in terms of gross income actually received less expenses actually paid, implying, therefore, a cash basis of income determination. The regulations, however, in effect ignored *paid* and *received.* These sound, convenient regulations "did little real violence to the law" but created the feeling that the regulations did vary from the law. Certain expenses could be deducted even if not actually paid, while others, such as interest and taxes, could be deducted only if actually paid. Despite objections, the 1913 law followed the language of the 1909 law.

The 1918 act provided that returns were to be prepared on the basis on which the taxpayer's books were kept, unless this basis did not clearly reflect income; in which case the Commissioner could prescribe the basis. "To most accountants the Act of 1918 seemed to dispose of the vitally important question of accounting bases for determining taxable income in a sound and satisfactory way."

*Reprinted in *Twenty-five Years of Accounting Responsibility.*

However, many misconceptions exist with respect to the cash and accrual bases of income determination. The Bureau has used the terms *accrual basis* and *an accrual* to describe almost any type of item which is not a cash item. Such usage of the above terms is unfortunate because accrual has now come to mean "grow up," "spring up," "fall in," "become due" and even "set up." Thus, accrual basis has become a meaningless phrase.

Income is a matter of estimate and opinion, and business practice with respect to allocation of income to time periods is entitled to great weight.

In a letter to the *Journal* (Vol. XXXX, December, 1925), attention is directed to the fact that the term *accrual accounting* actually originated in economics. Better accounting practice would restrict the use of the term *accrue* to items which grow by the mere lapse of time. Perhaps even more vague than the term accrue is the inconsistent use of the term *reserve*. One case decided by the Board of Tax Appeals disposed of the question of the deductibility of a reserve for discounts by holding that reserves are not deductible unless specifically provided for by statute. In reality, the reserve in this case was nothing more than a step in determining gross income. The Board was obviously misled by poor accounting terminology.

PUBLICITY OF ACCOUNTS, *New York Times*, August 27, 1926.* [129]

Professor Ripley's position that stockholders are entitled to receive adequate information on companies in which they are interested cannot be questioned. Unfortunately, in support of this obviously good cause, he has made certain inaccurate and unjust references to the annual reports of certain companies and to British practices. He is also inconsistent in that he praises a given procedure in one company and condemns it in another.

Professor Ripley's criticism of the new no-par value stocks from the viewpoint that at least the old par value stocks had a "bench mark solidly established — theoretically, at least" is invalid. Bench marks established only in theory are useless and may even be dangerous. Inclusion of the speculator as being among those entitled to information is to be questioned, since the investor-stockholder and the speculator by no means require identical information.

American stockholders receive more information than do British stockholders, yet Professor Ripley compares American and British practices to the detriment of American practice.

*Reprinted in *Twenty-five Years of Accounting Responsibility.*

CORPORATE PUBLICITY AND THE AUDITOR, *Journal of Accountancy,* XLII (November, 1926), 321-26.* [130]

Although the directors are primarily responsible for furnishing adequate information to stockholders, accountants should see that this information conforms to highest established standards.

Since the practice of having independent audits is now quite common, the Institute and other accounting bodies should undertake the task of outlining the auditor's responsibility, because the time has come for auditors to assume greater responsibility. A most valuable remedy for the defects now found in financial data is "the extension of the independent audit, accompanied by a clearer definition of the authority and responsibility of the auditor."

In England, where the independent audit is compulsory by English law, the auditor shares with the directors the responsibility for the published accounts. Because he may be held liable for damages, or even criminal prosecution, for the issuance of false statements, he is given powers of access to the records and of requiring information from officers and directors. He cannot be replaced until due notice has been given stockholders who elect the auditor at the annual meeting.

The position of the auditor in the United States can be the same as in England if cooperation can be secured between the Institute, stock exchanges, investment bankers and banks. The public would welcome a clearer definition of the auditor's responsibilities and position, and although the auditor's responsibilities may be increased, a long-run advantage would accrue to the profession.

Much is yet to be done to secure a fairer reporting of income, even though the essential points regarding the preparation and presentation of the balance sheet are fairly well established and followed by leading companies.

A PROPER COURAGE IN THE ASSUMPTION OF RESPONSIBILITY OF THE ACCOUNTANT, *Pace Student,* November, 1926, pp. 3-5.* [131]

Improved standards of corporate publicity might be obtained by extension of the practice of having accounts audited annually. However, auditors need a more real and definite statement of their responsibilities if such an end is to be achieved. Greater publicity of corporate financial data must come voluntarily, or bureaucratic control will come. The profession does not now have men capable of dealing with the problems of full disclosure, and it is even more true that no body of men exists outside of the profession to cope adequately with these problems.

*Reprinted in *Twenty-five Years of Accounting Responsibility.*

The profession will assume proper, defined responsibilities if given commensurate power. Some people now want the auditors to assume responsibility for verification of inventory, but this is not within the competence of the auditor nor has a real need been shown for such a verification.

Auditors should be elected by the stockholders. They should have the right to report to the stockholders regardless of their findings and should not be liable to supercession without having an opportunity to so report. Due notice should be given if an auditor is not to be reappointed.

DOUBLE TAXATION, *Foreign Affairs,* V (October, 1926), 69-79.*
[132]

The problem of double taxation is found primarily in the areas of income and inheritance taxation. The international aspects are by far the most important, although double taxation of inheritances by the states has resulted in an unsatisfactory situation.

Income can be effectively taxed at either its source of origin or its place of receipt. The United States at one time taxed its citizens residing abroad on income derived from foreign sources. England taxes non-residents' income derived from English sources. Which principle of taxation is to be emphasized depends upon the conditions prevalent in a country. Countries with relatively large resources, as compared to the foreign interests of their citizens, will tax according to the source of the income, while countries possessing large amounts of capital will emphasize taxation according to residence.

The Provincial and Financial Committee of the League of Nations presented the general principle that taxation at progressive rates should be levied according to place of residence. The Committee also apparently believed "that no state should levy on the profits of an enterprise owned by non-residents taxes computed at progressive rates, even if the scale were established entirely without regard to the status of the owners."

The Committee stated a number of rules for determination of the source of income, which have been approved by the International Chamber of Commerce, and which are substantially similar to provisions in our own federal legislation. Serious double taxation in the United States has been dealt with promptly, although the provisions have at times been arbitrary and the allowances, in some cases, obviously excessive.

Many improvements and changes must be made before state taxation is on a fair and sound basis, and there is room for improvement in the method of federal tax administration.

*Reprinted in *Twenty-five Years of Accounting Responsibility.*

A CONFUSION OF TERMS, *Journal of Accountancy*, XLIII (April, 1927), 310-11.* [133]

Many misconceptions surround the significance of the *reserve for depreciation,* and the majority of these center on depreciation rather than reserve. The depreciation reserve does not measure *overvaluation of assets,* but is based on exhaustion since depreciation is recorded despite increases in value.

Designation of profits withheld from distribution with the term *reserve* is becoming less and less popular in the United States. Surplus not available for dividends is sometimes designated as *appropriated surplus.* Rather than restrict the use of the term reserve to appropriation surplus, it would be easier and quite satisfactory to standardize usage of the term appropriated surplus. This usage of terms would be contrary to the suggestions of Professor Cole, and also contrary to his usage of *allowance* or *provision* in place of reserve. Withheld profits should preferably carry the title of *surplus* with an appropriate qualifying phrase or word. Reserve could then continue to mean "a reservation out of the gross proceeds of past business to meet charges which will or may arise in the future out of that business."

RAILROAD DEPRECIATION (Memorandum submitted in relation to the Report of the Interstate Commerce Commission in No. 15100 set for hearing November 9, 1927.) Pp. 23.* [134]

The Interstate Commerce Commission's proposal to require straight-line depreciation of carrier property and deduct accrued depreciation to arrive at fair value of the property for rate-making purposes raises three major questions: What is (1) the relationship of depreciation to valuation, (2) the relationship of depreciation to maintenance of property, and (3) the proper treatment to be accorded past depreciation, especially in view of the practices of the past.

According to the Supreme Court, the rate base must represent the fair present value of the property based primarily upon observation. The straight-line method of recording depreciation does not result in the net book value of the property fulfilling this requirement. The annuity method must be substituted for the straight-line method "or all suggestion of close relationship between depreciated values and fair value in service abandoned."

The practice of charging the replacement cost of an asset to operating expense can be defended, especially in periods of rising price levels. If the rate base is to be the fair value of the property, then consistency requires that fair value be employed in measuring property that is "used up." In some

*Reprinted in *Twenty-five Years of Accounting Responsibility*.

cases, especially from the viewpoint of the community being served by a new railroad, a strong case can be made against recording depreciation as now proposed by the Commission, since the proposed method creates the heaviest burden in the early years of life.

However, depreciation charges should be continued with respect to equipment and should be extended to include items, such as bridges, which were formerly handled under the so-called retirement method of recording charges for use of property.

Past depreciation should not be charged to profit and loss. The Commission proposes to charge profit and loss with past depreciation since it assumes that this is the account which benefited by past omission. This is not true, since the development of railroads and of the economy would have been retarded if a system of depreciation charges had been instituted in the early stages of railroad building.

CARRIER PROPERTY CONSUMED IN OPERATION AND THE REGULATION OF PROFITS, *Quarterly Journal of Economics,* XLIII (February, 1929), 193-220.* [135]

Whether a given rate structure is compensatory or confiscatory depends upon whether an allowance is made for use, and a second allowance is made for consumption of the carrier's property. A direct and vital relationship exists between the basis for determining charges for exhaustion of property and the rate base. The two major conflicting theories are the *prudent investment theory,* which stresses the capital employed in an enterprise and not the property, and the *present value theory* which holds that it is the property, not the original cost of the property, "of which the owner may not be deprived without due process of law."

The question is largely one of deciding what form of assurance of return is deemed most desirable. Many alternatives exist: (1) a fixed rate can be applied to actual investment, (2) current interest rates can be applied to actual investment, (3) a fixed rate can be applied to the actual investment in property adjusted for price level changes, and (4) current rates can be applied to the prudent investment adjusted for price level changes.

Should the charge for exhaustion of property be based upon original cost?

(1) "If the rate base is to be computed on the present value theory, then the balance of argument is slightly in favor of original cost as the basis of the exhaustion charge if provision is to be made as exhaustion proceeds,

*Reprinted in *Twenty-five Years of Accounting Responsibility.*

and slightly in favor of replacement cost if the charge is to be made when exhaustion is complete.

(2) "If the rate base is to be computed on the prudent investment theory, then the balance of argument is decidedly in favor of replacement cost as the basis of the exhaustion charge if exhaustion is provided for as it proceeds, and still more decidedly if the charge is to be made only in bulk when the exhaustion is complete."

A general system of depreciation for railroads is undesirable, especially if the prudent investment theory of the rate base is to prevail. Straight-line depreciation will not fulfill the objectives of the Commission, and, in addition, the Commission has not produced a satisfactory plan for handling past accrued depreciation.

Depreciation schemes for equipment should be continued and extended to movable property, as well as to plants of an industrial nature. The annuity method of calculating depreciation should be applied to large units replaceable as a whole. A maintenance equalization reserve should be established which, as a percentage, should not exceed "observed depreciation."

EXTERNAL INFLUENCES AFFECTING ACCOUNTING PRACTICE, *Accountant,* LXXXII (January, 1930), 83-87. [136]

Four major external influences upon accounting are regulation, new taxation, changes in the distribution of ownership of business and radical price level changes. More precise but at the same time less conservative accounting has resulted from regulation, which was counteracted by a trend toward greater conservatism as a result of new tax legislation. Mergers and consolidations resulted from the development of no-par stock which led to reincorporation of business. "Charter-mongering states" have engaged in keen competition to secure these reincorporated businesses. Rising price levels have caused questions to arise as to the desirability of restatement of assets values, the validity of profits derived by deduction of exhaustion of plant based on cost, and the desirability of fixed income bearing securities.

All of these tendencies have made the allocation of profits to various years more important and more difficult, and undue importance is frequently attached to the earnings reports for a year or even a quarter. The complexity of business makes it impossible to present a single statement, accurate in detail and in perspective. Modern corporate reports should include income and surplus statements, a classified statement of quick assets and liabilities, a statement of capital assets and obligations, and a statement of the resources made available during the year and their disposition.

FURTHER THOUGHTS ON DEPRECIATION AND THE RATE BASE, *Quarterly Journal of Economics,* XLIV (August, 1930), 687-97.* [137]

In the United Railways and Electric Company case the Supreme Court held that an allowance for annual depreciation based on cost rather than present value was erroneous. The yield from a given rate structure must be compared, to determine its reasonableness, against a total composed of amounts needed to cover (1) "a fair return on capital investment," (2) "exhaustion of property," and (3) "all expenses of or incidental to operation, except those of making good exhaustion of property."

The first of these amounts is compensation based on value and not on cost. The third is reimbursement of cost. Should the second be determined in the same manner as the first or the third? The Court's decision rules out original cost but does not choose between the determination of the allowance as "compensation based on value, or as a reimbursement of cost based on the actual or probable cost of replacing the property exhausted." Whether depreciation is based on original or probable cost of replacement is of relatively minor importance from a practical standpoint. However, it is imperative that depreciation "be recognized as a reimbursement of cost and treated accordingly."

Any depreciation scheme must be based upon reasonable estimates and assumptions, must be operated continuously, and provision for correction of error of estimate must be included. The scheme should also harmonize with the theory of rate base determination, and it is desirable that the scheme be equally suitable for current accounting as well as applicable in rate determination. These requirements can be met if depreciation is looked upon as a reimbursement of cost, prospective or actual.

The Supreme Court has held that in determination of present value, it is the present value of the existing plant and not some other plant that must be considered. But can the present value of a plant be determined without consideration of its relative efficiency, its construction and operating cost relative to an efficient and economical substitute? "The current theory of computation of present value is highly artificial and the results often lacking in reality."

INFLUENCE OF THE DEPRESSION ON THE PRACTICE OF ACCOUNTING, *Journal of Accountancy,* LIV (November, 1932), 336-50.* [138]

The importance of accounting in general, and the particular importance of independent audits in companies too small to maintain adequate systems of

*Reprinted in *Twenty-five Years of Accounting Responsibility.*

internal control and those who thought they did not need auditing, was made vivid by the depression.

Valuations based upon past or present earnings covering a relatively short period of time were found to be hopelessly in error. Investors did not realize that the value and significance of financial data depend upon the accounting methods employed and the wisdom and honesty displayed in applying such methods. There is a need for education in this area. Corporate reports need to be more fully explanatory so that interested parties will know what accounting methods were used and can thereby appraise the value of the data supplied.

A company's own stock is not, in most cases, an asset; and dividends thereon, or gains upon resale, are never to be treated as income.

Another practice resulting from the depression has been the writedown of property accounts so as to reduce future years' depreciation charges. Whether this procedure should be employed depends, to a certain extent, upon the circumstances of each case. In general, however, if the assets are revalued at fair figures, the writedown fully disclosed and made with approval of the stockholders, it can be accepted by accountants.

THE ACCOUNTANT AND THE INVESTOR, *Ethical Problems of Modern Accounting*. Lectures delivered in 1932 at the William A. Vawter Foundation on business ethics, Northwestern University, School of Commerce (New York: Ronald Press Co., 1933), pp. 26-54.* [139]

The banker offering securities is not informed on a corporation's financial status and earnings and is therefore likely to rely on the disinterested report of the accountant. The investor has the right to expect that financial data in a prospectus represent the accountant's own best judgment regarding such data. That financial data are matters of estimate and opinion must be continuously borne in mind. The investor, however, is "entitled to regard an accountant's statement in a prospectus as a little more objective and more clearly indicative of earning capacity" than similar data in the annual report.

Accountants must recognize, even under conditions which cause a division of loyalty, that their primary obligation is to the investor. The accountant should not present past financial data if, in the light of conditions internal to the company and not generally known, such data tend to be misleading.

The accountant must maintain a position of high character and complete independence. In cases of conflict of opinion, the accountant should never allow his judgment to be swayed by "the mere authority of the interested parties."

*Reprinted in *Twenty-five Years of Accounting Responsibility*.

There is no place in the accountant's report for "weasel words." Apart from the question of criminal or civil liability, the accountant has an ethical obligation to refrain from statements of half-truths from which ill-founded inferences can be drawn. The accountant, however, has no obligation to disclose "secret reserves" if such reserves were created in good faith and the amounts involved do not materially distort earnings.

The accountant, in addition to his legal and ethical duties, owes his entire practice in the financial reporting field to the investor whose confidence he must secure and maintain.

A firm position concerning ethical principles will bring "professional success as well as a consciousness of professional integrity."

The Position of the Accountant Under the Securities Act, *Journal of Accountancy*, XLVII (January, 1934), 9-23.* [140]

The Securities Act of 1933, especially Section 11, is of great importance to accountants in view of the liability that may be imposed upon them by this act. The act is unduly harsh in that it "deliberately contemplates the possibility that a purchaser may recover from a person, from whom he has not bought, in respect of a statement which at the time of his purchase he had not read, contained in a document which he did not know to exist, a sum which is not to be measured by injury resulting from falsity in such statement." Thus, thrown out by the act are the old rules of the burden of proof being upon the plaintiff, the doctrine of contributory negligence and the theory that there should be some relationship between injury and damages allowed.

The accountant's position under the act differs from that of other experts. He is liable for the truth of the statements, not only in his certificate, but also in the statements certified. The view that accounting is merely a fact-finding function is widely and erroneously held, as is the view that accounting data are facts and not opinions. To a certain extent accountants contribute to these beliefs by not doing as much as they should to counteract them.

Some of the harshness of Section 11 can be alleviated by the Federal Trade Commission making judicious use of the powers granted it in Section 19. Under Section 19 the Commission has the power to define accounting terms and to prescribe accounting methods. Statements of financial data could, if the Commission so decided, "be held to be true if they represented the application of honest judgment and acceptable methods of accounting to all the relevant facts which were known or ought to have been known to the person preparing or certifying them at the time of preparation or certification."

*Reprinted in *Twenty-five Years of Accounting Responsibility.*

TESTIMONY ON THE NATIONAL SECURITIES EXCHANGE BILL, *Stock Exchange Practices,* Hearings on Senate bill 2693, Senate Committee on Banking and Finance, 73rd Congress, March 10, 1934, Part XV, pp. 7175-88.* [141]

Recommendations for revisions to the proposed bill are that:

Section 12 be changed so as to (1) grant the regulatory agency power to dispense with quarterly financial statements if these are apt to be misleading, (2) limit the filing of certified statements to an annual balance sheet and income statement covering one year, and (3) make this provision regarding certified statements flexible enough so as to permit the distribution of the audit work over the year.

Section 17 be changed to provide for liability only in cases of willful misrepresentation rather than covering cases of honest error in judgment and in facts.

Section 18 be changed, or amended, so as to limit the authority granted the regulatory agency to prescribe uniform accounting systems and substitute therefor power to prescribe the information to be shown in balance sheets and earnings reports.

THE INFLUENCE OF ACCOUNTING ON THE DEVELOPMENT OF AN ECONOMY, *Journal of Accountancy,* LXI (January, February, March, 1936), 11-22, 92-105, 171-84. [142]

Accounting consists of the recognition of custom and convention and the exercise of judgment rather than strict adherence to rigid, unvarying rules. Because of the adherence to convention, the nature of the convention accepted may influence the development of an economy.

A problem of utmost importance to the accountant is that of distinguishing between capital and income. Accounting is primarily historical in approach and emphasis is placed on cost, although under certain conditions, as when an asset held for sale has a selling price less than cost, the lower figure may be substituted for cost. Accounting is not primarily concerned with the fluctuations in value of a capital asset, but is concerned with the exhaustion of the usefulness of such an asset and with making proper charges against income, based on cost, for such exhaustion. The goal is to have the asset on the books at its salvage value when its usefulness is ended.

*Reprinted in *Twenty-five Years of Accounting Responsibility.*

Conversely, in the borrowing of money, the amount actually borrowed forms the basis of accounting, and, if the amount to be repaid exceeds the amount borrowed, sums are periodically charged to income and added to the amount borrowed so that at maturity the full amount payable will be on the books.

The term *value* has many different meanings. However, the investor is interested in the value of the business as a whole, and this is dependent primarily upon future earning capacity. The accountant should shed some light on earning power, and in doing so he can ignore fluctuations in capital asset values.

The present view that gains or losses on the disposition of capital assets should be shown in the income statement is in marked contrast with the English view that such gains or losses increase or decrease capital. Affected by these differences in view are local taxation, income taxation and rate regulation. A study of the history of "legal" income leads to the conclusion that it is easier to determine annual income than to establish capital value, since such value is dependent upon prospective income.

The annual productivity of a country is its wealth. The real basis for economic security lies in annual productivity and not in capital value enhancement.

In the history of railroads two methods are found for providing for the expense of exhaustion of property. One method is the so-called systematic accrual of depreciation and the other the so-called retirement method. Depreciation accounting was not popular in the early development of railroads because of the added burden in expenses at a time when the railroads were earning only 5 percent on invested capital. Adoption of depreciation accounting would have been detrimental to the development of the railroads.

A noticeable change in the attitude of the Supreme Court toward depreciation can be found in the period 1878 to 1900. Under the Valuation Act of 1913, the Interstate Commerce Commission made the first serious proposal to apply depreciation methods to railroad fixed property. After the Transportation Act of 1920, the Commission supported straight-line depreciation based on original cost, while the Supreme Court favored "observable depreciation" based on present value.

No general economic advantage is to be gained from the depreciation method. There are no accounting principles governing accounting practice which supersede that of general economic advantage. Accounting should reflect that which is fair and in the best interests of those having a legitimate interest in the accounts and not that which is purely "metaphysical." No accounting rule, founded on an abstract notion of sound accounting, should be established contrary to the interests of all parties concerned.

STATEMENT OF GEORGE O. MAY ON THE REVENUE ACT OF 1936, *Hearings on the Revenue Act, 1936,* Senate Committee on Finance, U.S. Senate, 74th Congress, Second Session on H. R. 12395, May 6, 1935 (Washington: Government Printing Office, 1936), pp. 538-48. [143]

Two new proposals for taxation of corporate profits are (1) to tax the profits, when received by the individual, according to his tax status, or (2) to tax undistributed corporate profits on a steeply graduated basis. The first method is employed in England but suffers from serious problems of administration.

The proposed graduated tax on undistributed corporate profits is a "pressure tax" and does not rest on ability to pay. The analogy between a graduated tax on undistributed profits and one on individual income is "entirely specious and false."

American corporations, at least when compared to English corporations, do not withhold a larger proportion of their profits. Dividends paid in excess of current earnings during the depression exceeded the undistributed profits of the prior decade. Corporate profits are a source of capital, and serious economic effects will result if this source is eliminated. Numerous difficulties are encountered in determining income and especially in determining the income for a given year. If tax rates are ever-changing this periodic incidence becomes even more important and the possible source of great inequity.

The tax would also fall most heavily upon new companies whose growth and strengthening should be sought, not obstructed. Companies in liquidation or in the declining stage would not bear the tax, and they are the ones which are, economically speaking, of least value to society. The proposed tax simply does not recognize the varying needs of the various corporations.

In the field of personal income taxation, the nearest analogy to the proposed tax on undistributed corporate profits is a tax on income saved but not on income spent. The Treasury at one time gave consideration to an opposite type of tax, that is, a tax on spending with saved income exempt. Such a tax favors the accumulation of large fortunes by individuals and suffers from the lack of practical advantage.

EATING PEAS WITH YOUR KNIFE, *Journal of Accountancy,* LXIII (January, 1937), 15-22. [144]

Using financial data contained in annual reports and prospectuses for purposes for which they were not designed, and for which they are not appropriate, is inefficient if not dangerous. One report will not serve equally well for such purposes as taxation, regulation, annual reporting and security flotation.

Reports should be prepared with the purposes for which they are to be used clearly in mind.

The annual report is a chapter in a continuous history and is primarily an historical document. The importance of a prospectus lies in the implications that can be drawn from it with respect to the future. Accountants hesitate to adjust annual reports for inclusion in prospectuses, because they fear an inference will be drawn that the annual report was wrong and this may invite action against them. The SEC should recognize this difference between the two reports and state that simply because adjustments were made no implication should be drawn that the original report was erroneous. Reports could thus be prepared for one purpose and not be subject to the possibility of misinterpretation by the investor if used for another purpose.

WIDER HORIZONS, *Canadian Chartered Accountant,* XXX (April, 1937), 295-304. [145]

A review of the development of the accounting profession in Europe indicates strong professional development in Germany resulting from the demand induced primarily by American financing. A similar situation existed in South America, especially in the Argentine.

In Great Britain, where accountancy had been well established when business units were small, accountants naturally stepped into the administrative side of the law and filled such positions as trustee receivers and liquidators. In contrast, in the United States with its large business units and highly developed internal auditing, the accounting profession developed rather slowly as an important factor in economic life. The profession's position in Canada is similar to that in Great Britain.

The English audit certificate, commonly found in Canada, which states that "the balance sheet shows a true and correct view of the state of the company's affairs," should be revised to show more clearly what a balance sheet is, and what the auditors have done.

The prospectus issued under the United States Securities Act is too full of qualifications, reservations and footnotes to be of any real value to the investor. The valuable effect of the law has been to educate officers and directors in their own affairs.

The act will bring about changes in the form of financial statements. We may eventually see the day when the balance sheet ranks fifth in order of importance among the financial statements presented.

Canada has taken a wise course in following the example laid down by Great Britain in the field of taxation, especially with regard to capital gains and undistributed profits taxation.

GROWTH AND INCIDENCE OF TAXATION, *Accountant, Tax Supplement,* August 7, 1937, pp. 337-41. [146]

The Twentieth Century Fund report stated the objectives of taxation as being the raising of revenue and the control of production, distribution or consumption, while the famous Colwyn Committee report in England dealt primarily with the effect of taxation on savings and the development of new industries. American economists have not all overlooked the effect of taxation on savings. As desirable as redistribution of income or wealth may be, it has been repeatedly demonstrated how little this can accomplish. The greatest hope for our less fortunate people lies in increasing aggregate national income.

The principle of taxation of undistributed profits is unsound, and the law should be amended to exclude from taxation profits invested in productive plants, which would be a logical support to the pump priming theory of the present administration. And further, an amendment should be made allowing the offsetting of losses of one year against the profits of another.

Even under the new tax law, the budget remains unbalanced. The consequences of an unbalanced budget are so serious that it may be better to operate under an unjust tax law, at least for a while, than to allow an unbalanced budget to continue.

PRINCIPLES OF ACCOUNTING, *Journal of Accountancy,* LXIV (December, 1937), 423-25. [147]

The Oxford Dictionary defines a principle as a fundamental or primary truth or proposition on which others depend or as a general rule or law adopted as a guide to action. Gilbert Byrne, in the essay in which he discusses "accepted principles of accounting consistently maintained," has misunderstood the sense in which the word "principle" is used. He has attributed to the word the first meaning or sense given above, while history and the development of the auditor's certificate will show that the second meaning is intended.

Byrne has pointed out the apparent contradiction in the wording of the certificate in that the words "consistently maintained" in themselves "imply mutability" while the first of the two definitions above implies that principles are unchangeable.

Accounting is not and, as long as human conduct and judgment are involved, cannot be scientific. Accounting "is essentially pragmatic," and this pragmatism is indispensable to any real progress in accounting.

RECENT OPINIONS ON DEALINGS IN TREASURY STOCK, *Journal of Accountancy,* LXVI (July, 1938), 17-22. [148]

A serious defect exists in Montgomery's argument that treasury stock should be set up as an asset in those states which prohibit the reduction of legal capital by the acquisition of a company's own shares, and that gain or loss should be recognized upon the sale of treasury shares just as it is on any other capital asset. He also points out that in some states, such as California, where treasury stock may be acquired in certain cases out of stated capital, his views would be different.

The defect in the argument is to be found in "the very premise that when a company acquires its own capital stock, it does not acquire an asset and therefore should not be permitted to use for this purpose any funds except those which it is legally entitled to disburse without receiving valuable consideration therefor, as in the payment of dividends." The acquisition of treasury shares by companies governed by such laws is frequently spoken of as being "out of surplus."

The Institute has already adopted the view that dividends on treasury stock are not to be treated as income. If such were the case a company's income would be a function of its dividend policy and not the reverse. If dividends were income, a company could increase its income for a given period by an almost infinite amount by simply accelerating its declaration of dividends. If treasury stock is an asset and the yield therefrom is not income, how then can the gain from sales be treated as income?

Corporate executives would be in a position of "heads, we win; tails, we cannot lose," if the profession accepted the idea that the excess of sales proceeds over cost is to be carried to earned surplus. Shares are frequently acquired at less than par or stated value. If stock prices should rise, the shares could be sold and a credit to income secured; if prices fall, the stock could be retired and a credit to capital surplus secured. The adoption of such a position by accountants would be most unwise.

CONSEQUENCES OF INCREASING TAXES, *Accountant, Tax Supplement,* August 13, 1938, pp. 383-85. [149]

Any adverse deflationary effect resulting from financing only through taxation would be small compared to the benefits accruing from the increased confidence resulting from a balanced budget.

One of the lesser known consequences of high taxation is the uncertainty and instability of the tax revenue. Great Britain refrained from raising maximum rates to a level found in the United States, while at the same time taxing moderate incomes at higher rates. Benefits would accrue if the United States followed the English pattern of rates.

The growing complexity of the law, the increasing costs of administration and the constant attempts to prevent evasion by enactment of special provisions are further consequences of high tax rates.

Treating all forms of income alike may produce inequity under the ability to pay principle of progressive income taxation, as, for example, the earnings of a temporarily popular artist.

In estate and gift taxation, the combination of high rates and difficulties of valuation may result in complete confiscation, making the disposition of an enterprise as part of one's estate extremely hazardous. The danger point in taxation has already been passed, and a restrictive, prejudicial effect is being exerted on enterprise.

The undistributed profits tax law should be repealed, because it has and will discourage employment and the production of income.

UNIFORMITY IN ACCOUNTING, *Harvard Business Review,* XVII (Autumn, 1938), 1-8. [150]

Undoubtedly the desire for uniformity in accounting is but a part of a vague, widespread yearning for rules which will, it is hoped, eliminate complexities and uncertainties. Uniformity, however, should not be the goal in itself, but should be viewed as a means of making the accounts more informative and useful to unskilled readers having a legitimate interest in them.

If all accounts could be relied upon as being interpretations of relevant facts, understood and prepared by honest competent persons with an understanding of the uses to which the accounts are to be put, uniformity would be of minor importance. Since this ideal is not universally attainable, uniformity can provide a beneficially restraining effect. Uniformity can lead to rigid limitation, and if flexible rules or guides to action can be substituted therefor the aims of accounting will be better served.

INTRODUCTION TO DISCUSSION OF "A STATEMENT OF ACCOUNTING PRINCIPLES," *Papers on Accounting Principles and Procedure,* Fifty-first Annual Meeting, 1938 (New York: American Institute of Accountants, 1939), 1-2. [151]

Inventory valuation is an area in which least uniformity in accounting is to be found. An important question here is whether one method of determining cost, in the cost or market, whichever is lower, method, should be universally adopted.

A further important question relates to what constitutes a transaction, since accountants usually record charges and credits to income on the basis of completed transactions.

Although there is considerable demand for uniformity in accounting, accountants must guard against "the danger of unity in form which does not represent corresponding unity of substance."

VALUATION OR HISTORICAL COST: SOME RECENT DEVELOPMENTS, *Journal of Accountancy*, LXIX (January, 1940), 14-21. [152]

Accounting is, of necessity, conventional. Accounts are required for many different purposes, and the same conventions are not equally appropriate for all of these purposes. The SEC, for example, has been unwilling to concede that an accounting treatment appropriate for one purpose was equally appropriate for all others in the field of financial accounting. The chairman of the SEC has questioned the adequacy of "general purpose" accounts to meet all purposes for which accounts might be required. The needs of the public interest might be better served if the SEC were to call for "special reports."

Many of the difficulties and uncertainties in accounting arise from the fact that two principles, valuation and historical cost, are applied in drawing up a balance sheet; that two different principles, accrual and the completed transaction, are applied and presented in the income statement, and that the two statements must, in some manner, be tied together.

The application of these different principles was born of necessity, but the major problem of making clear why different principles are employed in different circumstances, and in what circumstances each is applicable, still remains.

The use of the *Lifo* method of inventory valuation is growing rapidly, and the adoption of this method "for inventories lends strong support to the use of the historical cost basis for fixed properties." ". . . balance sheets do not and should not reflect values of fixed assets," because "it is impracticable for them to do so, and, second, that such values are irrelevant."

THE RELATION OF DEPRECIATION PROVISIONS TO REPLACEMENT, *Journal of Accountancy*, LXIX, LXX (May and July, 1940), 341-47, 69-70. [153]

In their testimony before the Temporary National Economic Committee, Drs. O. L. Altman and A. H. Hansen stated that "re-investment of part of the present depreciation allowances will maintain productive capacity. Business can invest all of its depreciation allowances only by expanding its productive capacity."

The above views are based upon studies made by Drs. Kuznets and Fabricant of the National Bureau of Economic Research. Dr. Fabricant made the statement that "the economist, in estimating business facts, need not have the scruples of the accountant. The accuracy he strives for is related to a wider view."

This "wider view" of the economist may actually result in incomplete data and misunderstood facts. For example, current depreciation provisions, rather than being excessive, are actually inadequate to provide either for the amortization of capital invested or the replacement thereof when necessary. Nor are the depreciation deductions allowed under tax law sufficient to provide for new additions.

RECENT TRENDS IN ACCOUNTING, *Canadian Chartered Accountant*, XXXVII (September, 1940), 151-68. [154]

While the importance of the balance sheet has been declining and that of the income statement increasing, there is developing a growing recognition that these two statements do not supply all of the information desired by interested parties. This has led to the presentation of analyses of changes in reserve accounts and in increasing the use of some form of funds statement.

The question of allocation between the profit and loss account and surplus is receiving considerable attention with less use of the profit and loss account for items which might be allocated. Accounts are being more frequently presented in such a manner as to bring out clearly their interdependence.

Statements should not be presented which include expressions such as "deferred charges" and "unadjusted debits and credits." There is also a general trend against reporting a company's own securities as assets, and an attempt is being made to present financial data in a manner which can be understood by the layman.

There are essentially three schools of thought with respect to the substance of accounting. One group believes that there are some fundamental principles to which all sound accounting must conform. At the other extreme lies a group holding that accounting is essentially practical. The third group's position lies between the other two with the belief that while accounting must be practical, it would at the same time be desirable to develop some system of generally accepted principles on which a consistent theory of accounting can be built. The latter position is that of the Committee on Accounting Procedure of the Institute and the SEC.

The recommendation of the executive committee of the American Accounting Association, that corrections of previous estimate applicable to prior years should be included in the determination of net income, is questionable. The basic difficulty is that the income statement can not serve so many varied purposes equally well.

The stockholder's real source of income is the earning of income by the corporation, and a loss to the corporation is a loss to the stockholder. In view of this, ignoring undivided profits and losses of companies in which a corporation holds stock may not be as perfectly a consistent treatment as many suppose it to be.

The problems of reconciling the demands for uniformity and for flexibility have not been solved, although there has been greatly increased understanding of accounting and the difficulties it faces.

FUNDAMENTALS OF ACCOUNTING PROCEDURES, *New York Certified Public Accountant,* X (November, 1940), 73-83. [155]

The change in emphasis from balance sheet to income accounting has been followed by pressure for more uniformity in accounting. There are many dangers inherent in too much uniformity. The pressure for uniformity has come primarily from those who wish to regulate and those who wish to be free from responsibility.

Another noticeable trend is the shift from regulation by general law to the vesting of necessary powers in administrative agencies, as for example, the powers given to the Department of Justice with respect to monopolies and consent decrees.

As is true in law, accounting procedure problems lie in attempting to reconcile stability and adaptability. At a time when even the Supreme Court is shifting to adaptability, accounting is searching for fixed and fundamental principles which will remain valid despite changing business needs. The goal is unattainable, but the attempt may produce clearer understanding and more coherent rules.

Some of the basic accounting principles are consistency, conservatism, distinguishing between capital and income, matching costs against revenue and the allocation of charges to the period correspondingly benefited.

Illustrative of the different accounting treatments accorded an item are the varying treatments accorded taxes. Taxes may be viewed as (1) a cost of government services provided, (2) a governmental participation in income and loss to the extent of offset of losses against gains — this is the most reasonable view, or (3) related "to some business fact and to be guided in disposing of them by their relation to that fact." As for example, some taxes such as customs and excise duties are capitalized.

Fundamental accounting procedures may also be affected by the different treatments accorded certain items of expense and income in the accounts as contrasted to the tax return.

General and Special Purpose Statements, *Corporate Financial Statements,* Proceedings of the 1940 Accounting Institute, Columbia University (New York: Columbia University Press, 1940), pp. 155-57. [156]

One rather small group believes that valuation should be the basis for all items in the balance sheet. The majority, however, favor the view set forth by Paton and Littleton in their recent monograph, that cost should be the predominant if not universal point of view.

In spite of the great attention being placed upon the income statement, it would be a mistake to think that the balance sheet has no significance since it shows what has become of income, a question nearly as important as income itself.

The investor looks upon the income statement as a guide to (1) managerial efficiency, (2) probability of dividends, and (3) the capital value of the firm. In using the income statement for the third purpose the problem of recurring versus non-recurring items is frequently encountered. An increase in the size of the income stream is on a completely different basis than a gain resulting from an increase in the capital value of the income stream.

Of interest to the investor are a number of items which the accountant cannot measure, such as the quality of management and the labor policies of a firm. Regulatory machinery can do nothing in this area, no matter how carefully created or administered.

Paton and Littleton discussed and rejected the cost or market, whichever is lower, rule of inventory valuation. The rejection should not, however, be so complete. If costs cannot be recovered through sales they should be written off immediately and recognized as losses.

Profit and loss and *undivided profits* are better terms than *income* and *earned surplus.* The term *surplus* is vague and frequently includes items, such as discount on the discharge of debt, which cannot be considered earned.

Every effort should be made to secure recognition for depreciation as an actual cost.

ACCOUNTING PRINCIPLES AND REGULATORY EXPEDIENCY, *Journal of Accountancy,* LXXI (February, 1941), 116-18. [157]

In many instances alternative treatments may be accorded certain items, with such alternative treatments recognized as being within the limits of sound accounting. However, alternative treatments which are departures from sound accountancy should not be considered for the sake of expediency.

The Federal Power Commission has taken the position that unamortized bond discount on bonds refunded is to be charged off immediately. However, if such a charge would create a deficit, "a relaxing of the rule *not as a matter of accounting principle, but as a matter of regulatory expedient may be sanctioned.*"

Thus, the approach of the FPC to such problems differs considerably from that of the Institute which "recognizes that the practical consequences of accepting a rule should be taken into account in laying down principles, but they should be followed. . . . The Commission quite unnecessarily, as it seems to me, attempts to maintain the position that principles are something subordinate to administrative jurisdiction and to be departed from whenever such departure seems to be expedient."

GROSS INCOME, *Quarterly Journal of Economics,* LV (May, 1941), 521-25. [158]

Economists have been quite inconsistent in their choice of terminology. The term *gross* is used inconsistently in many different circumstances and with unfortunate connotations. The same is true with regard to the use of the term *income.*

The assertion by many economists, in their interpretation of gross income, that depreciation charges are "notoriously" and "grossly" excessive is quite untrue. In fact, the direct opposite is generally true; depreciation provisions are actually seriously inadequate.

SOME IMPLICATIONS OF ORIGINAL COST, *New York Certified Public Accountant,* XI (May, 1941), 481-85. [159]

Original cost is an unilluminating term by which cost is viewed from the standpoint of someone other than the present owner of an investment. *Enterprise cost* as a term would have revealed the distinction between enterprise cost and corporate cost, the latter being one of the first principles of accounting.

Under a *corporate cost* concept, the "property accounts are determined by values at the date the particular corporation which owns the property was created." Use of this concept has resulted in abuses through reorganization when prices were low or high depending upon the purposes of the corporation. The quasi-reorganization device has made it easier to secure the benefits of writeups or writedowns without going through a formal reorganization. The use of this concept has also made the capitalized earnings value of a corporation a function of the time of incorporation.

Under an enterprise cost concept, "the basis is determined on the prices which prevailed at a time when a real transaction between parties dealing at arms' length took place." Impliedly, a different position should be taken by accountants when reorganization takes place without ownership change as contrasted to when it is incidental to ownership change. Accountants should re-examine the concept of corporate cost as they are examining original cost and enterprise cost.

INTRODUCTION TO ROUND-TABLE DISCUSSION ON ACCOUNTING PROCEDURE AND RESEARCH, *Experiences with Extensions of Auditing Procedure,* Fifty-third Annual Meeting, 1940 (New York: American Institute of Accountants, 1941), pp. 45-46. [160]

The objectives of the Institute's Committee on Accounting Research are: (1) to help members in deciding what is best current practice, and (2) to take a broader view in exploring what changes in outlook may be called for by changed conditions.

The Supreme Court has gone through a period of reform in its shift in emphasis from stability to adaptability. Accountants need to proceed along similar lines and be willing to examine every old precedent and principle, seeking to bring about improvement and not merely change.

PREMIUMS ON REDEMPTIONS OF PREFERRED STOCKS, *Journal of Accountancy,* LXXII (August, 1941), 127-32. [161]

The position taken by the American Accounting Association in maintaining that premiums on the retirement of shares should be charged pro-rata against any paid-in surplus applicable to the class of shares being retired, and the balance of the premium, if any, should be charged to earned surplus, is questionable. The first basis for questioning this position is that it treats premiums on a different basis than discounts. To say that discounts may not be credited to earned surplus but premiums may be charged thereagainst is inconsistent.

The treatment of the retirement premium as a dividend is to be questioned, since the retirement of shares does not give the board of directors the power to enlarge the dividend. Charging such premiums to earned surplus might wipe out this account and work an injustice upon other holders of shares not retired, in that they may not then receive a dividend.

"Further, one of the most appropriate uses of capital surplus, it may be said, is to write off intangible values which are not elements in the production of income and do not have to be amortized out of revenues. Therefore, the appropriate accounting treatment would accord with the legally permissible treatment of charging the premium against any form of genuine paid-in surplus."

The problem of proper accounting for premiums on the retirement of common stock is complicated by the conflict between cost, in the accounts, and value, as paid for the stock. However, the same conclusion must be reached. Premiums on redemption or retirement of shares cannot be considered, theoretically or practically, to be dividends.

LOSSES AS A CAUSE OF GAIN, WITH A FOOTNOTE ON "VALUE," *Journal of Accountancy*, LXXII (September, 1941), 221-28. [162]

The depression brought with it situations wherein a company could retire some of its outstanding debt at an amount less than face value, thus creating the illusion of gain. Support for the position that gain results from the retirement of debt for less than the amount owed can be found in certain decisions in tax cases. However, it should be noted that redemption of debt for less than face value does not always result in taxable income.

The fact that a company can retire debt for less than the amount due at maturity is the result of two factors: change in interest rates, or change in the commercial value of the company or both. That which results from change in the interest rates can be considered gain and credited to income or surplus. With respect to the so-called gain resulting from the decline in the commercial value of the enterprise, "it is unsound accounting to consider these transactions as producing gains which can properly be regarded as income while the decline in the value of the enterprise is, under accepted accounting rules, rightly ignored."

The theory that the value of property consists of the expectations of income from such property leads down "a long and uncertain road." Valuation by discounting expected earnings depends upon the expected earnings, the degree of probability of realizing such earnings and the discount rate employed. However, actual situations have shown that the junior securities have a market value even in circumstances where, according to the application of this method, they have no value. "The more the question is studied, the more convinced accountants must be of the wisdom of avoiding valuation of enterprises or capital assets in corporation accounting as far as possible."

FUTURE TRENDS IN ACCOUNTING, *Papers and Addresses, Tenth Annual Meeting, Controllers Institute of America* (New York: Controllers Institute of America, 1941), pp. 37-52. [163]

The fundamental problems in accounting center around (1) the cost versus value question, (2) the need to allocate profits to short periods of time, (3) the varying purposes to which the accounts are put, (4) the time when income arises, and (5) the question of how far the motive for making an expenditure shall be employed in accounting for it.

The past decade has seen the trend to booking current values replaced by a strong trend toward adherence to cost. A question may be raised as to whether the emphasis placed on the income account has not gone too far. This emphasis has resulted in surplus charges being looked upon with disfavor. Consistency has been stressed and conservatism discredited.

A current regrettable tendency is found in regulatory agencies regarding accounting principles as being subject to change on the grounds of regulatory expediency. Of special note is the large amount of research and careful analysis of accounting's problems being undertaken currently.

As for the future, it would be desirable that the trend toward discrediting conservatism be reversed, and that the danger attached to emphasizing the results of a single period be recognized. ". . . the emphasis on the utilitarian view of accounting and on the investment approach, rather than the value approach, is likely to become even more pronounced." The future holds a possibility for more uniformity in inventory practices. Also to be recognized is the varying degree of importance attaching to varying kinds of income. Better terminology also lies ahead.

Accounting is a question of usefulness, not of right and wrong, and those who are to decide what is useful are those "who have had long practical experience as well as a knowledge of the theoretical aspect of the question."

RESEARCH AND TERMINOLOGY-RESEARCH, *Accounting, Auditing and Taxes,* Papers Presented at the Fifty-fourth Annual Meeting, 1941 (New York: American Institute of Accountants, 1941), pp. 86-89. [164]

"You cannot understand what are sound accounting principles without having a clear idea of the purposes of accounting." Accounting has shifted its viewpoint from that of continuing owners of securities to that of persons who buy and sell securities, and this shift may have already gone too far.

Greater effort should be expended to secure the ideas of persons who are not interested in listed securities so that the whole trend of accounting will not be dictated by considerations relating to companies under the SEC and other regulatory agency jurisdiction.

In the last bulletin on stock dividends the Institute's committee went further than in previous bulletins and discussed what is good corporate accounting policy. "The Institute ought to exercise an influence in regard to business practices in the general field of accounting even if they are not purely accounting questions."

TERMINOLOGY OF THE BALANCE SHEET, *Journal of Accountancy,* LXXIII (January, 1942), 35-36. [165]

The first goal of the Institute's Committee on Terminology in attempting to define *balance sheet, asset* and *liability* was to express the definitions in simple and popular language. "Simplicity was obtainable only at the sacrifice of accuracy." The committee was forced to consider definitions in the framework of accounting principles and rules. Since accounting principles and rules are not based on abstract theories, but on utility, "there seems to be a substantial advantage in defining balance sheet, assets, and liabilities so as to coordinate terminology with rules and principles as from time to time established." Because accounting is in part highly technical, the results derived from the application of certain techniques and conventions can only be defined in terms that take cognizance of these techniques and conventions.

WAR AND ACCOUNTING PROCEDURES, *Journal of Accountancy,* LXIII (May, 1942), 393-400. [166]

The hazards of war have increased the degree of uncertainty attaching to the determination of income and financial position, and the accompanying high taxation "makes these uncertainties of infinitely greater importance."

The Institute's Committee on Accounting Procedure faced the conflicting objectives "of making charges against revenue as nearly as possible in the same period as that in which the revenue is received," as opposed to the basing of "accounting entries as far as possible on definite evidence, or at least reasonably informed estimates." The committee believed the first objective to be controlling.

Management should be encouraged to set up contingency reserves, and charges should be deducted in arriving at net income as a practical matter even though, perhaps, not theoretically correct. This leads to questions regarding the usefulness of accounting data, because, in wartime, the principle uses of accounting are in connection with fiscal policy and taxation. For such purposes "conservatism is still the cardinal virtue of accounting."

Reserves should be established to charge into current operations costs which will be incurred in future years to convert production facilities back to peacetime operations. Reserves should be established in conjunction with inventories so that high wartime taxes will not be paid on profits which arise only because of inflationary trends. Reserves should also be established for separation allowances and pensions of wartime employees and for possible losses resulting from the actions of armed forces.

THE BRITISH TAXATION OF CAPITAL GAINS, *Journal of Accountancy*, LXXIII (June, 1942), 502-7. [167]

An important distinction between the tax law in the United States and England is in the different concepts of income. English courts, while not defining income, have held that accretion to capital — capital gains — is not taxable income in the absence of provisions specifically levying a tax upon it. The common American view, as expressed by the Supreme Court, includes capital gains as income. Misunderstanding of English tax law also results from the failure to distinguish between capital gains and casual profits. The latter term includes "speculative profits and profits on non-recurrent trading operations." Profits or losses on the sale of investments by English investment trusts do not enter into the determination of taxable income. Annuities and income from British natural resources are taxed without allowance for exhaustion of the asset, and British tax law allows no relief for losses not incurred in connection with a taxable business.

The casual profits section and the word *annual* in British tax law have caused a number of cases to be tried by the courts. Profits on the purchase and sale of linen in an eight-month period were deemed taxable, despite the assertion that they should not be taxed because of the "annual profits" provision of the law. Profit on the sale of Italian lira acquired in connection with a contract to buy Italian marble was deemed to be not taxable, while profits from trading in cotton futures were taxable. Profit on the purchase and sale, as a member of a syndicate, of two rubber plantations was held to be an accretion of capital and, hence, not taxable.

BRITISH AND AMERICAN TAXATION, *Journal of Accountancy*, LXXIV (July, 1942), 38-40. [168]

Prepared in connection with the annual budget, a recently completed British government white paper reveals the "smallness of the surtax collections in proportion to the yield of the income tax, and the fact that while the yield of the income tax is steadily rising, that of the surtax has become stationary."

The American income tax structure consists of a low normal tax and high surtaxes, while the British have a high income tax with abatements and surtaxes. Corporations are taxed on profits before deduction of interest, rent, royalties or dividends. Taxes are deducted from payments made for the above items and remitted to the government. If a corporation pays out all of its profits for the above items, it has no net tax liability.

The British do not tax capital gains because retained profits are taxed at the full personal income tax rate, and because the British place a very high value on profits re-invested to maintain industrial efficiency and future taxable capacity.

Other differences exist regarding charitable contributions, taxes, earned income and insurance premiums, so that a mere comparison of the rates between the two countries is apt to be misleading.

THE AMERICAN CAR AND FOUNDRY DECISION, *Journal of Accountancy*, LXIV (December, 1942), 517-22. [169]

The case of *Cintas* v. *American Car and Foundry Company* consisted of an action brought by a preferred stockholder to enjoin a dividend payment to common stockholders until the full dividend on the 7 percent non-cumulative preferred stock had been paid.

In 1936 the corporation suffered a loss in excess of the profits of its subsidiaries; however, it received a dividend from a subsidiary in the form of notes of another partially owned company, via yet another partially owned company.

The basic question then was whether or not there was a profit and, if so, in what year or years. The plaintiff's contention was that consolidated statements were a "figment" in spite of the increasingly widespread acceptance of such statements. The Court of Appeals rejected the defendant's contention that wholly owned subsidiary corporations must be regarded as departments or divisions of the parent company and affirmed a lower court finding for the plaintiff.

Because of the special facts involved and the manner of presentation, the case is not apt to have wide accounting significance. The court, however, had ample principles upon which to base a different decision.

REVOKE, *New York Certified Public Accountant,* XIII (January, 1943), 162-64. [170]

Although the belief has been previously expressed that "the enterprise theory" could be employed in public utility accounting, the accounting regulations of the Federal Power Commission are unacceptable. The primary reason for this lack of acceptability is the line of distinction drawn between (1) reclassification of expenditures, (2) reaccounting for expenditures, and (3) correction of errors in accounting for expenditures.

The Federal Power Commission is not adhering to accepted accounting principles even as defined by its own accountants. The FPC is resorting to accounting for expediency, and this is the same action for which it had previously condemned utility managements.

ACCOUNTING DEVELOPMENTS OF 1942, *Journal of Accountancy,* LXXV (April, 1943), 301-5. [171]

War has brought with it a demand for profit restriction and greater tax revenues. As a result increased importance is attached to the allocation of profits to the various years. Adding to the difficulties of measuring income for a year is the war contract renegotiation provision of the War Profits Control Act.

In the cost versus value problem area, the shift toward recognition of the cost basis continues. There is also a growing realization that accounts may be viewed from an enterprise point of view as well as a corporate entity point of view for purposes such as taxation, rate and price control, reorganization and prospective purchase.

The Interstate Commerce Commission accepted the "original cost" theory of accounting in railroad reorganizations, and special relief provisions for such reorganized railroads were included in the 1942 revenue act.

A Supreme Court decision stressed future earning capacity as the basis for value, and the Natural Gas Pipeline case decision supported cost as the basis of accounting for assets. The New York Court of Appeals, in interpreting a dividend provision of the state statute, held that unrealized appreciation should be taken into consideration. The SEC, in a decision, held that permanent declines in investments should be recognized by the holder thereof by writing down the investment, or establishing a reserve.

New tax legislation permits dividends on preferred stocks of certain public utility companies to be deducted in arriving at taxable income. The desirability of presenting a "profits before income and excess-profits taxes" figure is being increasingly questioned.

THE NATURE OF THE FINANCIAL ACCOUNTING PROCESS, *Accounting Review*, XVIII (July, 1943), 189-93. [172]

A review of the functions of financial accounting shows how accounting conventions have changed with time, social conditions, economic changes, etc. ". . . the most significant change . . . is the shift of emphasis from the balance sheet to the income statement."

A number of "alternative approaches to the problem of formulating or revising the conventions of financial accounting" exist. Should accounting follow the cost or value approach, or attempt to combine the two? Is accounting moving toward a more complete acceptance of the realization concept or of the gradual accrual concept? Accounting has a choice to make between the enterprise and the legal entity as its accounting unit.

Some accounting conventions may have to be revised because basic assumptions must be discarded — for example, the assumption of the stability of the monetary unit.

Accounting has long been looked upon as a valuation process, and only recently, because the complexity of business has become so great as to make valuation impracticable, has attention been turned to cost.

The credit grantor was the greatest external influence on accounting; now, however, statements are prepared to guide persons buying and selling securities.

Conservatism used to be the "cardinal virtue of accounting; now, the virtue of conservatism is questioned, and the greater emphasis is on consistency."

CORPORATE STRUCTURES AND FEDERAL INCOME TAX, *Harvard Business Review*, XXII (Autumn, 1943), 10-18. [173]

A number of differences exist between English and American tax law. English law levies a tax upon income, while we tax the income recipients. In England a corporation pays a net tax only on its undistributed income, with the tax thereon being much higher in normal times than our income tax on corporations. English tax law does not affect the building of the corporate structure, while our tax law places a premium on debt financing. In spite of this premium, the amount of debt of manufacturing and trading companies is surprisingly low.

Double taxation of both corporate profits and stockholder dividends is not sound and should be abolished. If this cannot be accomplished, the interest deduction for borrowed capital should be gradually eliminated and dividends should be exempted from personal income taxation.

ACCOUNTING AND REGULATION, *Journal of Accountancy,* LXXVI (October, 1943), 295-301. [174]

The present and future effects of the development of regulation of business and its resulting effects upon accounting "are matters of great importance to accountants and to those who rely on accounts. . . . Already we see commissions which are vested with policy-making, regulatory, and quasi-judicial functions seeking freedom from legal restraints by asserting the higher authority of accounting principles, old or new, laid down by them and based supposedly on considerations of equity or economic reality. They next undertake to relax the application of such principles as a matter of regulatory expediency or administrative policy. Thus with the aid of legal presumptions of administrative expertness and impartiality, accounting may be made superior to law but still remain the not too rigid implement of policy."

Investors should not fallaciously assume that uniformity will result from control by commissions. "Departures from principle on the grounds of expediency have long been an indicant of regulatory practice." The Federal Power Commission order in the Northwestern Electric Company case is illustrative of this point. The case centered around the issuance of $3.5 million par value shares without consideration prior to 1915. Present holders paid over $5 million for the shares. The Commission ordered the $3.5 million debit charged against net income after preferred dividends. This would result in obtaining the consideration not formerly received from present stockholders in the form of withheld dividends.

The accounting profession could do much more to influence legislative and regulatory bodies to comply with standards acceptable to the profession.

COMMENTS BY GEORGE O. MAY ON "ACCOUNTING PRACTICE AFTER THE WAR" (An Address by Joel M. Bowlby), *Accounting Problems in War Contract Termination, Taxes and Postwar Planning.* Papers Presented at the Fifty-sixth Annual Meeting. (New York: American Institute of Accountants, 1943), pp. 148-51. [175]

Accountants must demonstrate that their profession has status comparable to that of law in terms of the quality of its members. The stimulus given the accounting profession by the last war may have been too great because there are not enough qualified men to carry the responsibilities placed upon the profession by the public. Accounting may have developed too rapidly for its own good, and the securities legislation of the thirties was a blow to its professional standing. Today, however, there is no real need for anybody to dictate to accountants.

Accountants must guard against all threats to their independence, since "independence is the breath of life." The profession has shown a willingness to accept responsibility, but there may be too many opportunities thrust upon individual accountants which result in an unwarranted extension of activities.

ACCOUNTING IN THE LIGHT OF RECENT SUPREME COURT DECISIONS, *Journal of Accountancy*, LXXVII (May, 1944), 371-75. [176]

Reference is made to the Northwestern Electric Company case (see the author's article "Accounting and Regulation," §174) and to the brief filed by the American Institute of Accountants when the case was appealed to the Supreme Court. The Institute's brief specifically asked that the Supreme Court not sanction the writeoff of the debit balance against earnings after preferred dividends. The Court refused to agree with the Institute, stating that although the Commission's method may not have been in accord with the best accounting it was not "an obviously arbitrary plan. . . . The fact . . . is that the order was . . . the most punitive that could be readily conceived." It prevented the distribution of common stock dividends until an additional $3.5 million of earned surplus was accumulated.

In the Hope Natural Gas Company case the Commission fixed the rate base at original cost less depreciation, but described the method employed in its brief as the prudent investment method. The distinction between these two methods was understood by the Court, and it was then forced to "choose between approving the order of the Commission and approving the process by which the Commission arrived at its conclusion as being an application of the 'prudent investment theory.' " It chose the first alternative, holding that it could not say that the return allowed was not just and reasonable.

"The decision clearly constitutes a new chapter in the history of accounting as a factor in rate regulation. It indicates that the day of the appraiser has passed and the era of accounting has arrived. It seems certain that rate regulation will be almost completely a matter of accounting."

ACCOUNTING AS A SOCIAL FORCE, *Canadian Chartered Accountant*, XLIV (May, 1944), 274-80. [177]

One result of the growth in size of business enterprises has been the increase in the importance of the accountant. When business operations were conducted on a smaller scale the accounts were prepared primarily for the owner. Now the accountant must render more precise accounts to owners, management and the general public.

The new responsibilities of the accountant also require greater self-discipline on the part of the profession, which is far better than discipline by some form of commission. If a professional group does not discipline itself, the government will control or regulate it in some manner.

Accounting must be based upon principles. These principles derive their authority from their acceptance and are not fundamental truths. Since accounting is a language, it needs both stability and flexibility.

WHAT ARE CORPORATE INCOME TAXES? *Journal of Accountancy,* LXXVIII (October, 1944), 307. [178]

"The corporation income tax is not a true income tax. It is something of a hybrid; to the extent of the amount of normal tax of individuals it is a true income tax, because if a corporation pays that tax and then pays the dividend, the taxpayer gets corresponding relief [Ed. note — no longer true]; and, personally, I would not treat that part of the income tax as a cost, although some people might.

"As regards the balance, it is not a true income tax. It is merely an excise tax for the privilege of carrying on business as a corporation, and as such it is a part of the cost of doing business."

THE NARUC AND DEPRECIATION, *Journal of Accountancy,* LXXIX (January, 1945), 34-38. [179]

The 1944 report of the Committee on Depreciation of the NARUC clarified some of the issues of the 1943 report which had been severely criticized by many persons and groups including the Institute's Committee on Accounting Procedure.

The main issue centered on the adjustment of the books of public utilities to eliminate deficiencies in the depreciation reserves. The 1944 report set up three classes in determining adjustments: (1) those adjustments in which existing reserves are considered adequate, (2) those in which the deficiency is of moderate size, and (3) those in which the reserve is obviously inadequate. The Committee contemplates a gradual change to straight-line method depreciation for the cases in class two with the charges being made to operating expenses. Immediate adjustment, with the charge to surplus or capital, if necessary, is to be made in the class three cases.

A critical difference, however, still exists between the Institute and the Committee on Depreciation in that the Institute maintains that a properly calculated depreciation reserve is not the best evidence of actual existing depreciation. ". . . until the Committee has purged its definition of its defects, abandoned false inferences therefrom, and extended it to cover the significant concepts of 'depreciation for the year' and 'accrued depreciation' its reports, for all their many merits, will not be entitled to . . . general acceptance."

"All in all . . . the conclusion is that on the broad issue of adoption of depreciation accounting in the future . . . the Committee . . . reaches right conclusions on these points by the wrong reasoning."

INCOME TAXES AND INTANGIBLES — TWO SIGNIFICANT RESEARCH BULLETINS, *Journal of Accountancy,* LXXIX (February, 1945) 124-29. [180]

A review of the historical development of the accounting for income taxes reveals that in the period 1913 to 1936 the tax was treated as falling in the "intermediate classification between pure expenses and distributions." This type of classification resulted from the dual nature of the tax — a tax on income and an excise tax for the privilege of doing business.

After 1936 the tax was a pure expense to the company, since, as a result of the disallowance of tax relief to stockholders for taxes paid on dividends earned by the corporation, it was purely an excise tax. Bulletin No. 23 clearly states that "Income taxes are an expense which should be allocated, when necessary and practicable, to income and other accounts, as other expenses are allocated."

Bulletin No. 24 emphasizes management's responsibility to account for values in its care regardless of the mode of acquisition or whether tangible or intangible. Three types of intangibles are distinguished: (a) those with life limited by contract, law, etc., (b) those of indefinite life at the time of acquisition, and (c) those purchased in the form of a premium over book value of the capital stocks of subsidiary companies.

A further problem regarding the accounting for intangibles is the question of whether or not intangibles are subject to amortization, and if so, over what period. "It is frequently said that intangibles represent the capital value of superior earning power. Just how existence of superiority is to be determined is a question to which there is no established or ready answer. Therefore, when intangibles become worthless is a question on which there is room for wide difference of opinion."

The bulletin also recognizes that in consolidation the price paid in excess of book value in the acquisition of subsidiary company stock does not necessarily represent a payment for an intangible value. Some may question the wisdom of publishing this bulletin, but reaction to past bulletins shows that the value derived from stimulated thinking about a topic has been greater than the conclusions presented in the bulletin.

TEACHING ACCOUNTING TO NON-TECHNICAL STUDENTS, *Accounting Review*, XX (April, 1945), 131-38. [181]

The current period is one of great opportunity and responsibility for the accountant. Education concerning both the significance and the limitations of accounting statements must be given to all professions associated with our national income. "National income" should be an accounting concept, and "it is a task for accountants to make the term suitable as a central concept of our economic thinking."

All those engaged in the economic, statistical and financial activities of government should realize the significance of a given concept of income, while, at the same time, recognizing its limitations.

Most accountants will be bookkeepers or auditors, and accounting education in most schools is adequate to meet these tasks. However, a number of accountants will need to be more highly trained to master some branches of professional work. Education for the latter will require greater specialization.

Before attempting to teach an understanding of accounting concepts, accounting principles and rules will have to be dictated by powerful considerations and not designed to advance individual purposes. Research and re-examination of principles should be financed, if possible, by the American Accounting Association and the American Institute of Certified Public Accountants. One possible approach to the problem of formulating accounting principles would be historical. Corporate law, accounting history, and the evolution, foreign and domestic, of the various concepts of income should be examined. Such research, when combined with more practical terminology, would enhance the field of accounting as a profession and be useful in enabling the profession to bear its responsibilities.

DISTRIBUTION OF PROFITS, *New York Certified Public Accountant*, XV (May, 1945), 220-24. [182]

Whether profits should be distributed as dividends depends upon general corporate law, the corporate charter, ethical or prudent considerations, the needs of stockholders, eligibility of the securities as trust investments, and tax considerations.

It is impossible to draft a general law to protect the preferred shareholders and the directors against liability from the declaration of dividends when asset values fluctuate relative to stated capital. One possible solution would be to state, via corporate charter, capital at a low figure relative to assets and to allow dividends to be paid only out of profits as determined in accordance with generally accepted accounting principles.

The terms *current dividend* and *dividend* should be restricted to dividends paid out of current profits. It is as objectionable to pay dividends out of earned surplus created in entirely different circumstances as it is to pay dividends out of capital surplus.

Since accounting does not provide for the numerous contingencies that may arise, it is seldom prudent to disburse all profits as dividends. General goodwill should not be amortized. The amount of profits which should be retained will depend upon the treatment of war reserves and the accounting procedures followed, for example, whether *Lifo* or *Fifo* is used.

Stock dividends are not income to the recipient and should be capitalized at an amount bearing a reasonable relationship to market value.

Where the realization of income is controlled by the directors it does not have the same significance as in the case of an ordinary sale. Thus, accounting for interest and dividends may be based upon considerations different from those applicable to the income derived from manufacture or sale. The real source of income to the investor is the earning of a profit by the company in which he has invested. There is little difference between interest and dividends, especially in the case of income bonds. "In cases of companies owning wasting assets an investor cannot wisely treat the whole of the dividend as income merely because the corporation has provided amortization on the tangible assets on its books." The investor may have paid more or less for his beneficial interest in the wasting assets.

ORIGINAL COST AND CORPORATE COST, *Journal of Accountancy* (Official Decisions and Releases), LXXXI (April, 1946), 351. [183]

In the New York Telephone Company case the Supreme Court overturned a unanimous judgment of the District Court that the FPC could not retroactively enforce orders which conflicted with those receiving regulatory approval at the time of the consummation of the transaction. Involved was the treatment to be accorded the excess of price paid by the New York Telephone Company for equipment purchased over its cost to the seller, the American Telephone and Telegraph Company, such purchase being consummated in 1925-1928.

The Supreme Court deemed the action to involve an "accounting order" of the FPC and took the position, previously stated, that it would not upset such an order unless the order was an expression of whim. The real issue was not an accounting order issue, but, stated in question form, was: "May it properly be said that a public utility corporation has not made an investment in assets of continuing value to the extent of the purchase price thereof when it has purchased property of continuing value at a price which it would willingly have paid to a stranger — merely because the purchase was made from an affiliated company?" The Court's acceptance of the view that the above question was a question of accounting considerably enlarges the judicially determined area of accounting.

The real accounting issue was whether this "inflation" should be credited to depreciation reserves which were already adequate, since such "inflation" had already been removed from the accounts by charges to operations.

". . . the Commission made no effort to establish the facts but resorted to specious theoretical arguments based on obviously inadequate premises and made full use of its power to control the proceedings and of legal rules regarding burden of proof to avert an overthrow of a conclusion which it is hard to believe its own accountants would undertake to defend."

With Henry T. Chamberlain, NET INCOME FOR THE YEAR, *Journal of Accountancy,* LXXXI (May, 1946), 363-71. [184]

The concept of "net income for the year" is of vital importance for many purposes such as dividend payments, interest on income bonds, managerial compensation, and valuation of equity securities. Many other problems, including those of definition, are associated with income determination: whether it is to be determined from a current operating point of view, an all-inclusive point of view such as that recommended by the American Accounting Association, or an intermediate point of view as recommended by the Institute.

So many factors included in the "over-all" concept of income have such varying significance in the determination of capital value that a single figure for net income is of little value. Accountants should bear in mind the reliance placed upon net income per share. Accounting methods should be adopted to mitigate the dangers of such reliance, and attention should be drawn to the limitations of such a single figure. Rather than describe any balance as "net income for the year," it may be preferable to use terminology such as "income before extraordinary charges and income after extraordinary charges or income carried to surplus account."

Income determination is dependent upon the trend of prices and the method of inventory valuation employed, and a very vital question is when changes in the value of capital assets should receive accounting recognition.

"There are here whole new fields for analysis and for the development possibly of new concepts of net income for the year, a new form of arrangement of the income statement" and for reconsideration of the terminology employed.

AUTHORITATIVE FINANCIAL ACCOUNTING, *Journal of Accountancy*, LXXXII (August, 1946), 102-19. [185]

Accounting has suffered from the undue significance attached to legal views. However, today the accountant recognizes that he must subject even expert opinions to the test of reasonableness.

"Financial accounting is a modern art" and is governed not by natural but by conventional laws and must meet the test of social usefulness. Many commissions have jurisdiction over accounting and the purposes of accounts. Differences of opinion arise between the various commissions as well as between a commission and the profession. The accountant, of course, has the right to qualify his certificate if he does subscribe to the required procedures.

The 1932 letter from the Institute committee to the New York Stock Exchange "may be regarded as marking an almost revolutionary change in accounting outlook" in that it accepted the view that social usefulness was the test of good accounting. Three major shifts of emphasis followed: (1) "from balance sheet to income statement," (2) "from value to cost — or 'useful' cost," and (3) "from conservatism to consistency."

The Institute and the SEC have a history of cooperation. However, in one major instance, disagreement can be found. The conflict was between points of view expressed in the Accounting Research Bulletin No. 23 and the Accounting Series Release No. 53. The Commission eventually accepted what, in effect, was the Institute's second alternative — the first being categorically rejected.

Major differences of opinion have arisen between commissions and the profession. These differences have centered around such items as enterprise, tangible and intangible assets, cost, etc. Of special significance is the resolution passed by the Committee on Accounting Procedure which should prevent the FPC from asserting that its original cost doctrine is supported by accounting practice and theory.

ACCOUNTING IMPLICATIONS OF THE NEW YORK TELEPHONE COMPANY DECISION, *Journal of Accountancy*, LXXXII (December, 1946), 456-59. [186]

The decision of the Federal Communications Commission concerning the

New York Telephone Company case, as upheld by the Supreme Court, "is a sinister development in the use of accounting as an instrument of policy . . . the extreme point of a strange aberration — original-cost accounting as interpreted and applied by federal regulatory commissions." Past abuses in the public utility field have "formed the pretext for retroactive imposition of new ideas and for other oppressive acts for which they constitute no justification, though sophistry and factitious indignation have been freely employed in attempts to prove the contrary."

In the American Telephone and Telegraph Company case, the Supreme Court held that the Commission could require an immediate writeoff of only that part of the purchase price paid by a subsidiary company to its parent company for assets purchased which appeared "to be a fictitious or paper increment," and not "a true increment of value." In spite of this decision the Commission required New York Telephone Company to write off a part of its cost as representing profit of the selling parent company.

Under the Commission's own uniform classification, the excess over original cost should have been charged to Account 100.4 and not to surplus directly. The commissions have claimed that this rule is necessary as a matter of public policy, and that even if it operates to the detriment of the minority stockholder, he must be content to suffer in the public interest.

The facts in the case did not prove that the parent made a profit to the extent of the Commission's required writeoff, and whether or not there is a fictitious element in a transaction between affiliates is a question of law and not of accounting. On the whole, the decision is apt to cause greater abuses than those the commissions are seeking to prevent.

ANOTHER MILESTONE IN REGULATION, *Journal of Land and Public Utility Economics,* XXIII (February, 1947), 22-28. [187]

In the New York Telephone Company case, the Supreme Court upheld an order of the FCC requiring the writeoff, charging earned surplus and crediting the depreciation reserve, of an amount, allegedly in excess of the net cost of the assets, paid by the New York company to its selling parent company. This order was required even though it was not denied that the existing reserve was adequate and that the property for the most part was no longer in existence.

"A new ideology has triumphed, and those who successfully opposed it in the past are called to the bar and told that the new ideology was always the only true one, and that those who conformed to the old, even when it was the unquestioned law of the land, did so at their preference and must now have their acts judged according to the new dispensation."

Contrary to the Supreme Court's decision, the basic issue was not whether the Commission's order was an accounting order. The basic issues were (1) whether the Commission can hold the accounting for a transfer improper by retroactive application of laws and accounting principles which were not enforced when the transfer took place, (2) whether a real value entitled to recognition in the rate base can "be held to be fictitious because it was acquired from an affiliated company, which, as a result of the transfer, suffered a reduction in its own rate base of the full amount of the price," and (3) whether such transfer between affiliates "can be held 'inflationary' without a showing that the price exceed original cost less the appropriate reserve requirement for depreciation, simply because the transferer did not give the transferee the benefit of an excessive depreciation reserve which it had created."

For a further discussion of the accounting aspects of this case, see §185, "Accounting Implications of the New York Telephone Company Decision."

CURTIS-WRIGHT INCENTIVE COMPENSATION PLAN, *Journal of Accountancy* (Official Decisions and Releases), LXXXIII (March, 1947), 265-67. [188]

Proper accounting would not require the establishment of a reserve on the books of the parent company for probable taxes on the earnings of a subsidiary company when distributed, even though the earnings of the subsidiary company are included in the consolidated statement of earnings.

Current accounting practice does not require that depreciation be taken on assets previously written off even though these assets have been recalled for wartime service and are still being depreciated for tax purposes.

The past-service costs of pensions should be distributed over a reasonable, future period of years.

In distinguishing between income and earnings, the term " 'income' is more definitely associated with the realization concept, whereas 'earnings' is more definitely associated with accrual concept. What is earned is not necessarily measured by what is received, and I think that is particularly true in relations between parent and subsidiary."

The amount of incentive compensation should be deducted in determining income taxes, in arriving at the amount of incentive compensation when such compensation is to be determined as a percentage of the net earnings of a company, after taxes.

ACCOUNTING AND THE ACCOUNTANT IN THE ADMINISTRATION OF INCOME TAXATION, *Journal of Accountancy,* LXXXIII (May, 1947), 370-84. [189]

The first part of this article deals with early income tax laws and the administrative difficulties placed upon the Bureau of Internal Revenue and is similar to the author's "Taxable Income and Accounting Bases for Determining It" (see §128).

The Board of Tax Appeals created by the 1924 act, "was not constituted in the manner contemplated by the Treasury." The Board "appeared to deem it a part of its duty to reinterpret the law and decide anew upon the merits of regulations." Relations between the Board and the Treasury steadily became more unsatisfactory and, according to a report of a joint Congressional committee, "a field of administration has been turned into a legal battlefield." The recommendations of the committee resulted in the creation of a special group "charged with the duty of effecting settlement even at the sacrifice of meticulous accuracy and some revenue." Conditions improved steadily until the development of such depression measures as the abolition of consolidated returns and reduction of allowances for depreciation, and the practice of evaluating an agent's efficiency by the additional assessments he secured.

Throughout this period of time a number of cases were decided in a manner which seemed to completely ignore the provision that income could be determined on the basis on which the taxpayer kept his books. Many elementary and universally accepted accounting propositions, such as advance payments for goods and services are not income until the goods are delivered or the service rendered, have been completely rejected. The "accounting and economic cornerstones" of the tax structure were rejected.

Recognition must come in the United States of the fact, already recognized in England, that "what is business income is to be determined by the best practices of businessmen." More agreement in principle must be reached between the tax laws and the SEC. Accountants must actively participate in income tax work "in order that the accounting mode of thought shall receive more effective recognition."

The field of representing taxpayers is not the special province of either lawyers or accountants. "It seems wholly specious to argue that in the public interest a taxpayer in an administrative proceeding should be compelled to rely on the skill and artistry of a trained advocate dealing with facts at second hand rather than on the plain tale of the accountant who has determined the facts himself. . . . a good administrator should be immune to artistry."

Both the public and private interest is best served by "free and direct access by taxpayers to accounting as well as legal thought in income-tax matters."

In a letter to the editor (*Journal of Accountancy,* LXXXIV [August, 1947], 69-70) attention is directed toward a recently published book by Randolph Paul which illustrates many of the points made above. Especially interesting is a comparison of the accounting mode of thought with that of Mr. Paul, who in addition to stating what appears to be a number of accounting misconceptions, looks upon the income tax as a social tool, but does not consider how the tool works or what unexpected consequences might result from its employment.

THE FUTURE OF THE BALANCE SHEET, *Journal of Accountancy,* LXXXIV (August, 1947), 98-101. [190]

The usefulness of the traditional balance sheet can be seriously questioned, since it is only in part an instantaneous picture of position, and its use is merely historical and purely conventional. Rather than the balance sheet, attention should be directed to income determination, since it is earning power that is the primary criterion of investors in valuing a business.

The term *balance sheet* should be dropped and *financial position* substituted therefor. Such a statement would then be interpreted as "an accounting for the capital and profits that have become available to the corporation and its management." The basis for valuation of the assets should be shown and the reporting of capital simplified.

The order of presentation of the accounts should be reversed, with capital stock and profits employed in the business forming the first section. Secondly, a section would show that capital and profits are represented by current assets less current liabilities, plus long-term assets, minus long-term debt with the summation of this section being entitled "net assets."

INVENTORY PRICING AND CONTINGENT RESERVES: COMMENT ON NEW ACCOUNTING RESEARCH BULLETINS, *Journal of Accountancy,* LXXXIV (November, 1947), 361-67. [191]

Apparently the committee, in releasing Accounting Research Bulletin No. 29, agreed that little or no difference exists between the "cost or market" concept and that of "actual and useful cost," and that they might well make an explicit statement on this issue. The committee has agreed, insofar as inventory is concerned, that income determination is the primary objective or purpose in accounting.

Professor Paton correctly dissents from the opinion that "costs should in certain instances be written off even where there is no expectation of loss." The acceptability of *Lifo* can be questioned as can Professor Paton's dissent from "the requirement that the same principles should be applied to goods covered by purchase contracts as to goods already on hand."

Accounting Research Bulletin No. 28, dealing with contingency reserves, is also related, in part, to the inventory problems of Bulletin No. 29. In the problem of income determination, a statement should be prepared which reports income following accounting methods which the auditors could approve. The income figure could then be adjusted by reserve provisions deemed necessary by management in order to portray disposable income.

SHOULD THE LIFO PRINCIPLE BE CONSIDERED IN DEPRECIATION ACCOUNTING WHEN PRICES VARY WIDELY, *Journal of Accountancy,* LXXXIV (December, 1947), 453-56. [192]

The only accepted basis for charging revenue for amortization of capital assets is cost. Yet certain unmistakable problems arise with respect to capital asset cost expirations which are similar in nature to inventory costs chargeable to revenue. Accountants have devised *Lifo* as a method of handling the problem of changing monetary levels with regard to inventory. A more consistent approach to the problems of income determination would seem to call for recognition of a similar approach to the amortization of the cost of capital assets.

"It should not be forgotten that the adoption of LIFO has involved acceptance of the view that a meaningless figure in the balance-sheet (for inventories) is not too high a price to pay for a more informative income figure, a conclusion which is less open to question in regard to capital assets which are not intended to be sold."

A RESTUDY OF THE CONCEPTS AND TERMINOLOGY OF BUSINESS INCOME, *New York Certified Public Accountant,* XVIII (January, 1948), 9-17. [193]

The adequacy of financial statements can be questioned in view of the effects upon business of changing price levels. Many specific questions must be studied carefully for possible changes in accounting principles and techniques. Illustrations of some of the problems can be found in current data published by the United States Department of Commerce and in the recent quarterly report by the United States Steel Corporation. Basically, the major problem arises from shrinking corporate profits in terms of constant dollars. The reporting of net income with charges for depreciation being based on historical cost is grossly inadequate in periods of inflationary conditions.

Accountants and management could aid in the accumulation of more accurate statistics on a national basis by reporting income, before taxes, but with costs and revenues stated in terms of the same price level. To this income figure could be added certain adjustments for inventories and depreciation to bring the income figure to that which would result from following generally accepted accounting principles. Income taxes could then be deducted, and from the resulting net income after taxes figure, adjustments, carried to a special surplus reserve, could be made and the residual then carried to earned surplus.

PROPERTY AND INVENTORY ACCOUNTING AS RELATED TO PRESENT-DAY PRICE LEVELS, *Journal of Accountancy,* LXXXV (May, 1948), 406-12. [194]

The speakers at the Joint Accounting Conference held in Chicago in December, 1947 "reveal a profession facing difficult problems, created by new economic conditions." Their feelings range from frustration and inadequacy to calm assurance that new concepts have already been established.

Mr. Higginbotham's discussion of standard costs also contains a plea for recognition of standard cost as cost for financial accounting purposes.

Mr. Stans, in discussing ARB 29, "accepts wholeheartedly the residual character of inventory" and "discards the concept of *Lifo* as merely an assumption as to the flow of costs" and speaks of them as being " 'tools for two different concepts of income.' "

Mr. Blough, in discussing ARB 31 relative to inventory reserves, states that while it is the function of management to anticipate changes " 'it does not follow, however, that it is proper to reduce the reported earnings in a period of rising prices to provide for losses which may take place at some future time.' " This objection is sound so long as *Lifo* is available. The discussion of *Lifo* and reserves for replacement of *Lifo* inventories "reveals how imperfect *Lifo* is" and "to what strange results it leads."

Mr. McCluskey dwells upon the problems faced by management when its depreciation charges are inadequate, because of changes in the price level, to meet the cost of replacement. Mr. Duncombe presents the "orthodox view" with respect to the same problem and cites the need, in financial reporting, for adherence to generally accepted principles and for consistency. However, accounting clearly does, and must, contemplate change to more desirable methods.

The validity is questioned of two statements made by Professor Littleton that history repeats itself with variations, and " '*the ratio between money and goods usually changes so slowly and moderately as to afford a dependable factual platform for decisions.*' " However, the most significant statement of the day was Professor Littleton's assertion: " 'The germ of a very useful idea lies in managerially determined charges in the income statement.' "

Professor Van Ardell recommends adherence to cost and actual transactions in accounting and does not discuss the departure from this basis which has already taken place through the use of *Lifo.* Mr. Allyn's address must have been quite encouraging to young accountants as he left no doubt of his view of the accountant's role in our economy.

ACCOUNTING DEVELOPMENTS SINCE 1940, *Papers Presented at Fifty-fourth Annual Meeting of the Railway Accounting Officers* (Washington: Association of American Railroads, Accounting Division, 1948), pp. 11-20. [195]

Significant developments relative to railroad accounting since 1940 have been the extension of depreciation order of the ICC, the amortization of emergency facility provisions of the Internal Revenue Code and the inflation of the postwar period.

A system of replacement and renewal reserves to be recorded only on equipment should be employed to record property exhaustion charges and depreciation as such. Recording depreciation on the basis of use is theoretically superior to the straight-line method. Charges for the exhaustion of property are clearly inadequate, and "replacements which do no more than maintain the enterprise result in heavy charges to capital because of the inadequacy of depreciation based on cost to meet corresponding costs at today's much higher price levels."

The view that *Lifo* represents an attempt to bring about a better matching of costs and revenues in terms of the same price level has recently received support in a Tax Court decision. Since long-term depreciable assets are simply long-term inventories, the possibility exists that the *Lifo* principle might be extended to depreciable assets. Present tax law favors the investor in short-term rather than long-term inventories.

There is substantial agreement that the increased costs of replacement must be met. The question is should the increased charges come out of revenues or income, and should such a charge be borne by the users of the property. Such charges should be computed from a determination of replacement cost rather than original cost as modified by an index of purchasing power. Such a system of accounting has been employed by railroads for over fifty years.

Postulates of Income Accounting, *Journal of Accountancy,* LXXXVI (August, 1948), 107-11. [196]

One standard postulate of accounting is that income is "realized" gain. A natural result of this is the so-called cost principle, that is, that property to be consumed or used in production should never be carried at more than cost.

A second major postulate of accounting is that the enterprise's accounts should be expressed from a "going concern" point of view, that is, unless ample evidence points to the contrary, a business enterprise may be assumed to have an indefinite life.

Of the two postulates, "neither represents a scientific truth or even a completely rational assumption. Each is adopted for want of a better." The assertion made by some writers that there is historical support for the cost basis of accounting is untrue. Writers such as Dickinson and Montgomery support this position. In the Institute committee's letter to the New York Stock Exchange in 1932 listing accounting principles, the cost principle was not listed. The cost basis has no sacred tradition.

Numerous authorities can be quoted to show that even today it is acceptable to carry assets on a basis other than cost. Future economic changes may bring about a further evolution, but not a departure from a tradition of historical continuity of accounting records.

The going concern postulate is given its greatest recognition in England in the form of the statements presented and in the failure to take depreciation in railroads and utilities. The "base stock" method of inventory valuation, which created *Lifo,* is a natural result of this postulate. This concept has also produced the notion that the year to year value of long-term property is not materially significant. Balance sheets are then looked upon as reports of stewardship and not as statements of value.

Accounting Concepts and Standards Underlying Corporate Financial Statements, *Journal of Accountancy,* LXXXVI (November, 1948), 412-14. [197]

In the American Accounting Association's statement bearing the same name as the above title there are a great many "inaccuracies or misuse of language." The statement is inferior to the 1941 statement, and for a better view of the opinions and beliefs of accounting teachers the Paton and Littleton monograph should be read.

The statement sanctions "one-way street" accounting which was opposed by teachers such as Paton, Dohr and Sanders when it was imposed by the FPC.

The statement recommends the showing of only actual or estimated income taxes in the income statement; this is contrary to current practice which has followed the Institute committee's recommendation that allocation is desirable in certain circumstances.

Fortunately, "retained earnings" is used instead of "earned surplus," and recognition is given to basic accounting postulates. However, accounting is much too complex to be explained in such a brief statement.

ACCOUNTING RESEARCH, *Accounting Research,* I (November, 1948), 13-19. [198]

Accounting research may be related to three functions of accounting: (1) recording, (2) administrative analysis and interpretation, and (3) general financial accounting. In the latter area there is room for study of the adequacy of the unit of money in measuring economic change, the assumptions behind allocation of profits to years and shorter periods of time and the terminology and methods of presentation.

One specific problem — the declining value of the monetary unit — gave rise to the formation of a study group of some fifty persons to consider "the concepts and terminology of Business Income."

Specific topics or questions for study might, among others, be the declining value of the dollar and its effect on national statistics and the implications to the firm; the implications relative to the taxing of corporate income in view of the declining value of the dollar; the reasonableness of *Lifo* and whether it should be accepted; whether changes should be made in accounting methods of presentation; and whether greater reliance should be placed on supplementary information.

THE ECONOMIC AND POLITICAL INFLUENCES IN THE DEVELOPMENT OF THE ACCOUNTING PROFESSION, *Fifty Years of Service* (Newark: New Jersey Society of Certified Public Accountants, 1948), pp. 10-13. [199]

"A new era in accounting began in the closing years of the nineteenth century." Small enterprises were consolidated into large corporations. United States Steel, organized in 1901, followed from its inception a policy of presenting informative, annual stockholder reports, including the reports of independent auditors elected by the stockholders.

Depreciation and systematic cost accounting resulted from "concentration of groups of plants under single ownership." Valuation was replaced by methods of cost determination.

A powerful influence upon accounting was the passage of the 1909 excise tax law, and "the enactment in 1918 of Section 212 of the Revenue Act . . . was and will always be a landmark in the history of accounting in this country."

High taxes payable on death led to the conversion of many small privately owned companies into corporations. The New York Stock Exchange in 1933 required that listing applications include an independent public accountant's certificate. This was followed by the adoption by the Exchange, announced in 1933, of proposals made to it by an Institute committee. The Securities legislation of 1933 and 1934 has "undoubtedly proved beneficial to the public and to accountants."

World War II brought with it the problems of cost plus fixed fee contracts, renegotiation and contract termination. Since the war accounting issues have played an important part in labor relations. Changing price levels have also produced new problems for the accountant.

PROFITS AND HIGH PRICES: THE INSTITUTE'S RECOMMENDATION XII, *Accountant,* CXX (April 2, 1949), 258-60. [200]

Support should be given to the objectives and arguments advanced by the Council of the Institute of Chartered Accountants' Recommendation XII in which it is recommended that the basis of the property being exhausted be changed so that revenues and charges against revenues are stated in units of similar purchasing power.

Public utilities in England, by use of the estimated cost of renewal or replacement (renewal reserve method) as a basis for charges against revenue, have not felt the effects of a rising price level as much as industrial companies which have based charges against revenues on cost (depreciation methods).

No change may be necessary in accounting procedures in the case of English utilities. However, "I see no reason why a similar procedure should not be applied in industrial companies."

EFFECT OF RECENT PENSION PLANS ON INCOME, *Proceedings of a Meeting of the Study Group on Business Income, American Institute of Accountants,* December 3, 1949, pp. 76-78. [201]

Important problems are being encountered as a result of a pension agreement negotiated between the steel industry and its union. Under the terms of the agreement, pensions were to be paid to any worker retiring, certain other conditions being met, up to December 31, 1951 or for a period up to five years thereafter. The question arises, should the estimated costs of such a pension agreement be spread over two years, five years or some other period?

The crucial question in accounting for pensions centers around whether recognition is to be given to the past-service cost. For many reasons estimates as to amounts involved are almost conjectural. ". . . it doesn't seem to me possible to deal with it in any other way than you do with other entirely conjectural contingent liabilities."

The difficulties encountered in pension plans "are really very, very great, and the amounts of money involved are . . . colossal. The amazing thing is that corporations entered in these agreements with the unions with neither side having any clear conception of what was going to be involved. They started out to figure out the cost after they had made the deal."

THE CHOICE BEFORE US, *Journal of Accountancy,* LXXXIX (March, 1950), 206-10. [202]

Accounting principles need not and should not be codified. To introduce such rigidity is to diminish the great service which accountants can and do perform in the interpretation of freely transacted business. There is no reason to believe that accounting and accounting statements should be so simplified as to be readily understandable by one and all. A reasonable man does not expect all persons to understand the intricate details of the practice of medicine without being trained therein. It is equally illogical to expect everyone to fully understand all about accounting. This interpretive function is best left to the accountant.

The demand for uniformity and standardization in accounting systems arises from a distrust of business management. Uniformity and standardization will gain little "since management controls the form which transactions take." Accountants are challenged "to accept their interpretive function and show integrity, courage, and resourcefulness in discharging this function."

TRUTH AND USEFULNESS IN ACCOUNTING, *Journal of Accountancy,* LXXXIX (May, 1950), 387. [203]

"What is meant by truth in accounting and what is its relation to usefulness?

(1) Accounting must be true to the standards, principles, or canons by which it professes to be bound.

(2) Accounting determinations must not be 'proffered to the unlearned as representations of fact. . . .'

(3) There must be no concealment of the fact that accounting rests on a framework of assumptions, made up of a few fundamental postulates

> and a large number of minor assumptions, which are implicit in the treatment of specific items, and that these assumptions are acceptable and accepted as being useful, not as demonstrable truths."

The three most fundamental postulates of accounting are (1) "that the entire income from sales arises . . . when realization is deemed to take place," (2) fluctuations in the value of the monetary unit may be ignored, and (3) the enterprise may be assumed to have, in the absence of evidence to the contrary, an indefinite life.

CASE AGAINST CHANGE IN PRESENT METHODS OF ACCOUNTING FOR EXHAUSTION OF BUSINESS PROPERTY, *Five Monographs on Business Income,* Study Group on Business Income (New York: American Institute of Accountants, 1950), pp. 261-71. [204]

The need for change in accounting procedures because of changes in the price level is lessened as the years pass and the proportion of prewar plants in use declines. Profits in the last three years have been high enough so that no serious economic or financial harm has resulted from the use of old accounting methods. The public has discounted the significance of "Net Income for the Year" as reported. Furthermore, the problem of accounting under changing price levels is of less importance due to the development of other major problems such as pensions, lease-backs, and accelerated depreciation.

A change of the type presently contemplated is relatively unimportant compared to the need for clearer understanding of the significance and limitations of the accounts as now prepared.

However, a "regrettable disharmony in fundamental concepts" exists as a result of the use of *Lifo* and a refusal to adopt a similar concept with respect to capital assets. A better solution than change in present procedures would be to discard *Lifo* since it has been adopted primarily for tax reasons.

The contention that there is a basic stability in the price level is contradicted by the available evidence. "But it does not follow that a change in the accounting use of the monetary unit is the only remedial step to be taken." The evidence available does seem to support the claim that businessmen act upon the assumption of a stable monetary unit even when they know this is not the case.

No change should be made in plant assets for balance sheet purposes or in depreciation charges for income determination until all data are stated in common dollars.

An increase in allowable rates of earnings in public utilities may be a convenient way to protect invested capital and assure financial stability. Special tax relief might also be afforded less prosperous railroads, utilities and, perhaps, heavy industry. If not, no great harm would result from recognition of provisions for increased cost of replacement out of revenue or income as being necessary for preservation of capital.

BUSINESS INCOME, *Accountant,* CXXIII (September 30, 1950), 315-23. [205]

Accounting has developed sufficiently as a body of knowledge that it must now encourage valid criticism and investigation of its basic assumptions. The most basic postulates in accounting are those developed with respect to income realization, stability of the monetary unit and the permanence of the enterprise.

Current emphasis is placed heavily upon "administrative accounting" with the result that there is a lack of effort being made in the area of "financial accounting" for those interested persons outside of a given enterprise.

A review of the origin of the basic postulates indicates that certain events in history had a bearing upon them and in the changes or acceptance of them. For example, the first tax on income passed in 1913 in the United States had a distinct influence upon the income concepts, as did the utilities regulation.

A difficult question is that of defining income, especially in view of the many varied concepts of income as expressed by economists. Some economists, Professor Bronfenbrenner, for example, favor expressing charges and revenues in units of similar purchasing power. This view is to be preferred, although acceptance of this approach would not make it necessary to revalue all of the assets or to provide for inadequacies of the property exhaustion charges.

TASK OF FINANCIAL ACCOUNTING, *Accountant,* CXXIII (October 7, 1950), 343. [206]

In the financial accounting area there are many problems of conflict and compromise between theory and practice.

". . . financial accounting has faced . . . [the need for] certainty and simplicity in an economy which was moving rapidly in the direction of complexity and uncertainty, if not confusion. The task may be likened to that of the billiard player in *The Mikado* — to control, as it were, the cue ball (of accounting classification) to bring together in proper relation the two object balls (of revenue and cost) on a cloth untrue (of contractual relations indefinite or deceptive in expression) with the twisted cue (of ambiguous terminology and conventions) and the elliptical billiard balls (of an unstable monetary symbol). And this has to be done for an audience which is wholly unaware of the defects of the equipment provided, and which has been led to believe that the task is easy."

COMMENTS ON THE GREER-WILCOX ARTICLE "THE CASE AGAINST PRICE-LEVEL ADJUSTMENTS IN INCOME DETERMINATION," *Journal of Accountancy,* XC (December, 1950), 504-5. [207]

The Greer-Wilcox article presents only one argument that has not been anticipated and met. Capital expenditures are more apt to be made when prices and profits are high, and depreciation of such capital assets when based on the cost thereof may in some cases exceed depreciation in terms of current prices. While this argument may be valid and significant, it is not of major importance. The showing of depreciation in terms of both recorded cost and in current prices would point out the wisdom of those who might have made the expenditures when prices were low.

Accountants must recognize their responsibilities as interpreters of the financial affairs of big business for the stockholders. Their work would deteriorate to a meaningless level if they adopted a definition of business income so simple that its least competent members could implement it. Although certain deficiencies exist in the use of index numbers in financial accounting, it is doubtful that they are more damaging than the current practice of ignoring price level fluctuations. In reality, such an index may be more objective than many other criteria used at present in accounting.

STUDY GROUP ON CONCEPT AND TERMINOLOGY OF BUSINESS INCOME, *Accounting And Tax Problems In The Fifties,* Papers Presented at the Sixty-second Annual Meeting (New York: American Institute of Accountants, 1950), pp. 50-55. [208]

"The object of the Study Group is . . . to suggest a concept or concepts of business income that it regards as acceptable and capable of being implemented by accounting methods." A question arises whether accountants should attempt to implement more significant concepts of income, or adhere to concepts so simple that an intelligent layman will be able to appraise them — a so-called strictly factual determination of income. Some accountants want a more standardized, authoritative accounting.

Changing price levels, tax rules and new financial devices have resulted in more diversity in accounting — *Lifo* and some of the current expressions relative to depreciation are examples. Accounting cannot be standardized to the extent that some accountants desire. It is not possible to express, in all cases, the essence of the income account in a single figure. Management should be encouraged to use "common dollar" reports.

A witness testifying before the Flanders Committee erred when he stated that the Treasury Department caused the diminishing use of the declining balance method of recording depreciation in favor of an unrealistic straight-line method. The straight-line method should not be lightly dismissed and the declining balance method, while having some merit, is not widely used in America.

Suggestions have been made that greater flexibility should be allowed in the taking of depreciation charges as between years, because greater use or greater expectation of profitability is justification for higher charges in the early years of the life of the property.

Relative to the question of depreciation and changing price levels, "I am more than ever convinced that the most generally useful concept of business income in the foreseeable future will be one which contemplates charges against revenue being stated as nearly as possible in terms of units of the same purchasing power."

WHAT IS BUSINESS INCOME? FROM THE ACCOUNTANT'S VIEWPOINT, *What is Business Income* (New-York: Controllers Institute of America, 1950), pp. 18-30. [209]

A "composite" of accountants' views on business income would probably include (1) "realization as a prerequisite to the recognition of income," (2) acceptance of the going concern postulate, (3) a "desire to make income reporting as factual as possible," (4) a "reluctance to abandon the postulate that fluctuations in the value of the monetary unit . . . should be ignored," (5) "an almost superstitious reverence for a 'cost principle,' " (6) "a widespread feeling that in so far as financial statements were not factual, they should be based on 'objective' evidence," (7) a preference for a single net income figure determined under an "all-inclusive" concept, and (8) "a strong emphasis on uniformity."

Controllers should supplement or revise statements prepared in accordance with accepted assumptions and concepts so that (1) the accounting methods employed are disclosed, (2) the statements are enlightening and free from ambiguous terminology, (3) the income reported is classified into that arising from price level changes and that arising from conversion, purchase or sale, (4) "information regarding price changes and other important economic developments" is disclosed so a comparison can be made with operations of prior years, and (5) "inescapable limitations on the significance of [the] accounts" are stressed.

WHAT IS BUSINESS INCOME? *Journal of Accountancy* (Official Decisions and Releases), XCIX (January, 1951), 142-44. [210]

The Study Group on Business Income limited its considerations to business income as differentiated from personal service or investment income. Any definition of business income must be framed so as to indicate the time period covered and the recipient.

Business income may be called "activity profit," that is, sale or production profit in contrast to a change in wealth concept. Implementation of the latter concept is impossible except in rare cases, such as marketable investments.

From the postulate of permanence flows the notion that valuation of individual assets is immaterial. Only the collective value of the business as a whole is important and this rests upon earning power. The assumption that fluctuations in the value of the monetary unit may be safely ignored needs to be re-examined. Within a certain range of fluctuation it is likely that the problems of adjustment would be greater than the benefits derived. With respect to the future trend of prices, accountants should keep their eyes on the "middle distance" rather than on the very short or very long-run point of view.

Distinctions should be made in the requirements for income determination for the large corporation with widely held stock ownership as compared to the small, close corporation. Disclosure is of far greater importance than uniformity, as the latter may not change with need. Since income determinations are widely used in wage negotiations and taxation, changes in price levels ought, as in labor contracts, to be given consideration.

PERIODIC BUSINESS INCOME AND CHANGING PRICE LEVELS, *Report of the Proceedings of the Fifth Tax Conference* (Toronto: Canadian Tax Foundation, 1951), pp. 115-25. [211]

Two of the basic postulates of accounting, the "*monetary postulate* [and] the *postulate of permanence* . . . were well established at the beginning of this century." Income was the "*increase in monetary net worth between two points of time.*" The one exception to this concept of income was found in enterprises which were regarded as permanent, such as utilities and railroads, where income was determined by deducting from revenues the cost of maintaining the enterprise. Depreciation was not recorded as an expense, while current expenditures for maintenance of the enterprise were expensed. The third basic postulate of accounting is the so-called *realization* postulate. To the economist realization is of no great importance. Realization merely makes measurement more precise.

Strong opposition has been expressed to extending the concept that the proper charge against revenue in a permanent enterprise is the cost of maintaining or replacing an asset at the time of the exhaustion. To avoid this, writeups of property have been made to get higher depreciation charges and depreciation has been "accelerated." It is time now for a reconsideration of our attitude toward property exhaustion.

Opponents of price index adjustments of property exhaustion charges use a price index in *Lifo* inventory determinations while holding that such a device cannot be applied to property exhaustion even though the British railways have been using such a device for years.

The Study Group on Business Income recommended that the accounting framework be modified so that the two component parts of business income be recognized and the distortion resulting from changing price levels be separately stated. The Group also recommended, in view of the "tolerances" in accounting, that the accounting methods employed by a company be made known to stockholders upon request, and that a substitute be found for the words *value* and *valuation*.

THREE DISCUSSIONS OF FINANCIAL ACCOUNTING AND INFLATION, *Journal of Accountancy*, XCIII (March, 1952), 294-99. [212]

Three recent discussions of the impact of changing price levels upon financial accounting are: the report of the Study Group on Business Income, statements of the American Accounting Association's Committee on Concepts and Standards, and a discussion conducted by the Controllers Institute.

Improvements which will result in more adequate disclosure of the results of business activity and "the distorting effects of inflation" are needed in financial reporting.

A number of faulty assumptions exist relative to the balance sheet. These are that "(1) the introduction or withdrawals of capital, or (2) the creation of income or loss and distributions of income" are the only sources of change in net assets. Although the procedure may be too complex to be readily acceptable, it may be well to recognize changes in the purchasing power of money. Balance sheet problems are complex and should perhaps be studied separately; improvement in the reporting of income should not be delayed. The form of the income statement should be changed so as to show income under generally accepted accounting principles as well as in terms of current purchasing power.

Accounting in the Time of Inflation, *Accountant,* CXXVII (October 18, 1952), 442-46. [213]

A revision of the postulate that changes in the value of the monetary unit may be ignored could be approached logically in three steps. The first phase would uphold the postulate because of the minor change in the value of the monetary unit, but would point out the deficiencies resulting from such adherence. The second phase would also uphold the postulate, but the effects of inflation would be isolated. The third phase would probably require abandonment of the postulate.

Ample evidence exists to show that the traditional cost principle is not a valid excuse for accountants to refuse to change their approach to financial accounting. For example, the lower of cost or market inventory rule is a deviation from historical cost. Accounting is concerned with a pool of costs, and emphasis may be placed upon those costs charged against revenues or those carried over in the balance sheet.

Agreement may be expressed with the principles of stated costs and revenues in terms of current purchasing power, while at the same time objections are voiced as to the method of implementation. This position indicates a typical human weakness — reluctance to change from accustomed methods to something new.

Limitations on the Significance of Invested Cost, *Accounting Review,* XXVII (October, 1952), 436-40. [214]

Disagreement must be expressed with Professor Littleton's views relative to the significance of invested cost. In his earlier writings the problems involved in accounting under changing price levels were recognized as was the accountant's role in dealing with these problems.

The belief is often expressed that historical cost is traditional, when in reality it is not. Dickinson, in 1904, wrote about the increased attention being paid to cost by accountants.

Public accountants have a duty to point out to stockholders the inherent defects in the concepts underlying published corporate financial reports. Until an adequate and realistic definition and concept of business income is secured, the profession should make the shortcomings of financial statements known and make an effort to remove these deficiencies.

SOME THOUGHTS ON INCOME ANALYSIS, *Analysts Journal,* VIII (November, 1952), 9-13. [215]

The various disciplines (such as accounting and economics) should use the term *income* with care since so much significance is attached to it. As a bare minimum, a qualifying adjective should be used to describe it. Business income in itself is not homogeneous. The concept of business income is based upon important postulates regarding the permanence of the enterprise, realization, and the stability of the monetary unit.

These postulates have had an influence in the development of ideas on personal income. Advocates of personal income tax who desire drastic redistribution of income disregard or dislike the realization postulate, but find the monetary postulate most satisfactory.

Several factors, such as capital gains and the corporate form of business enterprise, have had an effect "on the significance of the available statistics of income." Changes in tax rates and applications have influenced many financial decisions of corporations and individuals and, consequently, will have a disturbing effect on all income statistics of the future.

STOCK DIVIDENDS AND CONCEPTS OF INCOME, *Journal of Accountancy,* XCVI (October, 1953), 427-31. [216]

Dividends on common stock do not represent income to the individual who receives them. Income determination with regard to stock dividends is primarily a question of law. ". . . the general concept of income adopted by the Supreme Court is closely in accord with the accepted accounting concept."

Use of the word *dividend* in Accounting Research Bulletin No. 43 may not be wholly satisfactory when discussing stock dividends because it carries so many implications. Stock dividends can reasonably be distinguished from stock splits although the exemption of the close corporation is of doubtful validity.

Any redefinition of income (as is being considered by the Treasury Department) must give adequate consideration to economic and legal concepts of income. Accountants should seek to improve income determination for both tax and general purposes, thus seeking to remove emergency and incentive tax provisions. They should also oppose any effort to tax undistributed earnings of the widely-held corporation.

CONCEPTS OF BUSINESS INCOME AND THEIR IMPLEMENTATION, *Quarterly Journal of Economics,* LXVIII (February, 1954), 1-18. [217]

A century ago business income was considered the net increase in the net worth of the enterprise while the economic concept viewed business income as the fruit of the capital tree. Dickinson, just after the turn of the century, also recognized income as the excess of revenues over costs incurred and ascertained; at the same time he recognized the need for explicit treatment of appreciation, for provision for anticipated losses and for declining values of assets such as inventories.

The first attempt to promote uniformity in business accounting was made by the American Institute of Accountants in 1917. Business practices determined the accounting for income taxes. Reluctance to capitalize expenditures for the creation of intangible assets was and is an established characteristic of accounting.

Three major postulates of accounting are (1) the stability of the monetary unit, (2) indefinite life, and (3) realization of income. Two other major factors are that (1) income statements must be integrated with balance sheets, and (2) income determinations must be made by corporations of varying size, objectives and types of ownership.

Prior to World War I, accounting did take cognizance of the cost, maintenance and exhaustion of physical construction but did not deal with costs of research and experimentation, creation of demand, or "lessening or cessation of demand causing partial or complete obsolescence of the industry or major parts thereof" and changes in price.

Depreciation on the straight-line basis became the general practice following World War II. One of two methods of determining straight-line depreciation was employed, depending upon whether the asset was short-lived or long-lived and whether it required major rebuilding or renewal.

Fluctuations in price levels should be recognized in the measurement of depreciation and depletion charges, at least in a supplementary manner. The effects resulting from the application of this concept to regulated industries are of great importance as can be shown by a detailed analysis thereof.

With James L. Dohr, BOOK VALUE: A BRIEF COMMENT ON THE STANS-GOEDERT ARTICLE, *Journal of Accountancy,* XCIX (April, 1955), 42-44. [218]

The definition of book value given in the Stans-Goedert article must be rejected in favor of that in Accounting Research Bulletin No. 9 which "establishes a clear rule" and "gives effect to the intention of the parties affected by it."

The preferred definition is not in accordance with the 1932-1934 correspondence between the Institute and the New York Stock Exchange. The concepts therein established that accounting "is neither absolute rule nor anarchy but a system that has elements of stability and adaptability, and that stresses disclosure and significance — not strict uniformity."

Since the balance sheet merely reflects what has been invested and not the value of anything at a given date, book value might better be called "book investment."

COMMENT ON "PRESTIGE FOR HISTORICAL COST," *Illinois Certified Public Accountant,* XVII (June, 1955), 30-31. [219]

Professor Littleton, in his article "Prestige for Historical Cost" (*Illinois Certified Public Accountant,* XVII [March, 1955], 23-27), relies upon assumptions, explicit or implicit, which are not well founded. Accounting should not be "wedded to tradition" and its supreme virtue is its usefulness and capacity to adapt to new conditions. The proposals currently advanced along the lines of so-called purchasing power accounting will not destroy accounting's usefulness since only supplementary information is to be provided.

There is no tradition supporting historical cost. "Not only the cost or market rule, but the whole history of accounting seems to me to dispute the claims made by the historical cost tradition, claims which are made plausible only by its ambiguity in the use of the words 'historical' and 'cost.' "

All accountants should join together in developing a more adequate philosophy of accounting in view of the growing importance of the problems facing accountancy.

THE ROYAL COMMISSION ON THE TAXATION OF PROFITS AND INCOME: DISCUSSION OF "AN ACHIEVEMENT OF MAGNITUDE," *Accountant,* CXXXIII (December 24, 1955), 701-4. [220]

Acceptance of *Lifo* by the Commission is incompatible with its refusal to adopt a similar proposal with regard to wasting capital assets. The *Lifo* method can be defended in that while it does not provide business with more spending power, it does reduce the amount of capital which management must accumulate to support inventories, accounts receivable and pay taxes. Furthermore, since price levels fluctuate, the value of the tax liability of one period may be quite different from the actual payment (much later) made in monetary units of a different value.

Tax laws should be framed so as to accept the accounting methods of the taxpayer within certain limitations. Accountants' opinions with regard to the provisions and form of new tax laws should have great weight. However, the organization of the accounting profession is such that changes in accounting rules are not easily made. Thus, accounting seems to need the impetus of regulation in order to make the necessary changes resulting from rapidly changing conditions.

The assumption of the Commission relative to the stability of the price level is certainly questionable in view of the policies of maintenance of full employment and redistribution of income.

A FURTHER LOOK AT LAWYERS AND ACCOUNTANTS, *American Bar Association Journal,* XLII (June, 1956), 582-83. [221]

Contrary to many opinions expressed, the growth of large, national accounting firms is not connected in any significant way with the increasing number of situations in which the practices of law and accounting are combined. Such a combination of practices is to be deplored. The growth of national accounting firms developed from the needs of large companies. In such companies, the accountant frequently works on tax and other matters with lawyers employed by the client.

The practice of law in the United States is not a profession in the traditional sense of the word; nor is accounting. "Neither the lawyer nor the accountant is necessarily dependent for his status or privileges on membership in a body of learned persons bound by mutual obligation to maintain high standards of skills, ethics and conduct."

In the tax field the issue of combined practice must be left to the discretion of the Treasury Department. Accountants should not appear before either the Tax Board or the Tax Court.

A COMMENT ON MR. GREER'S BENCHMARKS AND BEACONS, *Accounting Review,* XXXI (October, 1956), 581-83. [222]

The previously published address of Howard C. Greer "must surely be one of the strangest articles that ever appeared in an accounting journal. The substantive part of it is a recommendation that the Association endorse an approach to the problem of corporate financial reporting that has been in existence for nearly a quarter of a century."

Greer has erroneously claimed that for many years practitioners " 'denied the necessity of a code of principles or standards' " while at the same referring in their opinions to generally accepted accounting principles. This latter phrase was first suggested in the Institute - Stock Exchange correspondence, and its meaning was clearly defined, contrary to Mr. Greer's statement. The Institute's "Audits of Corporate Accounts" was issued seven months before the passage of the law creating the SEC, and not afterward as Mr. Greer suggests. Thus, rather than bringing pressure to bear upon the profession, the SEC "*harvested* the fruits of the earlier activities of the Stock Exchange and the Institute."

Greer also spoke disparagingly "of two . . . teachers of accounting . . . Professor Sanders and Professor Hatfield for having adopted in 1935 an approach to a problem which he has now himself adopted." Greer also quotes the Institute president, out of context, as noting a "reluctant trend" toward the adoption of an all-inclusive income account.

BUSINESS COMBINATIONS: AN ALTERNATE VIEW, *Journal of Accountancy,* CIII (April, 1957), 33-36. [223]

The term *pooling* in pooling of interest has, in law, long been used to describe an arrangement for sharing profits from property pooled without change of ownership. In Accounting Research Bulletin No. 48, the transactions described represent an exchange of interest.

The validity of an accounting procedure which allows a company to start with a deficit, a possibility if one of the merging companies had a large deficit, may be seriously questioned.

However, the really important question is what "monetary ascriptions" should be attached to the existing capital assets. Security allotments in combinations are presumably made on the basis of current values. Future charges to revenues will presumably be based upon the amount assigned to the assets. It follows that such charges will be more significant and useful if based upon present day costs rather than costs to the stockholders a generation ago. Securities issued in a combination are assumed to be all issued at the same price, and the burden of proof is upon those who hold otherwise.

There is merit in the suggestion of Dr. T. S. Adams that the monetary ascriptions on which future revenue charges are based be revised periodically, perhaps every 25 to 30 years. This time period, however, might well be cut in half.

INCOME ACCOUNTING AND SOCIAL REVOLUTION, *Journal of Accountancy,* CIII (June, 1957), 36-41. [224]

It is very disturbing to find reports of a utility corporation prepared in accordance with generally accepted accounting principles, according to the independent accountant, which show a dividend to have been earned by a substantial margin and at the same time to be substantially tax-free.

The accountant has for a considerable period of time been concerned with the problem of determining what is business income. To him it is an excess of revenues over costs, in contrast to the economist's definition of "income as an accretion to economic power between two points of time" — a concept which cannot be implemented by accounting means.

The Institute committee's "Audits of Corporate Accounts" has come closest to reducing the subjective concept of income to a reasonably narrow range of meanings. The cooperative attitude of the SEC brought further progress toward the goal of a clearer definition of income, until the war and other causes brought about realization that either the definition or significance of "business income" was changing significantly.

Many major events have influenced accounting and the accountant's role in meeting changes in social conditions. Accountants have learned that one analysis cannot yield a significant statement of costs and revenues and change in stockholders' equity. Accountants "have reached the point at which they can afford to admit the limitations of their art."

GENERALLY ACCEPTED PRINCIPLES OF ACCOUNTING, *Journal of Accountancy*, CV (January, 1958), 23-27. [225]

Much discussion has resulted from the adoption, in 1932, of the phrase "generally accepted principles" in auditors' opinions. The key word in the phrase is "accepted" and acceptance may be based on law, regulation, or it may be voluntary. That regulatory commissions are not bound by principles accepted in the non-regulated area is now clearly established.

The question of what accounting principles are to be accepted by the ICC is once again raised by the Commission's proposal to extend depreciation accounting to grading and track material. Depreciation need not be recorded on grading in view of its perpetual life, assuming proper maintenance. With respect to track material, the present practice of charging replacements to expense yields results similar to those that would follow from adjusting depreciation charges for changes in price levels. The validity of the accounting postulate that changes in value of the dollar may be ignored is questionable. In British practice adjustment of depreciation for changes in price levels is accepted while *Lifo* is not. No change should be made at this time in the method of accounting for track material.

Causes of current problems in accounting are changes in the purchasing power of the dollar, technological advances creating intangible assets and accelerating obsolescence of others and vast promotional expenditures for distribution.

Accounting has not kept pace with changes and a rapidly changing Committee on Accounting Procedure cannot render the services required of it. There is a pressing need for "continuous research at a high level."

IV. WILLIAM A. PATON

U. of Mich. News Service

WILLIAM A. PATON

William A. Paton was born in Calumet, Michigan in 1889. He earned three academic degrees from the University of Michigan, including the Ph.D. received in 1917. In 1944 he was awarded an honorary Litt. D. by Lehigh University.

He began his teaching career at the University of Michigan in 1914 and was appointed professor in 1921. There, in 1947, he became Edwin Francis Gay University Professor of Accounting, a position he held until his retirement in 1958. He was an instructor at the University of Minnesota for one year, was a visiting professor at the University of Chicago and the University of California, was Dickinson Lecturer at the Harvard University Graduate School of Business Administration in 1940, and a lecturer at the Case Institute of Technology's Economics in Action Program in July, 1952.

Mr. Paton's great interest in accounting theory and economics and accounting education has had a profound influence upon the theory and practice of accounting and has brought him recognition as "a teacher of teachers."

He is the author of twenty books and monographs and nearly one hundred articles. He has appeared as an expert witness in many industrial, public utility, and governmental investigations and hearings and has delivered a great many speeches. For some time he was a member of the public accounting firm of Paton and Ross. He was editor and major contributor to the 1932 and 1943 editions of the *Accountants' Handbook.* He also wrote *Principles of Accounting,* with R. A. Stevenson (1918), *Accounting Theory* (1922), *Accounting* (1924), *Corporate Profits as Shown by Audit Reports* (1935), *Essentials of Accounting* (1938 — which has recently appeared as a revised edition, with R. L. Dixon), *An Introduction to Corporate Accounting Standards,* with A. C. Littleton (1940), *Advanced Accounting* (1941), *Asset Accounting,* with W. A. Paton, Jr. (1952), *Shirtsleeve Economics* (1952) and *Corporate Accounts and Statements,* with W. A. Paton, Jr. (1955).

Mr. Paton has been a member of the American Accounting Association since its formation, and has served it as President, Research Director and editor of *The Accounting Review.* He has been a member of the American Institute of Certified Public Accountants since 1930, and has served as a member of its Council as well as on several committees, including the Committee on Accounting Procedure of which he was an original member. He is a member of the

American Economic Association, the National Association of Accountants, the Michigan Academy of Science and is a fellow of the American Academy of Arts and Sciences.

Mr. Paton is a member of Phi Beta Kappa, Beta Gamma Sigma and Beta Alpha Psi. In 1950 he was selected a charter member of The Ohio State University's Accounting Hall of Fame.

At the present time Mr. Paton is a trustee of the Foundation for Economic Education and the Earhart Foundation. Since his retirement, he has continued to serve as a visiting professor at several universities.

IV. *WILLIAM A. PATON*

SUMMARIES OF PERIODICAL WRITINGS

THEORY OF THE DOUBLE-ENTRY SYSTEM, *Journal of Accountancy*, XXIII (January, 1917), 7-23. [226]

The double-entry system of keeping accounts is founded logically in the nature of the facts with which accounting deals, namely, property and equities (rights to property). These two classes of facts are always equal, since one deals with the objective items of property while the other represents the situs of ownership of this property and the same measuring unit is used in both cases.

Business operation involves a constant process of shifting of both property and equity items. Arbitrarily, property balances are maintained in the left hand side of an account and equity balances in the right. In each case, the opposite side of the account is used for subtraction. The guiding principle is the maintenance of equality of the original equation (property = equities).

All possible transactions can be classified under four headings: (1) one property is exchanged for another of equal value, (2) an increase or decrease of property takes place through an equal increase or decrease of equities, (3) an equity is exchanged for another equity of equal value, or (4) a combination of the above.

THE SIGNIFICANCE AND TREATMENT OF APPRECIATION IN THE ACCOUNTS, *Twentieth Annual Report of the Michigan Academy of Science* (1918), pp. 35-49. [227]

The array of opinion against recording appreciation in the accounts should not be given much weight in view of the fact that fifteen to twenty years ago the validity of recognizing depreciation as an expense was seriously questioned.

Since perhaps the most important function of modern accounting involves providing data for management, the accounts should show the fact that is most significant to management — present value.

In spite of the objections of accountants, indirect recognition of appreciation in the accounts occurs, for example, when an asset is used and depreciated over a twenty-year life as compared to an original estimate of fifteen years of life because costs of replacing it have increased substantially.

The argument that simply because an asset has appreciated in value does not make it more efficient confuses utility with value. ". . . the function of the accounts is to show economic facts." Recognition of appreciation will in some cases make the accounts more effectively serve as "an index of efficiency to guide directors and owners in their judgments."

Because "many of the individual owners in a modern corporation are transient," failure to correctly determine net revenue ("net increase in the status of the equities") for a given period results in their rights being impaired. "From the standpoint of the immediate interests of the equities, therefore, a net revenue figure which reflects *all* asset variations, is the important amount."

Accruals are made to maintain the integrity of the accounting period and appreciation could likewise be readily accrued. The practice of establishing secret reserves has been soundly criticized and condemned, yet failure to recognize appreciation results in exactly the same understatement of assets.

The argument that recognizing appreciation would call for recording "unrealized profits" is not correct, since all accruals are "based on 'unrealized' transactions in the same sense." Furthermore, appreciation can in many instances be estimated more accurately than depreciation or decline in value due to deterioration or handling.

Original cost figures do not show the sacrifice of investors because of changes in price levels, and "in accounting there is no propriety in the assumption of static prices."

The argument that recognition of appreciation would not be conservative fails to distinguish between "conservatism and downright concealment." Listing at a nominal sum assets which have a value of many thousands of dollars is not desirable accounting practice.

The cost or market rule of inventory valuation should be discarded and cost used unless market is considerably different, in either direction.

SOME PHASES OF CAPITAL STOCK, *Journal of Accountancy,* XXVII (May, 1919), 321-25. [228]

". . . a stock discount is neither an asset nor a loss, but is rather a valuation item — an offset to a capital stock figure which is largely nominal as far as the balance-sheet is concerned." The stock discount account should always be read in conjunction with the appropriate capital stock account to determine the status of the proprietary equity.

Stock discounts, if recorded, should be retained as long as the original stock issue involved is not disturbed. If such discounts are written off, two important classes of proprietorship are obscured, proprietary investment and accumulated earnings, although total proprietorship is still correctly stated. Stock discounts should not be eliminated by charges against gross revenues since such a procedure would disturb the integrity of the net revenue figure.

It would be entirely possible to omit the recording of discounts and record the proprietary equities on the basis of actual valuation. The investor may attach undue importance to par value, and "if par is more likely to deceive than instruct it may well be omitted." Such a position does not deny the legal significance of par value, "but the fact that par has a meaning in certain cases does not justify its inclusion in the balance-sheet."

Although "it is generally agreed that unissued stock is not an asset in any sense, and if brought into the books should be viewed as nothing more than an offset to total authorized capital . . . treasury stock on the other hand — especially in certain circumstances — is held to be a bona fide asset." Treasury stock, however, is not an asset but merely an offset to capital stock and surplus. The purchase of its own shares by a corporation is not an exchange of one asset for another, but simply a reduction in the shares outstanding. Reissuance does not represent an exchange of assets, but rather new investment.

The fact that treasury stock may be re-issued at any price does not in any way change its basic nature. ". . . it is illegitimate to count as an asset any condition which merely makes possible or convenient the raising of capital."

Preferably, all treasury stock items should be excluded from the balance sheet, thus promoting intelligent interpretation. If, however, such items are to be presented in the balance sheet they should be shown as valuation accounts or as deductions from the gross balances of the main proprietary accounts.

TRANSACTIONS BETWEEN PARTNERS AND FIRM, *Journal of Accountancy,* XXVIII (July, 1919), 33-38. [229]

Transactions between a partner and the firm should not be viewed or handled in the same way as transactions between the partnership and outsiders.

In the case of a partner borrowing from the firm through the giving of a note, the note should not be set up in notes receivable, since partner borrowings are in essence equivalent to partner drawings. Such a note cannot be considered an asset from the point of view of the firm as an entity, but should be viewed as a proprietary adjustment and charged to an account entitled "Loan to A."

Interest on partner borrowings should not be credited to a revenue account, since no revenue is involved. The transaction is an adjustment between the partners. The borrowing partner's capital account should be charged with the amount of the interest and all partners' capital accounts should be credited in accordance with the profit and loss sharing ratio.

PROPRIETORS' SALARIES, *Journal of Political Economy*, XXVIII (March, 1920), 240-56. [230]

What constitutes a "reasonable" salary for proprietors in close corporations became an important question as a result of the enactment of the excess profits tax provisions of the Revenue Act of 1918, which allowed the deduction of a reasonable allowance for salary or other compensation for personal services actually rendered to proprietors in determining net income.

Only in the sense of a rough approximation based on a broad statistical analysis is it possible to develop a general test of the reasonableness of salaries. The actual situations encountered are apt to vary widely, including that where the department is likely to allow the proprietor a "living wage" as minimum allowance even though, in an unsuccessful company, his real economic contribution may be nil. There will always be unusual cases requiring special consideration.

The practice of establishing salary allowances for owners of single proprietorships, partnerships and close corporations has been rather imperfectly developed because the significance of the contributions by such owners has varied widely. Net income might in one case consist entirely of interest and profits on capital invested, and in another almost entirely of compensation for personal services rendered. For this reason, from the proprietary point of view all payments to the majority-stockholder manager, even though called a salary for tax purposes, are distributions of income.

SOME CURRENT VALUATION ACCOUNTS, *Journal of Accountancy*, XXIX (May, 1920), 335-50. [231]

"Among questionable accounting procedures and usages are certain practices in the treatment of two kinds of discounts: (1) cash discounts, and (2) those discounts on promissory notes which are sometimes labeled 'prepaid interest.'" Cash discounts are simply current valuation charges or credits, and present practice with respect to statement presentation is not correct.

Sales discounts and returns, rebates and allowances are deductions from nominal revenue figures and not expenses or losses. Strictly speaking, expense is the cost of producing revenue for a given period, and since sales discounts are not costs of revenue they are not expenses. Similarly, purchase discounts are deductions from nominal cost figures, as are returns, allowances and rebates, and not an element of income analogous to interest earned.

It is unfortunate that in the widespread and legitimate use of valuation or offset accounts such accounts are frequently misinterpreted by laymen and improperly placed in financial statements. While some progress has been made toward presenting genuine offset accounts as deductions from the appropriate accounts in the balance sheet, accountants have failed to recognize that it is equally important that offset accounts be correctly interpreted in the construction of the income statement.

Unaccrued discounts on notes payable and other obligations are also valuation items and should be presented as such. "Prepaid interest," in the proper sense of the term, does not exist, and such items as discounts cannot be considered assets from any reasonable point of view. These discounts, rather than being assets, are offsetting items to the face or par of the outstanding obligation, in any case to the extent to which this par or face is not yet the effective liability.

DEPRECIATION, APPRECIATION AND PRODUCTIVE CAPACITY, *Journal of Accountancy,* XXX (July, 1920), 1-11. [232]

"Accountants deal with an unstable, untrustworthy index (the dollar); and, accordingly, comparisons of unadjusted accounting statements prepared at different periods are always more or less unsatisfactory and are often positively misleading." The instability of the accountant's yardstick is one of the fundamental limitations of accounting. ". . . the apparent improvement in the financial position of the typical enterprise in recent years is in no small degree a matter of the change in the value of money."

Several suggestions relative to accounting procedures which could be adopted in periods of fluctuating price levels have been advanced in previous issues of the *Journal.* However, the problems created by fluctuating price levels cannot be dealt with merely by recording depreciation on replacement cost. "To charge costs of replacement to revenues instead of original costs, without further adjustments, would build up depreciation reserves in excess of book values of property retired. We would then be confronted with the unreasonable situation of having an offset or valuation credit balance on the books, although the property to which this credit was supposed to apply would have been replaced with new equipment which had suffered no depreciation. This balance in the reserve account would evidently constitute surplus; and a belated recognition of proprietary or capital increase would be forced."

If a reserve for depreciation is built up by charging operations with depreciation on replacement cost and a part of the cost of the new asset is charged against this reserve, the new asset would be stated on the books at the cost of the old even though it cost more. This procedure would not be good accounting.

Appreciation could be recorded by charging the asset account and crediting an appreciation capital account. There is much to be said, from the viewpoint of management, in favor of recognizing appreciation in the accounts. On the other hand, it should be noted that asset values are conjectural at best and subject to continuing change.

THE DRUG STORE'S OVERHEAD, *American Druggist and Pharmaceutical Record,* LXVIII (September, 1920), 17-24. [233]

Care must be exercised to avoid being victimized by the belief that a cost system is a cure-all. However, as a minimum, a drug store should have a double-entry system of accounts to permit easy preparation of periodic statements. A certain amount of classification of accounts is feasible and such a classification should assist in cost analysis and the detection of abnormalities.

In retailing, all costs of doing business other than merchandise costs are overhead. Such overhead costs should be classified into well-defined accounts. Percentage analyses should be made. Certain types of so-called expenses should not be included, for example, "no recognition should be given . . . to interest, rent, or any other item which is not an actual expense." In other words, imputed expenses should be excluded.

INTEREST DURING CONSTRUCTION, *Journal of Political Economy,* XXVIII (October, 1920), 680-95. [234]

While economic theory supports the view that interest on investment is a cost element, the concept has almost no support in accounting practice because of practical difficulties and theoretical objections. To the accountant, cost is represented by purchased goods and services expired, and services furnished by the owners cannot be considered as costs to the owners.

Acceptance of the arguments for recognition of interest on investment during the construction period is undesirable because (1) it leads to the conclusion that all investments inevitably increase in value over time, (2) it would lead to a lower rate of return in later years by increasing present capital value, and (3) such recognition of interest would be incomplete in the sense that it does not measure all the services contributed by the owner which presumably are represented in the difference between cost and possible selling price.

It is further argued that a business cannot start with a deficit. This is not true, since losses may result from accident, inefficiency, or illegitimate expenses. A further problem encountered is what rate should be used if interest is to be recognized.

In many cases invested capital is contributed, in part, by preferred shareholders and bondholders. Preferred dividends and interest paid during construction might be carried in a contra-capital account until closed against future earnings. Such payments are not losses to the common stockholders since they accept this concession now in the hope of higher future earnings.

DISCUSSION OF "AIM AND SCOPE OF GRADUATE AND RESEARCH WORK IN ACCOUNTING," *Papers and Proceedings of the Fifth Annual Meeting* (1920), American Association of University Instructors in Accounting, V (1921), 26-29. [235]

There are at least four possible areas of respectable graduate study involving accounting. A graduate student may labor profitably in the field of accounting systems for special branches of industry; in corporate finance and the history of a particular enterprise or groups of enterprises; in statistical research on corporate profits and surplus, including costs for different lines, turnover statistics, the effects of changing price levels on apparent profits, and many similar topics. Also, there are many opportunities for study in the theory area. For example, the whole area of valuation is in need of factual study and theoretical research.

METHODS OF MEASURING BUSINESS INCOME, *Administration,* I (April, 1921), 509-26. [236]

The determination of net business income for relatively short periods of time is necessitated as a matter of equity between different classes of corporate security holders and between individual owners of the same class of security. The levying of taxes upon business net income and differential profits also makes imperative the determination of income.

Many problems are encountered in measuring business net income, including those of definition, recognition and measurement. These difficulties are such "as to tempt one to say that the periodic expression of net income for the particular business is, under the most favorable circumstances, no more than a good guess."

The many difficulties faced in cost determination and allocation have been generally recognized. It is generally assumed that the assignment of credits to income accounts is a routine matter. However, this is far from the truth and many problems are encountered in determining what should be the "signal" for a credit entry in an income account.

The receipt of cash is one possible basis of revenue recognition. "Cash is the asset excellent." Under such a basis, the credit sale would not be formally recorded until collected. Even if such a basis is employed, cash disbursements would not be the measure of the proper deductions in arriving at net income. Expense must be recognized as the cost of producing a particular volume of revenue. To look upon income as the change in the cash balance would be wholly unreasonable. The installment sales basis of recognizing income as permitted for tax purposes is, under the circumstances, a logical employment of the cash basis of revenue recognition.

The most widely employed basis of revenue recognition is the credit sale. In a credit sale, passage of title is the characteristic that distinguishes the sale from the securing of an order or a contract. The credit sale is valid evidence of the existence of revenue if the account receivable arising therefrom is reasonably sure of collection.

Revenue may also be recognized on a technical completion basis. This method may have validity in those situations where securing the finished product is the significant goal of the enterprise, and where sale is merely routine. Examples of such situations are found in agricultural products and coal mining. Goods would be priced at selling price less estimated marketing costs. The objection to this method is that it is said to involve recognition of unrealized profit, since the sale is the true test of realization. However, it can also be argued that profit evaporates if the sale is not collected.

Revenue may also be recognized on a percentage of completion basis. From a broad economic standpoint the idea of accruing income gradually has much to commend it. However, since there is no assurance that income is accruing as expenses accrue, this method is limited in its use to long-term project accounting, such as the building of a ship.

The changing value of the dollar produces one of the most serious limitations to accounting data. Even if a satisfactory plan of income determination is employed, the accountant's figures must be adjusted to show the real change in economic status.

ASSUMPTIONS OF THE ACCOUNTANT, *Administration,* I (June, 1921), 786-802. [237]

The accountant almost universally assumes the existence of a business entity, not only for corporations legally viewed as separate entities, but also in sole proprietorships and partnerships.

The accountant assumes a continued existence for the business entity. Assets are thus valued on the "going concern" basis.

The accountant assumes the equality of the assets to the total equities. Stating the equities in this manner is a matter of convenience, and, in cases of liquidation, the common stockholder is entitled to that which is left over and not the nominal amount shown on the balance sheet.

The accountant assumes that a statement of assets and liabilities shows the financial condition of an enterprise on the date of the statement. This assumption can be readily disproved, but the accountant, for lack of a better approach, continues to use this method. He also assumes that the value or significance of the measuring unit remains unchanged. This is also unsound. However, he does have the right to assume that first cost and value are the same.

The accountant assumes cost transference, that is, that the cost of goods and services utilized are transferred to the resulting products and services and constitute the latter's cost. He also assumes that costs accrue, but that income appears only in terms of specific transactions. Depreciation is assumed to accrue ratably through time.

Another assumption is that asset expirations extinguish first current earnings, next retained earnings, and then the original capital investment. And finally, the accountant assumes that the inventory is composed of the latest acquired lots (*Fifo*).

DIVIDENDS IN SECURITIES, *Administration,* IV (October, 1922), 394-402. [238]

So-called corporate dividends paid in securities of the declaring corporation are not true dividends. Only those dividends requiring the disbursement to the shareholders of cash or other corporate property are true dividends. In the latter case the corporation's assets and equities are decreased while in the former case only the equities are reclassified.

Until the recent Supreme Court decision exempting stock dividends from taxation at the time of receipt, all dividends, except those out of capital or from earnings accumulated prior to March 1, 1913, regardless of the mode of payment, were considered to be taxable income.

Many reasons are advanced for the declaration of stock dividends, among the more valid of which are the desire to permanently retain income in the corporation and to reduce the market price of a stock to a more desired trading range. Less valid reasons sometimes advanced are to hide the amount of accumulated surplus or undivided profits, to manipulate stock prices for the benefit of insiders, to hide increasing cash dividends and occasionally to aid in fights for control of a corporation.

To the shareholder there is no real significance in a stock dividend. His fractional interest in the corporation remains unchanged, although divided into more parts. He can sell his dividend shares to realize cash only at the cost of losing a part of his fractional interest, a transaction into which he could enter without receiving dividend shares. To some shareholders expecting cash dividends the receipt of a stock dividend is a discouragement in that it postpones cash dividends. It should be borne in mind that it is not the payment of a dividend, per se, which enhances the shareholder's wealth, but the successful operation of the corporation.

Dividends in bonds, stock of another class, notes and scrip are of essentially the same significance to the shareholder as stock dividends, except that in the case of the former he may be able to realize cash by disposing of the securities received without giving up a part of his proportionate interest in the control of the corporation. Dividends in short-term scrip are best viewed as postponed cash dividends.

From the standpoint of taxation dividends in bonds, stock, notes and scrip should be treated alike and not be subject to possible taxation until the security is sold or paid by the corporation.

A much more fundamental question relative to the taxation of dividends is that of the double taxation of corporate earnings.

VALUATION OF INVENTORIES, *Journal of Accountancy,* XXIV (December, 1922), 432-50. [239]

One possible basis of inventory valuation is actual cost. This basis should not be rejected simply because it does not reflect current market value to acquire. Actual cost is the rational valuation method if one looks upon a sale as necessary evidence for income recognition. In trading enterprises actual cost as a factor in income determination is so important that its deficiency as an indicator of present value in the balance sheet is outweighed.

Because of the extreme difficulties encountered in the determination of actual cost, a number of approaches to the computation of cost have been developed. Among these are the pricing of inventory on the basis of a weighted average price or at the cost of the most recently acquired goods. The latter method is to be favored because of the simple, systematic way in which it can be applied; the inventory value approximates current value, and the method of determination is in harmony with the physical flow of goods in most well-run businesses. Another approach to the computation of the cost of inventory items is the base-cost scheme of pricing, which has been strongly urged by several large corporations and which yields "a kind of long-term or standard cost."

Replacement cost, even though use of this method in a period of rising prices may result in the recognition of some unrealized income, has merit in that it (1) is more logical than actual cost, because it assigns the same value to various units of homogeneous goods, (2) is consistent with the fact that replacement cost has a significant effect on selling price, (3) requires a minimum of clerical effort to use, and (4) is the most reasonable portrayal of financial condition in the balance sheet.

The lower of actual cost or replacement cost, a compromise between the above two methods, should be rejected because it (1) is difficult to apply, (2) violates the fundamental canon of consistency, and (3) recognizes unrealized losses and can result in the recognition of unrealized income.

Valuation of inventory at selling price may have merit in situations where productive activity is of overwhelming significance, and the selling activity is quite insignificant, as, for example, in the case of wheat farming. Here selling costs are nominal, sale is assured at a market price, and costs are difficult to determine.

". . . business conditions are so varied and complex that no single valuation rule or principle can be relied upon for application to every case. . . . We must take a broadminded attitude, condemning no rule or principle purely on the basis of tradition and prejudice, but testing every method primarily on the grounds of reasonableness and expediency."

EDUCATIONAL VALUE OF TRAINING IN ACCOUNTING, *Papers and Proceedings of the Seventh Annual Meeting* (1922), The American Association of University Instructors in Accounting, VII (1923), 66-73. [240]

An "intellectual revolution" is taking place in education at the collegiate level, especially with respect to the ever increasing number of universities and colleges offering training in business administration and, in particular, accounting.

Three tests may be applied to determine whether an area or subject is suitable for teaching at the university level:

(1) Is the subject matter important and of fundamental and general interest?

(2) Does the subject matter include knowledge which an individual would not automatically acquire from a lifetime of everyday experience?

(3) Is the subject matter sufficiently recondite and difficult to escape understanding from casual contact?

Economics and accounting, especially economics, fare well when these tests are applied. However, there are serious grounds for criticism of university work in business, such as the lack of good texts, stressing of superficial aspects, and the scramble after practical trivialities rather than an emphasis upon the fundamentals of economics.

SIMPLIFICATION OF FEDERAL INCOME TAXATION, *Certified Public Accountant,* II (June, 1923), 141-43, 152. [241]

Successive revisions of the income tax laws have increased the complexity of the individual tax return. Taxation procedure "should not be unreasonably inequitable, but neither should it be unduly elaborate." Several features of the Revenue Act of 1921 are unnecessarily complex in the devices allocating taxation between the large and small incomes. Rather than disguising and complicating "discrimination between large and small incomes . . . we should have simply a clear-cut graduated tax with no trimmings."

Provisions relating to depletion allowances, capital gains, taxation of corporate income and loss recognition only when a security is sold are either inequitable, questionable, or based upon doubtful lines of distinction.

TENDENCIES IN ACCOUNTING LITERATURE, *Papers and Proceedings of the Ninth Annual Meeting* (1924), The American Association of University Instructors in Accounting, IX (1925), 66-69. [242]

In recent accounting literature, a trend toward a broader and more rational point of view with emphasis upon the underlying aims and purposes of accounting can be noted in the area of principles and theory. More rational explanations of the double-entry system have been presented, and the sole use of the mercantile point of view is disappearing. Greater emphasis is being placed on income accounting with increasing emphasis upon the points of view of the private accountant and the business executive.

Attention has also been directed toward the application of accounting techniques and methods to the operating problems of the large enterprise and the needs of the business executive and his assistants. The current auditing literature shows a recognition of the widening scope of the professional accountant's function and exhibits less rigidity in rules of valuation.

ACCRUED DEPRECIATION ON SEASONED PROPERTIES, *Certified Public Accountant,* VII (July, 1927), 206-10, 214-17. [243]

Depreciation, a problem involving value, can never be determined with absolute accuracy, even though it is now generally recognized as an operating expense.

The question of whether there is depreciation on "property that has reached more or less settled operating conditions . . . and for which replacement and maintenance charges are occuring rather uniformly" arises especially in public utilities and railways. The arguments against recognition of depreciation on seasoned properties are based on the theory that efficiency or potential service is the measure of value, and that recognition of depreciation will result in the accumulation of funds of no use to a business.

On the other hand, if maintenance charges increase throughout the life of an asset, it must have greater value in the early years. Depreciation must be accrued in order to avoid impairment of the funds of the security holders. The maintenance of service argument does not take into consideration the quality of the service, nor the fact that new properties are likely to be more efficient than seasoned properties.

An important argument against non-recognition of depreciation is that 100 percent service does not indicate 100 percent basic value. Also, substitution of replacement charges for depreciation misstates the original cost of existing properties. The "abandonment and acquisition of property are two different transactions, and . . . ought to be accounted for as such, through independent entries."

Depreciation accounting will never become thoroughly rational until such time as large complex units of property are divided into smaller units according to service life which are followed individually.

DISTRIBUTION COSTS AND INVENTORY VALUES, *Accounting Review,* II (September, 1927), 246-53. [244]

More attention should be directed toward the development of methods whereby costs that do not have a direct relationship to specific sales, such as advertising costs, may be assigned to sales of specific periods.

The present practice of charging distribution costs directly into operating expenses without passing them through the regular cost system and thus into inventory, or a special type of asset, is questionable. What is the cost of sales? Strictly speaking, any charge to revenue or a cost properly applicable thereto is a "cost of sales." The conventional line of distinction between cost of sales, on the one hand, and all other expenses, on the other, is unfortunate. There is no fundamental economic distinction between trading and manufacturing, and there should be no fundamental difference in the methods of accounting for costs developed in the two fields.

LIMITATIONS OF FINANCIAL AND OPERATING RATIOS, *Accounting Review,* III (September, 1928), 252-60. [245]

The use of financial and operating ratios as interpretative devices to make financial statements more intelligible and significant has increased substantially. However, the enthusiasm for ratios as such seems at times to go beyond reasonable bounds. Ratios are, at best, merely supplementary devices, useful and worthwhile only insofar as their limitations are clearly perceived.

Although a myriad of ratios can be calculated from an enterprise's financial statements, only relatively few have any considerable significance to business management. Ratios of the first order of significance are: (1) net return to investment, (2) proprietary equity to total assets, (3) expenses to gross earnings or volume of business. The ratio of current assets to current liabilities may be a fourth ratio of the first order of significance. Other ratios, such as accounts receivable to sales, fall into a second order of significance while yet others, such as the the ratio of cash to accounts payable, fall into a third order of significance.

Ratios in themselves have little significance and are, at best, nothing more than clues or starting points for study and investigation. Standards are needed against which to compare ratios. Such standards may be based upon the past history of the enterprise, more importantly upon the records of other concerns in the same line of business, and should include "a trace of the ideal."

With respect to a number of ratios, "we have widely accepted impressions as to standards . . . [which] must not be taken too seriously in the particular case if errors are to be avoided. . . ." For example, it does not follow that the ideal ratio of proprietary or residual equity to total assets is one to one, "and the more nearly this ideal is approached the more favorable and to be commended the situation." This ratio will vary widely in different fields of endeavor. "If it is feasible to use borrowed capital to the extent of fifty percent of the total assets, for example, is it not good management to maintain this proportion continuously?"

Generalizations with respect to the significance of even the more important ratios are dangerous. Each situation is unique and requires independent study.

SPECIAL APPLICATIONS OF DISCOUNTING, *Journal of Accountancy*, XLVI (October, 1928), 270-82. [246]

From the viewpoint of accounting and business, discounting is "the process of reducing one or more future considerations, certain in amount and in money or its equivalent, to effective present market value, a value which may appropriately be recognized in the statement of financial condition."

By attaching undue, legalistic significance to par or maturity value, accountants fail to recognize that (1) there is an imputed interest element in all contracts regardless of terms, (2) neither the amount due at maturity nor the total of the amounts due under the contract is the measure of initial value except coincidentally, (3) initial value or principal accumulates due to unpaid accruing interest, and (4) discount is not prepaid interest — it is *unpaid* interest.

Discounting techniques can be applied to such items as wages payable, accounts payable and receivable, notes receivable and other evidences of indebtedness, land contracts, contract prepayments such as insurance and leaseholds, in addition to bonds and notes payable.

HOW MICHIGAN TRAINS HER YOUNG MEN FOR ACCOUNTING CAREERS, *American Accountant*, XIV (September, 1929), 495-96. [247]

Accounting was first taught at the University of Michigan in 1901 in the Department of Economics. By 1929 between 30 and 40 hours of accounting were offered, requiring the services of five or six instructors.

The student usually begins his accounting work in his second or third year by taking the elementary course. The fourth and fifth years are devoted to specialized and professional courses, and the MBA degree is awarded at the end of the fifth year.

The principal objectives of the work in accounting have been to train students for administrative or managerial accounting or for public or professional accounting. In 1926 an internship program was developed under which selected students spend six to eight weeks with a public accounting firm.

A college graduate may write on all subjects of the state CPA examination except "practical accounting" and, if successful, receive a "certificate of examination." After two years of practical accounting he may take the balance of the examination and, if again successful, receive his CPA certificate.

THE DIVIDEND CODE, *Accounting Review,* IV (December, 1929), 218-20. [248]

A number of points should be given consideration by the drafters of the dividend code provisions of the various state corporation acts. With respect to basic conceptions and definitions, the dividend code provisions should be clear and concise on such matters as: (1) the source and measure of dividends, (2) the method of determination of current and undivided profits or surplus, (3) the treatment to be accorded increases in asset values not related to regular operation, (4) the essential conditions which must be met from an accounting standpoint, (5) the act of appropriating or declaring a dividend, and (6) the types of dividends — that is, dividends payable in cash or other property (the only true dividends), and so-called dividends represented by the issue of evidences of indebtedness or shares of stock.

In addition, specific rules should be laid down governing dividend appropriations with respect to: (1) legality insofar as the articles of incorporation and other contracts are concerned, (2) limitations on the amount of dividends regardless of the mode of payment, (3) losses which must be recognized, (4) types of surplus adjustments which may or may not be required in determining the dividend base, (5) treatment to be accorded special profits, such as those arising from capital structure change, (6) whether stock discounts or initial overvaluations of assets must be "made good," (7) what amount of a holding company's consolidated surplus is available for dividends, (8) the dollar amount at which stock "dividends" or longer-term evidences of indebtedness should be recorded, (9) what items of capital surplus may be included in the dividend base, (10) the interpretation to be placed on surplus indirectly capitalized as a result of a capital structure change, and (11) returns of capital (liquidation payments).

ECONOMIC THEORY IN RELATION TO ACCOUNTING VALUATIONS, *Accounting Review,* VI (June, 1931), 89-96. [249]

All assets may be classified as (1) "repositories of funds," or (2) "summations of costs." Valuation problems arise chiefly with the developmental and operating costs of the enterprise which are included in the second category. In determining the treatment to be accorded these costs, reference may be made to propositions and reasoning found in economic theory.

"To the economist, all market costs are homogeneous in their effect upon values." However, the accountant in dealing with such costs as organization costs finds himself entangled "in a legal structure, a body of engineering considerations, and a slowly developing network of business traditions." From the standpoint of economics, absurd solutions follow.

To be an effective cost, an element of cost incurred must be of such character that the presence of the factor or condition represented by such cost makes it possible for the enterprise to avoid incurring another similar cost which would otherwise be required in the production of revenue. Although all effective costs are homogeneous, economic uselessness must be recognized. In the case of land, cost may approximate value, but carrying costs do not increase that value: supply and demand do.

To the economist, effective costs are not only the money units of the original charge, but include "costs to date, potential costs and costs of replacement." Also, the economist will distinguish between appreciation due to general price level changes and that due to change in the status of the particular object being valued.

ACCOUNTING PROBLEMS OF THE DEPRESSION, *Accounting Review,* VII (December, 1932), 258-67. [250]

Distinction must be drawn between operating costs and non-operating charges to reduce the tendency during the current period of reduced business activity to charge all types of items directly to surplus on the theory that they are non-operating items. The income account is thus relieved of considerable pressure. Certain tests can be established to aid in distinguishing operating from non-operating charges. Such tests include regularity of occurrence, whether a service has been received and used in the usual way, whether the item is under the control of management, and whether the item is necessary for legal or social reasons.

Depreciation and similar charges are not a matter of convenience, to be recognized or not as the volume of revenues appears to make feasible.

There is no valid reason to apply smoothing techniques to the determination of corporate net income in order to eliminate the peaks of prosperity and valleys of depression.

Clarity is to be sought with regard to the source of dividends. Dividends should not be charged directly against surplus reserves. If cash is available and a desire to pay dividends exists but there is no surplus against which to charge such dividends, it would be proper to reverse the stock dividends of earlier boom periods if such action were properly controlled and explained.

Caution should be employed in plant writedowns. Cost of replacement means little if anything in the case of obsolete or semi-obsolete property which is not being reproduced in the form of a constant flow of new plants and new machines. Sweeping writedowns of assets are also to be condemned for their non-conservative effect on later income reports. Writedowns of assets handled through creation of trick surplus accounts are to be deplored.

WORKING CAPITAL IN PUBLIC UTILITY REGULATION, *Journal of Accountancy*, LIV (October, 1932), 287-99. [251]

In cases involving the determination of public utility rates, working capital is viewed from the standpoint of what it ought to be and not what it is. A question arises whether the rate of return should be computed upon total capital employed or total capital employed less current liabilities which do not carry an explicit rate of interest. It would be incorrect to deduct accrued payroll from current assets for rate-making purposes, because employee services are usually charged directly to operating expense rather than to an asset account. On the whole the evidence in support of deducting "current non-interest-bearing obligations" from current assets for rate-making purposes is inconclusive.

The amount of working capital to be included in the rate base can be determined from prior years' experience and supported by reference to representative firms in the same field.

Certain items should not be considered working capital items. For example, cash received from the sale of securities and held for construction or debt retirement purposes and temporary investments of idle funds in marketable securities should be excluded. Materials in inventory held for construction may be included in current assets if wisely purchased and not extraordinary. Ordinary prepayments are elements of working capital. Interest on bank accounts, call loans and other liquid securities (and other assets of ancillary nature) should be included in income and the assets in working capital.

SHOESTRING BANKING, *Certified Public Accountant*, XIII (June, 1933), 333-38. [252]

Despite all the discussion of the banking system in recent years, little or no mention has been made of the basic problem of weaknesses in the capital structure as related to maintenance of solvency. Banks are an extreme example of "trading on the equity" as evidenced by the report of the Comptroller of Currency for 1931 which shows that liabilities of banks average over 86 percent of the book value of the resources. No substantial buffer or cushion of proprietary equity exists in a size approaching that deemed desirable in other lines of endeavor.

Extreme liquidity is an unreasonable goal in bank management. Depositor confidence cannot be obtained in this fashion. Therefore, in order to function in a more normal manner, maintenance of a liquidity position to enable meeting the demands of 20 percent of the obligations is a reasonable goal.

A capital and surplus ratio of 10 percent may not be adequate in a time of shrinkage in the value of a bank's resources although undoubtedly the yield, earnings-wise, will be greater in "fair weather" than if a 25-30 percent ratio is maintained. The lower return to a 25-30 percent equity would be offset, however, by more stable and sound practices and conditions, thus reducing the risk of loss of capital.

PUBLIC OWNERSHIP UNNECESSARY, *Public Service Magazine,* LVI (February, 1934), 41-42. [253]

The growing demand for the construction of municipal utility plants has been based upon the desire for lower rates, the possibility of obtaining federal funds on low, easy terms, and the general attitude of the administration — witness TVA. Many of the arguments for public ownership are based on false assumptions and data which break down under careful examination.

The assumption that unbridled exploitation is the only alternative to governmental ownership is unwarranted. Rate regulation has been relatively successful. Municipal ownership is no mysterious source of superior economic efficiency and service. Government has no monopoly on human talent. With respect to the question of rates, the fact that taxes take between one-third and one-sixth of the total receipts of privately-owned utilities is frequently overlooked. Also, if governmentally owned plants were called upon to earn a fair rate of return, another advantage would disappear. All public utilities have been unjustly tarred by the brush of scandal applicable only to some holding companies.

The large integrated utility has a number of sources of power and hence can render better service in the event of disaster. Many municipalities are on the verge of bankruptcy now, and house cleaning is in order before additional borrowed funds can be sought. Care must also be taken to ensure that the rights of individual investors are not destroyed, especially in view of the demand for the construction of competing plants.

SHORTCOMINGS OF PRESENT-DAY FINANCIAL STATEMENTS, *Journal of Accountancy,* LVII (February, 1934), 108-32. [254]

Present-day balance sheets can be improved in many ways. Asset valuation accounts should be deducted from their respective assets and not from a hodgepodge of assets. Treasury securities are not assets, but should be shown as contra liability or equity items. All forms of security discounts should be shown as separate items, not lumped together with issue costs, and deducted from their respective securities. Items in the catchall "deferred charges" classification should be detailed, more aptly titled and classified. The capital and surplus section of the balance sheet is in need of new, descriptive titles. A calculation of book value should be shown. Classifying asset valuation accounts, liabilities and surplus reserves as "reserves" in the balance sheet is most improper.

Present-day income statements can also be improved in many ways. The showing of gross profit should be eliminated, since there is no need for an intermediate figure before the all-important net operating income figure. Interest is a distribution of earnings, not an expense. Depreciation, a perfectly valid operating expense, should be included in operating expenses. Purchase discounts are not income, but adjustments of nominal cost. A combined statement of income and surplus should be presented, in view of the tendency to charge many items to surplus. Current dividends should be shown in the income statement as a charge against current earnings.

Accountants should make greater use of cumulative reports, statistical devices such as index numbers and funds statements. Accountants could also prepare a balance sheet in two segments — first, the current account data which would take the liquidation point of view, and secondly, the capital account section which would take the going-concern point of view.

ASPECTS OF ASSET VALUATIONS, *Accounting Review,* IX (June, 1934), 122-29. [255]

Accountants record the acquisition of technical cost factors — inventories, structures, equipment, etc. — at cost incurred because this measures historical outlay, which the accountant must report, and because cost can be assumed to approximate effective economic value. However, changing circumstances may make later revision of cost desirable.

Revaluation would be appropriate in case of insolvency, except where liquidation is expected to occur over a long period of time. Revaluation to scrap value is appropriate in circumstances where an asset has lost its economic value sooner than expected, even under the going-concern point of view.

The existence of short-run or temporary excess capacity would not appear to warrant revaluation. Revaluation would be justifiable in cases of long-run excess capacity, although such a revaluation would face a number of practical difficulties.

Revaluation because of changes in the level of prices may be accomplished by the use of an index of the price level as a whole or by the use of replacement cost. It is questionable whether use of the latter method results in more desirable economic data, and the argument that the employment of this method will insure adequate funds for replacement is not valid.

Accountants can use supplementary statistical procedures such as index-number techniques, separate from the accounting records, to provide management with useful information on the effects of price-level changes.

COSTS AND PROFITS IN PRESENT-DAY ACCOUNTING, *N.A.C.A. Bulletin,* XVI (October 1, 1934), 123-39. [256]

Modern accounting measures costs and revenues under a doctrine of periodic apportionment. Costs and assets are related, assets being either (1) money and representatives of money, or (2) a pool of cost factors. The accountant's task, in dealing with this pool of cost factors, is to assign an appropriate amount to a particular period. In attempting to accomplish this assignment, accountants place undue stress on the physical, technological side of the business as opposed to the economic side.

The accountant also places undue emphasis upon the balance sheet and balance sheet valuations. The primary goal should be a sound determination of periodic income. In the accounts revenue may be recognized at any of a number of different points in the cycle of operations. Revenue may be recorded (1) when cash has been collected from the customer, (2) at the time of the making of a legal sale, (3) when physical output or production has occurred, or (4) according to the accumulation of costs incurred.

VALUATION OF THE BUSINESS ENTERPRISE, *Accounting Review,* XI (March, 1936), 26-32. [257]

Of the two approaches to problems of valuation in business — cost or income — the cost approach could be used satisfactorily with respect to an individual asset. However, assignment of a segment of a firm's income to a particular asset on a reasonable basis is a next to impossible task.

In the valuation of the enterprise, the income approach is far more significant and proper than the cost approach. Such a process of valuation involves the following processes:

(1) Past earnings for a period of, perhaps, not less than three nor more than ten years should be studied, especially with regard to the accounting policies followed for organizational and developmental costs, inventory, maintenance, depreciation and depletion charges, and unusual profits or losses.

(2) The carefully studied and interpreted past earnings should be translated into an estimate of future earning power, by establishing estimated ranges into which earnings will probably fall in the next five to ten years. The approach to be followed is that of viewing earnings from the all-capital point of view rather than from the proprietary position.

(3) A critical appraisal must be made of the tangible assets and a valuation attached thereto.

(4) A fair rate of return must next be estimated. The rate chosen should be one that maintains capital and attracts additional capital as needed, plus a small margin for safety.

(5) The rate of return should be applied to the tangible assets which are to be associated with the production of the earnings. The amount so computed should then be compared with the expected earnings in order to determine whether the enterprise has any superior earning power.

(6) To determine their present worth, the superior earnings, which should probably not be viewed as lasting for more than five to ten years, should be discounted at a higher rate of return than that associated with the tangible assets. The value of the enterprise is then the present worth of superior earnings plus the valuation attached to the tangible assets.

Problems requiring special study and consideration in the valuation of an enterprise include those of excess working capital, nonessential physical properties and the treatment to be accorded liabilities not calling for explicit interest payments.

PRESENTATION OF BOND DISCOUNT, *Accounting Review,* XII (September, 1937), 285-90. [258]

The American Accounting Association's "Tentative Statement of Accounting Principles" has taken the only proper position in recommending that unaccumulated bond discount be reported in the corporate balance sheet as a contra to the face or maturity amount of outstanding obligations.

Of the three possible amounts at which the original liability on the bonds issued could be reported (total amount payable — principal plus all interest payments, maturity amount, or actual amount received) only the actual amount received is acceptable.

The American Institute's Committee on Accounting Procedure includes prepaid interest under the caption *deferred charges.* Presentation of bond discount as an item separate from prepaid interest does not correct the error. Interest is a charge for the use of funds through time and in a strict sense cannot be prepaid since any advance by the borrower would merely serve to reduce the amount of the loan. Discount represents unpaid or future interest. The true liability is the actual amount received or invested, and this liability grows with the passage of time as the discount accumulates.

Adherence to the traditional method of presenting bond discount also leads to the mistake of combining bond discount with the "genuine costs of raising capital."

While there is not great significance in the point under discussion, "the issue of straight thinking and sound classification and procedure versus adherence to customary practice has real significance."

COMMENTS ON "A STATEMENT OF ACCOUNTING PRINCIPLES," *Journal of Accountancy,* LXV (March, 1938), 196-207. [259]

". . . my general reaction to this statement . . . is one of keen disappointment." The statement makes it appear that the accountant is subservient to management and has little or nothing to offer business management in the way of positive and constructive advice.

The treatment accorded a number of important topics such as depreciation "is feeble, and lacking in consistency and clarity." The replacement cost basis of recording depreciation is dismissed simply because of difficulty in estimating replacement cost. The only alternative to the straight-line depreciation mentioned is the reducing charge method; no mention is made of allocation according to output or service. According to the statement, depreciation may or may not be an operating charge, and such a position is certainly detrimental to the profession.

"Gross profit" is accorded a place of prominence in the income statement, although there has been a trend in recent years to eliminate this definitely misleading balance.

The authors apparently believe that attempts to equalize earnings are contrary to recognized accounting principles. Yet, they support the last-in, first-out method of inventory pricing, which is essentially the European base-stock method, and "which represents nothing more nor less than a major device for equalizing earnings."

The terminology in the report is quite inconsistent. For example, expenses are charges against income, charges to earnings, charges to revenue, and charges to gross revenue.

Conservatism is worshipped merely because of its age and its tradition. This is not sound conservatism. Conservatism "is not a determined allegiance to prevailing practices, regardless of their merits." An "outstanding example of unsound and nonconservative practice masquerading under the guise of sainted conservatism is the 'cost or market, whichever is lower' rule of inventory valuation." The objections to this method are clear-cut and overwhelming, and not a single point has been advanced to indicate that this method is a sound accounting rule.

Other defects in the report include showing bond discount added to cost of raising capital as an asset, showing prepaid interest along with other genuine prepayments although it does not exist, and the suggestion that treasury stock might under some "mysterious circumstances" be shown as an asset. On the whole, the report does not represent a clear-cut, coherent statement of accounting principles.

IS IT DESIRABLE TO DISTINGUISH BETWEEN VARIOUS KINDS OF SURPLUS? *Journal of Accountancy,* LXV (April, 1938), 285-89. [260]

"Ignoring legal complications for the moment, it seems clear that the ideal definition of capital stock, in dollars and cents, is the following: Capital stock represents the amount of money actually invested by the stockholders. Similarly, corporate surplus should be defined: Surplus is measured by the amount of recognized profits retained by the enterprise and validated by existing assets."

"Since the law is quite ready to call capital 'surplus' and surplus 'capital,' the accountant who has a lingering desire to present a clear picture of net worth has found himself in a somewhat embarrassing position. On the one hand, he is faced with the necessity of avoiding any appearance of ignoring the legal conditions attaching to the corporation; on the other hand, he wishes to recognize the objective economic and administrative situation, and meet the needs of those who are thinking primarily in these terms. As a way out, he has adopted — not altogether fortunately — the practice of classifying surplus into two divisions, (1) capital or paid-in surplus and (2) earned surplus."

The stockholders' equity should be reported in such a manner as to make clear the "extent to which the business to date has been financed with stockholders' capital investments on the one hand and undisturbed profits on the other."

Some further classification of surplus, in the sense of undistributed profits, may be in order although "the practice of sub-dividing surplus account under fancy titles has been carried much too far in some cases, and quite generally the importance of the process of earmarking surplus has been exaggerated." It is neither necessary nor desirable to classify surplus in the balance sheet according to the source of profits.

PRINCIPLES RELATED TO "DEFERRED CHARGES" AND "PREPAID EXPENSES," *Papers on Accounting Principles and Procedures,* Fifty-first Annual Meeting (New York: American Institute of Certified Public Accountants, 1938), pp. 26-30. [261]

There is no basic distinction between deferred charges and prepaid expenses except, perhaps, that of long-term versus short-term. The use of the caption *deferred charges* as a catchall for unexplained odds and ends "is decidedly poor practice." Such a collection of items may contain current prepayments which are current assets, contra equity items which should be reported on the other side of the statement, and losses which should be written off. Only long-term items not reportable elsewhere should be shown as deferred charges.

Use of the term *deferred charges* implies a sound income statement point of view in that it assumes a flow of costs through the business and raises the problem of which costs should be currently absorbed and which deferred.

The basic question is whether the charge under consideration is reasonably applicable and significant to future periods. More attention should be paid to economic significance than to tangibility and "the homogeneity of all classes of legitimate costs in their relation to the activities of the enterprise must be recognized." There is no justification for deferring recognition of losses. Such a practice may be based upon too narrow a concept of business and its division into operating and non-operating categories.

THE "GROSS PROFIT" CONVENTION, *Accounting Forum,* X (October, 1938), 19-20. [262]

A questionable practice in accounting today is that of drawing a sharp line of distinction between cost of goods sold and operating expenses and displaying prominently in the income statement the difference between total revenues and the cost of the goods sold as gross profit.

The implication of this practice is that certain costs have a preferential ranking insofar as being recoverable from revenues, and that certain costs are recovered 100 percent while others are only partially recovered in an enterprise operating at a loss. In reality, all costs are on the same level as charges against revenue.

Accountants also place too much stress on physical factors to the detriment of service factors. ". . . a dollar of service cost is just as significant *in every respect* (including inventoriable quality) as a dollar of goods cost."

"There can be no profit in any legitimate sense until *all* costs have been taken into account." Presenting reports in which gross profit is stressed will result in misunderstanding, and changing terminology from *gross profit* to *trading margin* will not remove the basic defect of the implication of ranking of cost.

There is much merit in the single-step income statement. This does not mean that the drawing up of a statement showing the excess of departmental revenues over costs definitely assignable may not be of significance for internal management purposes.

RECORDING REVENUE ON OTHER BASES THAN SALES, *Accounting Ledger*, IV (April, 1939), 22-24. [263]

The three major methods of recognizing total revenue are "physical production, delivery accompanied by sale, and collection from customer." The second is commonly employed in business and is generally quite reasonable.

Current recording practices with respect to the first and third methods are objectionable in that they both fail to record and disclose the total volume of business of the enterprise. In the construction field the typical practice, when the percentage of completion method of recognizing revenue is employed, is to accrue a "semi-net" figure of income calculated by expressing costs incurred as a percentage of total expected costs and applying this percentage to the expected income from the job. Thus, "semi-net income" is recorded but total revenue is obscured.

The same defect is found in current practices relative to recognizing revenue on installment sales. In the typical installment sale situation a receivable is established for the contract price, the asset sold credited and an unrealized gross income account established. At the end of the period a portion of this unrealized gross income is transferred to earned income according to the collections made. Here again gross revenue is not reported.

In each case it would be entirely possible to record the transactions in such a fashion so as not to obscure gross revenue and bury costs by a process of cancellation. Illustrative examples of possible procedures for recording revenue on the physical production basis and the installment sale (collection from customer) basis are presented.

OBJECTIVES OF ACCOUNTING RESEARCH, *Papers on Auditing and Other Accounting Subjects*, Fifty-second Annual Meeting (New York: American Institute of Certified Public Accountants, 1939), pp. 229-33. [264]

"Any systematic, sustained analysis or investigation of phenomena may be called research. Research need not necessarily be purposive; nor need it have an objective, although much research of a highly organized and subsidized nature with an objective is being undertaken at this time. In such circumstances the danger of bias, partiality, and lack of independence must be recognized."

Research undertaken in accounting must "not accept, either deliberately or unconsciously, the objective of merely trying to sustain the time-honored concepts and practices of accounting."

Works such as Fabricant's *Capital Consumption and Adjustment* are indicative of one type of research that accountants can do. However, the Institute is more interested in a second type of research — "work designed to render accounting procedures more effective for whatever purpose the results may be used." There is a crucial need for accountants "to crystallize the most significant and useful concepts and procedures as a framework or backbone for accounting practice."

LAST-IN, FIRST-OUT, *Journal of Accountancy,* LXIX (May, 1940), 354-60. [265]

An analysis of the technical application of the *Lifo* technique reveals that the method yields different results when applied on a periodic basis as contrasted with a continuous accounting for goods utilized. Results quite similar to those obtained from the use of *Fifo* may emerge in certain circumstances in applying *Lifo* on a continuous basis.

The argument that *Lifo* yields a "true profit" by charging against revenue costs prevailing near the end of the period is not free from objection. Costs of the past cannot be ignored in determining income of the past. Nor does this method offer assistance to management in forward planning; it is the current inventory costs that are significant in planning utilization of the inventory.

Although programs to minimize business fluctuations are desirable, it does not follow that accounting methods purporting to show a "purely specious, artificial stability" are desirable.

The assumption of the flow of costs under *Lifo* is contrary to the actual flow of goods in almost all situations. Nor is there any merit in the argument that *Lifo* accounts for inventory in the same manner in which accountants account for fixed assets. The use of *Lifo* often produces a balance sheet showing a current position that is not even roughly reliable.

ACCOUNTING REPORTS, *Proceedings of the Third Annual Institute on Accounting,* The Ohio State University, College of Commerce and Administration, College of Commerce Conference Series Proceedings, May, 1940, pp. 5-12. [266]

Accounting reports must above all be useful to management; secondarily, they must be of interest to the investor. The dominant goal of accounting is that of income measurement. However, the shorter the time period the greater the difficulty of drawing significant conclusions relative to the business enterprise.

Accountants have failed to indicate the basis of balance sheet valuations clearly. For example, inventory writedown under the cost or market, whichever is lower, rule of inventory valuation and the recording of plant appreciation must be clearly disclosed. "Deferred charges cover a multitude of sins."

The striking of intermediate profit balances in the income statement is objectionable. Preparation of this statement under the all-inclusive concept is to be recommended. Stabilizing techniques, such as the "deferred charges habit" and operating reserves, are inherently dangerous. Reserves for insurance are examples of operating reserves. The *Lifo* method of inventory valuation should be critically reviewed from the point of view of a stabilizing technique. Business fluctuations are not imaginary and vary from one enterprise to another, but the goal of accounting should always be the full disclosure of such fluctuations. Comparative, cumulative and average income statements should be presented so that such movements may be viewed in their proper perspective.

ANALYSIS OF FINANCIAL STATEMENTS, *Cost and Management* (Canada), XXII (September, 1940), 303-19. [267]

". . . the function of accounting is to furnish at least a large part of the ideas and techniques which will enable us to understand our economic system." The amount of misunderstanding and misinformation on the elementary facts of business is staggering.

Consolidated statements are based upon assumptions that are not strictly true; therefore, they should be published, if at all, as supplementary statements.

Improvements in terminology are urgently needed and these improvements may aid in understanding such items as surplus, reserve for depreciation, and contingency reserves. Drawing up a "profits before taxes" figure is "like leaving Hamlet out of the play."

The failure of accounting to recognize changes in the value of its measuring unit, the dollar, also results in misleading financial statements and earnings ratios calculated therefrom. Investors in long-term corporate bonds are frequently looked upon as being conservative investors when in reality they are engaging in a hazardous speculation — speculation in the value of money.

Rigid adherence to the so-called cost basis of recording has also in many cases resulted in failure to recognize the most significant event occurring in the life of a business organization. The accounts in many companies are so inadequate, especially with respect to depreciation, as to justify employment of the quasi-reorganization device. In "a system of accounting that is based upon recorded cost, as our system is bound to be, a system that has limitations that are unavoidable to some extent, we should have techniques for making controlled and disclosed adjustments in circumstances where it has become clear that the figures that are recorded are misleading."

Accountants and management tend to confuse the process of measuring performance via income with that of administering the funds flowing in and out of a business. In this respect, a well prepared statement of funds may add considerably to the amount of information available relative to a given enterprise.

BASIC CONCEPTS OF PROPERTY ACCOUNTING, *Edison Electric Institute Bulletin*, IX (March, 1941), 93-96. [268]

Accounting is concerned with the economic attributes of property as opposed to the tangibility aspect. The question of tangibility versus intangibility is merely "a matter of classification of economic costs." Organization cost and plant overhead are equally valid costs and must be recognized.

Accounting is primarily concerned with the matching of costs and revenues, and plant accounting is a part of this process. Undue preoccupation with the view that the property account is a determinant of the rate base has given way to emphasis on systematic absorption of costs. Adequate classification of property is vital and there must be a careful "tracing of property, in and out."

The relationship between depreciation and maintenance must be given careful study. Utility property should not be viewed as one mass of indivisible property, with depreciation eliminated and property renewals charged to maintenance costs. Depreciation accounting should be employed, using the straight-line or production methods.

The new "original cost" concept is unacceptable when one recognizes that a utility is not a risk-free business. Property accounts, as a result of arm's length transactions, should be revised to embody new prices and conditions.

THE COST APPROACH TO INVENTORIES, *Journal of Accountancy*, LXXII (October, 1941), 300-7. [269]

"What costs attach to the physical movement of goods?" At one extreme are those who advocate inventorying only the net invoice cost of the goods plus direct costs of conversion or manufacturing. At the other extreme is the view that virtually all costs of operating the business attach to the physical product. An almost infinite number of views fall between these two extremes. A stamp of approval must be placed upon the trend toward a broader concept of cost. However, this does not mean that all types of selling and office costs should be inventoried.

"What is the order or pattern of the flow of tangible goods through the representative enterprise?" Any assumption of flow should be systematic and not "hit or miss" and should result in financial statements that are reasonable and meaningful to the intelligent, experienced reader; it should not be at odds with empirical evidence or be unduly complex or expensive.

"When should costs which were originally associated with particular physical units, or aggregates of units, be absorbed as operating charges (or losses) prior to the final disposition of such physical units or aggregates?" The "cost or market" rule consists of "doctoring accounts this year" to assure a "pleasant picture . . . next year." Too much attention is being directed toward "normal profit," whatever this may be. Maintenance of profitability is the task of management, not of the accountant.

Merchandise that has made an economic contribution (display merchandise) and is less saleable as a result should be written down. Physically deteriorated or obsolete goods may also be written down. Only rarely (and the burden of proof is upon those who advocate so doing) should standard goods in unimpaired condition held with expectation of regular disposition be written down. The proof required should be more than simply the fact that prices have been moving downward during the period of acquisition.

COMMENTS ON THE COST PRINCIPLE, *Accounting Review,* XVII (January, 1942), 10-19. [270]

The statement of the Executive Committee of the American Accounting Association, with respect to the proper occasion for recognizing costs, does not cover the situation in which it is necessary to accrue expected costs. For example, the cost of restoring leased property should be accrued throughout the life of the lease, even though the actual expenditure will be made at the end of the lease.

There is, however, no justification for accruing so-called losses on firm purchase commitments since there is no actual liability, and because there may in fact not even be a loss.

The position taken by Walter Staub in his article, "The Cost Principle" (*Accounting Review,* XVII [January, 1942], 3-10), is quite untenable with respect to a number of points. "The inclusion of bond discount in assets is an accounting error, supported by nothing but habit." Bond discount is unpaid, not prepaid, interest. The position taken by Mr. Staub that bond discount, which represents an amount so far undeposited by an investor, can appear as an asset, and that tax warrants, "a good realizable asset, for which money has been paid," should preferably be shown as contra liability is "utterly inconsistent" and "quite wrong."

In debt refunding operations, unabsorbed discounts, redemption premiums and similar items should be written off immediately. "Each generation of borrowings . . . [should] be accounted for in its own right, without being burdened by the ghost of earlier transactions."

The *Lifo* supporters' argument that inventory profits are not real profits because they have to be re-invested in inventory confuses income determination with income administration. It is no more invalid to say that funds brought in by profits are re-invested in inventory than that such funds are re-invested in plant assets.

ADAPTATION OF THE INCOME STATEMENT TO PRESENT CONDITIONS, *Journal of Accountancy,* LXXV (January, 1943), 8-15. [271]

If classification of sales revenue is to be reported in the general condensed income statement, such classification should be detailed in a supporting schedule. Current practices with respect to reporting other income may be questioned. The showing of such other income after a figure purportedly reporting the results of primary operations results in an unduly elaborate statement being prepared, fosters an unduly narrow concept of operations, and implies that such earnings or gains have been secured free of cost. Preferable treatment would be to report all revenues first with reasonable classification.

The reporting of gross profit as a figure of significance is purely conventional and without merit. Such a practice implies a ranking of costs, when, in reality, all costs are homogeneous as revenue deductions.

The practice of reporting net profit before depreciation is slowly dying out. However, the practice of reporting net profit before depletion continues to be very common. This practice is no less objectionable than the older practice of reporting profits before depreciation, or than that of reporting profits before the deduction of any valid, actual cost.

"Back-door" recognition of losses — direct charges to surplus — is fortunately on the wane, with such losses being recognized in the income statement. Care must be exercised that a too narrow view of operations, resulting in the unwarranted classification of operating charges as losses, is not taken.

The present practice of deducting income and profits taxes resulting from a profits figure implies the view that taxes are a sharing in the net income by the governmental unit. Under the preferred alternative view, taxes of all types are viewed as being homogeneous and as deductions from revenue. Corporate profits do not emerge until taxes have been deducted.

The preferred form of income statement is one showing classified total revenues, revenue deductions classified into expenses, losses and taxes, and with the total of these three categories deducted in one step from total revenues to arrive at corporate net income. Interest is then deducted from corporate net income to arrive at the net income to the stock equity. Dividends are then deducted and a surplus statement is tied directly into the income statement.

CLASSIFICATION AND SEQUENCES IN FINANCIAL STATEMENTS, *Accounting Problems in War Contract Termination, Taxes, and Postwar Planning,* Papers Presented at the Fifty-sixth Annual Meeting, 1943 (New York: American Institute of Certified Public Accountants, 1943), pp. 57-67. [272]

A fourfold classification of assets is suggested — namely, working capital or current assets, long-term fund accumulations or investments, long-term cost commitments and prepayments for services, and intangibles. Internal arrangement within each category is of little significance. The effects of writeups or writedowns should be clearly shown.

There is no major objection to the usual method of segregating short-term and long-term liabilities so long as blind adherence to a rule can be avoided. Other possible bases of liability classification are the purpose for which funds acquired from creditors are used, the method of repayment and legal ranking.

No real need for a "reserve" category exists, as each reserve should be shown according to whether it is a contra-asset, liability, or stockholder equity item.

The two main classifications of equity are the amount invested by stockholders and retained earnings or deficit. Ideally, if more than one class of stock is outstanding, the amount paid-in by each group of investors should be shown.

The offsetting of assets and liabilities is an unacceptable practice. Almost without exception all revenue credits should be shown in a revenue section at the beginning of the income statement. Costs applicable to revenues should not be reported in too much detail; supplementary schedules should be used. Losses should be included as revenue deductions, shown separately and appropriately captioned if desired. Taxes are also revenue deductions. There is no "true net to private capital" until taxes are deducted. Interest should be deducted in the distribution of income section, and the resulting balance should be given prominence. There is also virtue in showing how much the current income stream exceeds dividends. Incorporation of the statement of earned surplus into the income statement may also be desirable as a means of tying the income statement to the balance sheet.

SIMPLIFICATION OF FEDERAL TAX ADMINISTRATION, *Accounting Review*, XIX (January, 1944), 11-19. [273]

A basic weakness in the present tax structure is the taxation of the business corporation as an entity. Corporate income is basically the income of its stockholders. Taxation of corporate income and of stockholders' dividends is double taxation. The results are: (1) an inequitable burden is placed upon stockholders, (2) an obstacle is placed in the path of business development and full employment, since our most effective institutional mechanism for the carrying on of large-scale production is penalized, and (3) the tax structure is made increasingly complex and the total cost of financing governmental functions is increased.

Two possible methods of correcting this inequity are to tax corporate income only when it is received as dividends by the stockholders, or to treat the corporation as a partnership for tax purposes and tax the stockholder upon his computed share of the earnings.

The special treatment of capital gains is justifiable in part because of the decrease in the value of the dollar. However, this special treatment is so full of loopholes that it would be preferable to treat capital gains as ordinary income and to recognize losses as proper deductions without limitation.

ACCOUNTING POLICIES OF THE FEDERAL POWER COMMISSION — A CRITIQUE, *Journal of Accountancy*, LXXVII (June, 1944), 432-60. [274]

The *original cost* classification rule of the Federal Power Commission's Uniform System of Accounts is of doubtful value. Cost to preceding owners is not pertinent, useful information to present owners and there is no support in generally accepted accounting principles for this rule. Also, due to inadequate past records, determining original cost usually means resorting to an historical cost appraisal.

It is unfair to claim that Account 100.5 contains nothing but intangibles, since it may also include a portion of the actual cost to the present owner of land and water rights, structures, and equipment costs, as well as organization, financing, and development costs. The proposition that intangibles in utilities are incompatible with reasonable rate regulation is unsound, as is the assertion that intangible values are created by the public. Amortization of Account 100.5 against net income or surplus is directly contrary to established accounting principles, which hold that intangibles—where properly subject to amortization—should be charged against revenues.

The Commission's rule relative to *re-accounting* is not compatible with its expressed desire to have utility accounts show the cost, or approximate cash equivalent, of property devoted to utility service. The Commission's improper interpretation of the term *writeup* has resulted in arbitrary elimination of actual costs; the attitude taken that transactions between affiliated or associated companies can never be on a sound commercial basis is unreasonable and unrealistic.

The Commission is expecting too much from accounting, since accounting "has important limitations as a basis for equitable settlement of rights of stockholders, bondholders, consumers, and other parties at interest."

MODERN REPORTS TO STOCKHOLDERS, *Current Considerations for Controllers,* Annual Meeting Proceedings, 1944 (New York: Controllers' Institute of America, 1944), pp. 116-24. [275]

With respect to the annual corporate report, there are grounds for believing "that the typical small stockholder's understanding can be improved by non-technical, 'humanized' presentation." Considerable progress in improving corporate reporting has been made, but skepticism must be expressed over attempts to frame reports from the point of view of a normal year. " 'Normal operation' has become a mirage."

Lifo enthusiasts tend to regard this method of inventory valuation as being a key to succesful operation. This method, in effect, adds another step to the operating cycle of cash to cash in that it calls for making provision for maintenance of the basic physical inventory before recognizing net earnings. An important and unanswered question is: If we go beyond the conventional cash to cash cycle in accounting, where do we stop? Actually, *Lifo,* if it is the proper approach, has much more applicability in the field of noncurrent assets than in the area of inventory.

Accountants report far too many intermediate figures in the income statement, and frequently use the term "net" to describe four or five of these figures.

All costs are homogeneous in relation to the revenue stream, whether assignable to a product or not. Terminology such as *productive labor* and *non-productive labor* has hindered "understanding of essential economic relationships." Greater attention must be given to the charging against current revenues of costs which are applicable, although not, in a literal sense, yet incurred. A familiar example is the cost of the required back-filling of an excavation made in extracting gravel or other mineral deposits.

RESPONSIBILITIES AND TRAINING OF THE POSTWAR ACCOUNTANT, *Proceedings of the Seventh Annual Institute on Accounting,* The Ohio State University, College of Commerce and Administration, College of Commerce Conference Series Proceedings, 27-29, 1944, pp. 6-18. [276]

The responsibilities of the postwar accountant will vary according to the trend of our postwar economic environment. Accounting attempts "to facilitate effective management, effective administration of economic conduct, particularly in the organized business area," and to promote "equity between the parties at interest in this area of business activity."

If the trend is toward socialism, both of these objectives would still exist although income accounting would be minimized, cost accounting stressed, and clerical red tape increased. If socialistic tendencies should prevail, it ought to be noted that the accountant would play an important part in the liquidation of private business. The responsibilities of the postwar accountant will be even greater if private enterprise is rehabilitated.

TRANSACTIONS BETWEEN AFFILIATES, *Accounting Review,* XX (July, 1945), 255-66. [277]

Although accounting is generally based on cost, this does not mean that financial statements continue to show acquisition cost. The recording of depreciation, depletion, accretion, discovery value, etc., all tend to modify cost. The standard of cost measurement is "bargained-price" negotiated on a commercial basis between distinct entities. Cost is valid for accounting purposes only when it is not seriously out of line with economic significance in the market situation in which the transaction is consummated.

"Transactions between affiliated corporations or other related parties should be conducted *on the same basis as transactions between wholly independent parties* — namely, the basis of actual economic significance, actual value, at date of transfer." Substantially all accountants subscribe to this proposition, although it is opposed by the Federal Power Commission and its staff. Transactions between affiliates are held by the FPC to be of nominal significance only and are to be recorded at the cost to the furnishing party or last preceding affiliated party. This doctrine is to be applied retroactively to companies under FPC jurisdiction, even though such transactions may have been consumated on a cash basis, equitable to all, and approved by the regulatory agency having jurisdiction at the time. The implication is that all transactions between affiliates are invalid.

The Commission and its staff disregard the corporate entity and attempt to justify this treatment with a reference to consolidated statement theory. Accounting writers agree that consolidated statements are secondary supplementary statements and not substitutes for the statements of the legal entity. The FPC staff has attempted to apply consolidated statement principles and procedures in circumstances where the degree of affiliation was so slight that no professional accountant would ever consider consolidation justified. The position taken by the FPC on transactions between affiliated companies does not square with its original cost requirement.

CURRENT ECONOMIC FALLACIES, *Commercial and Financial Chronicle,* CLXII (August 23, 1945), 825, 843. [278]

Five current economic fallacies are that: (1) prosperity can be secured by maintaining a shortage of economic goods; (2) efficiency in output should be restricted in order to create more jobs; (3) economic security can be obtained for all merely by the paying out of government funds; (4) under wartime illusions, people can live on their wartime savings without producing; (5) a government can continually capitalize deficits.

COST AND VALUE IN ACCOUNTING, *Journal of Accountancy,* LXXXI (March, 1946), 192-99. [279]

In most situations the actual price paid is the most dependable evidence of fair market value at acquisition date, and is certainly a more reliable indicator of value than the opinion of an outsider who does not make an expenditure. In all questionable situations, whether involving transactions between affiliated or completely unrelated parties, if the stated price is not a reliable indicator of value the accountant should encourage adjustment and insist upon clear disclosure of the limitations of the stated price.

If cash is not exchanged in a transaction, then the fair market value of the property transferred expresses the cost of the property acquired. If stock is issued in exchange for property, then the amount of credit to the capital stock account (and the amount invested by the stockholder) is shown by the fair market value of the property received. In some circumstances, clearer evidence of the value involved in such an exchange may be found in the market value of the stock.

Thus, "cost and value are not opposing and mutually exclusive terms. . . . In fact *cost is significant primarily because it approximates fair value at date of acquisition.*" Cost is generally a reasonable approximation of the value of materials and services as they flow through the enterprise, because prices rarely change substantially in short periods of time. The rule of matching revenues against current cost factors is therefore particularly defensible. However, any substantial loss (for example, unusual damage to inventory), convincingly demonstrated, is subject to recognition in the accounts even though the goods in question may not have been sold.

With respect to long-term cost factors, departure from adherence to the cost basis should be considered only when a change has occurred which renders accounting on this basis *"inadequate and invalid in view of the recognized purposes of accounting."*

ACCOUNTING POLICIES AND MANAGEMENT, *Accounting as an Instrument of Management* (Proceedings of the Accounting Conference, 1946, Sponsored by Loyola University and the Illinois Society of Certified Public Accountants), pp. 11-16. [280]

"If accounting is to serve management ably it must be *free to serve.*" This freedom to serve is being obstructed now by "(1) the development of arbitrary and rigid government rules and controls," and "(2) the unreasonable and restrictive conventions and fetishes that have been a millstone around the accountant's neck for years, particularly in the field of public accounting."

Especially objectionable are the fallacious ideas "(1) that some costs are peculiarly under managerial control while other types of cost are entirely outside the pale and hence should not be viewed as true operating costs; (2) that some costs are superior to others in economic potency and accountability; (3) that suppression of resources and premature absorption of costs are desirable practices; (4) that use of hindsight and consequent revision and correction are improper."

Treating certain kinds of taxes as a distribution of profits is "nonsense." All taxes are charges against revenue in income determination. The practice of showing "gross profit" and deducting therefrom other "expenses . . . as a sort of necessary evil . . . is sheer humbug." Other equally objectionable practices of the accountant are his failure to reinstate assets which have been fully amortized although still being used; his practice of suppressing assets, especially intangibles; his expensing of minor improvements; and his slavish adherence to cost even when cost has become useless as a measure of economic significance.

RESTORATION OF FIXED ASSET VALUES TO THE BALANCE SHEET — SECOND AFFIRMATIVE, *Accounting Review,* XXII (April, 1947), 198-200. [281]

Prematurely written off fixed asset values of substantial amount should be restored in the accounts because:

(1) private enterprise and private property are still dominant factors in business operation;

(2) accounting's primary function is to provide useful, significant information regarding the activities of a business enterprise;

(3) accounting neither destroys nor creates assets; rather, the existence of assets is a matter of economic and legal fact;

(4) "business enterprises are not a series of cost-plus contracts with specific customers or customer groups";

(5) prices in a competitive market are the same regardless of the varying costs of the producers;

(6) neither past history nor method of acquisition controls the future use or future accounting for fixed assets;

(7) accountants and businessmen, by denying the existence of assets, play into the hands of those who have already used distorted accounting to impair property rights;

(8) past entries should not prevent accountants from making the necessary revisions resulting from attempts to fulfill the complicated matching process of accounting;

(9) absorbed costs may be misstated for a number of reasons; however, the effects are the same and the origin of the misstatement does not affect the propriety of making corrections;

(10) the purposes of accounting are incompatible with a policy of deliberate misstatement to cancel out past errors.

THE ACCOUNTANT AND PRIVATE ENTERPRISE, *Journal of Accountancy*, LXXXV (January, 1948), 44-58. [282]

Accountants, who have a vital interest in maintaining a free enterprise system, have certainly not distinguished themselves as defenders of this system. Accountants should take greater advantage of their special position and knowledge to explain the operations of private business enterprises. In order to do this and to assist in combating current fallacies and misrepresentations, an understanding of the basic features and requirements of the competitive market economy is needed. Of particular importance is an understanding of the nature of cost records, and the relationships, or lack of relationships, between costs, prices and profits. Monopoly and governmental interference can both lead to collectivism and the accountant, by explaining the operation of the free enterprise system, can help to check movements toward this undesirable goal.

WHAT IS ACTUAL COST IN DEPRECIATION ACCOUNTING? *Journal of Accountancy*, LXXXV (March, 1948), 206-7. [283]

Accounting Research Bulletin No. 33 tends to bar serious consideration of a major problem of accounting — that is, the problem of measuring depreciation under changing price levels.

In a period of advancing prices, those who advocate replacement cost depreciation are more truly supporters of *actual cost* depreciation than those who would record depreciation on the basis of recorded dollars of varying values without conversion to the common denominator of the current dollar.

Two possible lines of attack are available: (1) supplementary explanations and calculations may be included in the annual report which will show the limitations of conventional accounting, or (2) the fresh-start or quasi-reorganization approach may provide the "safety factor necessary to make the so-called 'cost basis' of accounting really work."

ACCOUNTING PROCEDURES AND PRIVATE ENTERPRISE, *Journal of Accountancy*, LXXXV (April, 1948), 278-91. [284]

If accounting is not providing owners and managers with pertinent, useful economic facts, the accountant should explore methods whereby he can make accounting fulfill this goal. Adherence to tradition or convention should not prevent the exploration of such new methods.

"The most objectionable and obstructive tradition of accounting is conservatism. . . ." To most accountants this means understatement of assets and of income, although these two goals are not always consistent. Accounting should stress *"careful, competent measurement* not conservatism, in the sense of understatement."

Supported in the name of conservatism has been the practice of suppressing certain asset costs, such as the absorption against capital surplus of organization and financing costs, the immediate chargeoff of intangibles, the expensing of additions under the guise of maintenance expense, and the expensing of a part of the cost of new facilities because current prices are "extraordinarily high."

Premature writeoff of assets is another device closely akin to suppression of assets. Premature writeoff can result from either a deliberate plan of action or, in effect, by mistakes made in choosing rates of depreciation or amortization. The injury is compounded by taking the position that assets prematurely written off cannot be restored to the accounts. Supporters of this latter position, by using the so-called double recovery of costs argument, indicate an amazing lack of understanding of basic economics.

Failure to recognize assets acquired without cost often results in substantial understatement of property. Strict adherence to the cost basis of accounting when cost has lost all significance is undesirable accounting. Recording depreciation on a basis other than recorded cost can be accomplished by conversion of recorded dollars through an appropriate general price index, or by using the replacement cost approach.

DEPRECIATION AND THE PRICE LEVEL — SECOND AFFIRMATIVE, *Accounting Review,* XXIII (April, 1948), 118-23. [285]

Arguments in accounting based solely upon precedent, materiality and expediency are invalid. Clear thinking is necessary when dealing with the problem of original cost versus replacement cost depreciation.

The objective of accruing depreciation is to match costs with related revenues, not to provide funds for replacement, which depreciation, in itself, cannot do.

The case for depreciation based on replacement cost has merit when depreciation is viewed as a measure of actual economic sacrifice. Net income can emerge only after the economic costs of producing revenue have been covered.

There are three practical solutions to the problem of conveying pertinent information with respect to replacement cost. First, income can be reported on the conventional basis, with the need for retaining "earnings" to cover the depreciation deficiency explained in a footnote. Second, appreciation and depreciation on appreciation can be incorporated in the statements. Third, resort can be made to the quasi-reorganization procedure, with the capitalization of the amount of the net adjustment of the plant account.

SOME COMMENTS ON GROUP AND SECTIONAL INTERESTS, *Michigan Alumnus Quarterly Review,* LIV (May 8, 1948), 203-8. [286]

The use of propaganda has led people to believe that the standard of living can be increased by reducing efficiency and the number of working hours. People have also been misled into believing that the government can give "security" to all, and if such security is not forthcoming that capitalism has failed.

Attention must be directed toward the interdependent relationship of the various sections of our country. Together we constitute one great enterprise, and we will "sink or swim" together. This does not mean that there should be a lessening of competition. A free enterprise system cannot exist without competition.

Our common interests must be recognized. Many statutes, interfering with the free flow of goods, would not have been enacted if it had been realized by most people that our economic progress has in large part been due to a free flow of goods across state lines.

The individual states should not expect to be subsidized by the federal government. If the states had to go directly to their citizens for all tax revenue to meet state needs they would be more conservative in their spending programs. Attention of the citizens would also be focused directly on the fact that government costs money.

WHY CORPORATE PROFITS ARE OVERSTATED, *Commercial and Financial Chronicle,* CLXVIII (December 16, 1948), 2490, 2521-23. [287]

Profits are essentially "the wages of the stockholders, the persons who provide the risk capital which is the life blood of private business enterprise." The stockholder's position is one of risk in the sense that there is no guarantee of earnings. We have a profit and loss system rather than simply a profit system. Profits are an important source of risk capital. The only real alternative to a flow of private risk capital is governmental funds, raised through taxation or borrowing.

Corporate earnings are overstated due to the failure of conventional accounting to recognize the effects of inflation upon the measurement of income. Earning rates based upon reported data are also overstated, but here the error is compounded in that overstated earnings are related to understated book values.

LACK OF VENTURE CAPITAL REACHING STAGE WHERE IT AFFECTS OUR ECONOMY, *National Savings and Loan Journal,* IV (September, 1949), 23-24. [288]

Many people feel that a corporation is, per se, wicked or immoral, and that when a corporation becomes large "then unquestionably it is wicked or bad." Actually a corporation is nothing more than "a piece of institutional machinery . . . just as an automobile is a piece of machinery in the more technical field."

The term *profits* in itself is misleading; the term *earnings* is to be preferred. The "profits of a corporation are the earnings of its common stockholders." Stockholders certainly have the right to expect earnings. The very nature of common stock and the economy is such that fluctuations in earnings will occur. Consequently, substantial earnings in some years are needed to offset the poor years.

Evidence is available in the form of a lack of equity funds to show that stockholders are not faring as well as they would like, and that the prospects are not good. This lack of flow of equity funds "is gradually approaching the critical stage." The only alternative to private investment is the substitution of tax funds and, at least, a form of public ownership. In reality, there is no truth in the assertion that the public is being exploited by the common stockholders of business corporations; the reverse is literally true.

ACCOUNTING PROBLEMS RELATING TO THE REPORTING OF PROFITS, *Accounting Problems Relating to the Reporting of Profits,* Proceedings of a Public Forum Sponsored by the Economic and Business Foundation (New Wilmington, Pa.: Economic and Business Foundation, 1949), pp. 8-13. [289]

The *cost basis* of accounting has serious limitations in the periodic matching of costs and revenues if the term is too narrowly interpreted. Cost is given prominence in accounting because it "expresses initial *value,* and as such is a datum of importance."

For assets acquired by means other than purchase, the orthodox basis of recording is fair market value at time of acquisition. ". . . the basic data of all economic analysis are values . . . [and] . . . it must be recognized that accounting is a primary source of valuation data." Consequently, the common conception of the cost basis of accounting must be modified and interpreted "as a means of recording and bringing periodically to our attention the significant economic data of the business enterprise."

At present there is serious mismatching of costs and revenues because of changes in the value of the dollar, especially with respect to amortization, depletion and depreciation. Clearer thinking concerning this problem might result if the name of the present monetary unit were changed to "zollar."

Of the various methods proposed for removing this deficiency in accounting, the quasi-reorganization device is preferred.

The article by John Kennerly in the December, 1948 issue of the *Accountant* describes the laws, decrees and orders of the French government in its attempt to cope with a serious problem of inflation. These laws permit the revaluation of fixed assets into current francs, and permit depreciation on the revised values. The increase in assets amounts is credited to a "revaluation reserve" which is not taxed unless distributed. The effect of such revaluations, in some cases, was to show that taxes had been paid on profits when profits did not exist, and that dividends had actually been paid out of capital.

CORPORATE PROFITS, *Hearings Before the Joint Committee on the Economic Report, Congress of the United States, December 6–21, 1948* (Washington: Government Printing Office, 1949), pp. 53-77. [290]

"Indeed, if the total reported earnings of all stockholders of the United States were to remain constant or decline in a period of large production and sales, such a development would be cause for alarm as far as the future of private business enterprise was concerned."

There are many dangers inherent in carelessly formed opinions based upon "aggregate figures representing earnings of stockholders, earnings of factory employees, or any other group."

The pertinent questions relative to the current level of reported corporate profits are whether such profits are large relative to other factors, whether such profits represent an increasing share of the national product, and whether current developments are enhancing the economic position of the risk capital providers to the detriment of other important groups. A careful study will show that a negative answer must be given to any such question. The "forgotten man of the present era is the common stockholder," and he has fared badly whether his "showing" is measured in terms of his share of corporate profits or in "take-home pay" — dividends, less personal income taxes.

Corporate earnings are overstated due to the practice of "basing certain expenses on recorded dollar costs that are out of line with current prices expressed in a new and cheaper monetary unit." The error is magnified when earning rates are computed from overstated earnings and understated book value of stockholder investment.

THE BASIS FOR ADEQUATE FINANCIAL REPORTING, *Organization Controls and Executives Compensation* (American Management Association: General Management Series, 141-148, 1948), pp. 34-44. [291]

The basis for adequate financial reporting can be improved in a number of respects. The desire for fast write off of asset costs should be curbed because of the "secret reserves" thus developed and the resulting understatement of operating costs. Adherents to the fast writeoff policy apparently believe that one can be placed in a better economic position by figures placed on paper.

Value is the real basis of accounting, and accounting ideally should show the current value of the assets, not the cost. The impact of price-level changes should be recognized. The cost basis of accounting can be carried to extremes. Assets acquired by the process of investment or inheritance should be recorded initially on the basis of fair market value at date of acquisition, and assets resulting from discovery or accretion should not be excluded from the accounts. Accounting should not adhere to the so-called cost principle if this means disregarding its inadequacies.

Fully amortized war plants should be re-instated in the accounts and depreciated, if still being used, with depreciation thereon considered an operating cost even though not allowed on the tax return.

While the matching of costs and revenues is an important process in accounting, it can be overemphasized. Terms such as *surplus* and *profit* should be discarded because of inappropriate implications drawn therefrom. Experimentation with the form of the statement of funds may lead to better reporting to stockholders and the general public.

THE 1948 REVISION OF THE AMERICAN ACCOUNTING ASSOCIATION'S STATEMENT OF PRINCIPLES: Comments on Item 5, Under "Expense," *Accounting Review*, XXIV (January, 1949), 49-53. [292]

One provision in the 1948 "Statement of Principles" holds that reversals should not be made of entries assigning asset cost to expense, except in cases of error of a mechanical or non-judgmental nature.

This provision is "a complete departure from common sense, straight thinking and established procedure. The proposition that they have dug up is novel, stultifying, and discreditable to this Association. It flies in the face of reason, scientific attitude, and professional competence. It is at odds with most of the material in the revised draft."

"According to the proposal the accountant cannot correct an excessive accrual of depreciation, made in good faith, even if the original estimate of service life proves to be only a fraction of the actual life. Apparently it would prevent correction even in those extreme cases where the major existing resources of a company have been written off in full, prematurely."

STATEMENT OF W. A. PATON REGARDING THE OVERSTATEMENT AND MISINTERPRETATION OF CORPORATE EARNINGS UNDER CURRENT CONDITIONS, *In the Matter of United Steelworkers of America—C.I.O. and Republic Steel Corporation, et. al.*, before the Presidential Steel Board, August 19, 1949, 35 pp. [293]

See summary of the author's statement before the Wage Stabilization Board, § 299.

FINANCING PROBLEMS AS SEEN BY THE ACCOUNTANT, *Credit and Financial Management*, LI (September, 1949), 18, 20. [294]

Reported corporate profits for 1948 of $20 billion were approximately 8 percent of the gross national product of $253 billion. If allowance were made for the overstatement of profits due to failure to recognize changes in the value of the dollar, the percentage would be even smaller.

While corporate profits may be viewed as stockholder earnings, they do not represent what the stockholder receives. Much of the earnings must be kept in the corporation to finance expansion. Also, the earnings distributed as dividends are taxed as part of the income of the recipient. These two factors explain why the flow of new risk money is decreasing. The real earnings of farmers and factory workers have increased 75 percent over the last ten years, yet no substantial increase in real income has been realized by the investor group.

Government ownership of business will inevitably result if conditions are not made more favorable to the investors of risk capital. One way to remove this threat of socialism is to allow depreciation expenses to be expressed in current dollars in tax returns. Foreign countries which have experienced severe changes in their monetary units have provisions in tax law to premit measurement of depreciation charges in current monetary units.

THE SEMANTICS OF ANNUAL REPORTING, *Proceedings of the Annual Report Forum,* University of Michigan, School of Business Administration, 1949. (Report prepared by the Detroit Trust Company in co-operation with the School of Business Administration.) [295]

To a great many people *surplus* is a word which implies something other than the accountant's intended meaning. Preferable terminology would be "retained earnings" or "retained income" or, more radically, surplus could be designated as a part of the capital of the company. In spite of legalistic ideas, accountants might well use one word *capital* to describe "the stockholders' stake in the business." Dividends are a matter of cash or working capital position, not of total retained earnings.

"Profits," because of unfortunate connotations attached thereto, might be relabeled "earnings applicable to stockholders' equity."

Desirable and achievable simplification can be obtained in both statements by reducing the number of headings.

The showing of "gross profit" is ridiculous, as is "net profits before taxes."

MEASURING PROFITS UNDER INFLATION CONDITIONS: A SERIOUS PROBLEM FOR ACCOUNTANTS, *Journal of Accountancy,* LXXXIX (January, 1950), 16-27. [296]

The argument that accountants need do nothing about accounting under rising price levels since prices will probably be lower in the future is "wishful thinking." The large volume of postwar construction does not alter the fact that the great bulk of plant assets of American companies was acquired a number of years ago. Nor should accountants adopt a "do nothing" attitude because revisions of recorded cost data would not be acceptable for tax purposes. Accounting has other and even more important objectives than tax determination. The most ridiculous argument, and the one usually advanced, is that a revision of recorded data would not be conservative.

In periods of major change in the general price level, book costs, especially of plant assets, no longer represent "actual," significant costs. "Cost is not merely a figure on a piece of paper." In speaking of the *actual cost* of an asset, the number of dollars attached to the asset in terms of the current price level must be increased proportionately with the decline in the economic significance of the dollar.

Corporate profits currently are being substantially overstated. The Securities and Exchange Commission is failing to fulfill its responsibilities by not requiring disclosure of this overstatement.

Various methods are available for use in recognizing the effects of changes in the value of the dollar including the use of replacement cost, the common dollar approach, the "compromise" method of recording appreciation and depreciation thereon, and the quasi-reorganization approach.

The issuance of bonds and other contractual securities is primarily "a speculation in the value of money." Changing price levels also affect working capital items and in this respect the existence of short-term liabilities in effect constitutes a hedge against bearing the full burden (or securing the full gain) from changing price levels in this area.

ECONOMIC AND ACCOUNTING ASPECTS OF PENSION PLANS, *Michigan Certified Public Accountant,* II (September, 1950), 5-6. [297]

Since retirees can live only from the current output of goods in the years after retirement, funds deducted from workers' pay checks should be invested in productive assets, and not in government promises to pay.

The basic accounting question with regard to pensions is the treatment to be accorded past-service accruals. Any plan which requires immediate recognition of a definite liability is to be questioned since it in effect transfers a part of the existing stockholder equity to the employees. Because of the many difficulties involved in computing past service accruals (number, ages, length of service of employees, interest rates, etc.) there is much to be said for a footnote showing of the plan with no definite estimate of the liability.

If it is necessary to recognize a liability, one possibility would be the setting up of the estimated present value of the obligation to make payments during the estimated life of an employee after he has retired. On the other hand, there is something to be said for the overall group concept with financing on a strict pay-as-you-go basis. There may also be some merit in the suggestion that an intangible asset of equal value to the estimated present liability is acquired. The most reasonable assumption is that a pension plan is a method whereby present workers as a group will be compensated for services to be rendered in the future.

THE USE OF ACCOUNTING DATA IN ECONOMIC ANALYSIS, *Accounts and Taxes* (University of Kentucky, Bureau of Business Research, Bulletin 21, 1950), pp. 66-83. [298]

No sharp line of distinction can be drawn between economics and accounting. Accountants record economic data from a "microeconomics" point of view.

In recent years, a definite trend can be noted toward the substitution of accounting figures for the mechanism of the market place. Specific examples of such substitution include the stress placed on accounting data in public utility regulation and the ability-to-pay theory of wages. If such substitution occurs, the accountant must be especially careful that the data he presents are suitable for such purposes. Accounting practice with respect to plant assets, and especially intangibles, is generally unsatisfactory due to the tendency to minimize these assets.

Attempts are being made to bind accountants with accounting conventions. The "no reaccounting" and "original cost" rules of the utility commissions are examples.

Accountants have failed to take into consideration the changing value of the dollar. The Dow-Jones averages, and other similar computations, are not high when the change in the value of the dollar is considered. The small amount of new equity financing in view of the huge demand suggests that investors with funds understand that earnings are actually low.

In order to get realistic, significant reports, it may be necessary to go through a quasi-reorganization at the start of each year.

STATEMENT OF W. A. PATON REGARDING THE INTERPRETATION OF CORPORATE EARNINGS AND THE POSITION OF STOCKHOLDERS UNDER CURRENT CONDITIONS, *In the Matter of United Steel Workers of America — C.I.O. and Various Steel and Iron Ore Companies,* Wage Stabilization Board, Steel Panel, Case No. D-18-C, February 14, 1952, 39 pp. [299]

Corporations are in fact entities only in the legal sense. Consequently, it is the interest of actual human beings, the stockholders, which is at stake if corporations do not receive an attractive return on the investment made.

"In the last ten years the accounting data of corporate enterprise have been peculiarly subject to misinterpretation as a result of the impact of a material change in the price level. The measuring unit employed in accounting, the dollar, has been cut in half, and this condition must be taken into account if reasonable conclusions as to earning power and financial condition are to be drawn."

"The major effect of ignoring the change in the value of the dollar in corporate accounting and reporting has been serious *overstatement* of corporate earnings during the last decade. . . . The overstatement results primarily from two causes: (1) failure to charge revenues with a sufficient number of dollars to represent the cost of materials and supplies consumed, in *current prices;* (2) failure to adjust depreciation cost to a *current basis.*" The first difficulty has been, to a certain extent, met by the adoption of the *Lifo* inventory pricing procedure. "In the case of depreciation cost, however, nothing has yet been done with respect to the measurement of taxable income or accounting procedures generally to make the necessary adjustment. In France and other European countries, where in some cases the devaluation of the monetary unit has gone much farther than the debasement of our dollar, there has been governmental recognition of the problem, and the use of index numbers to convert depreciation cost to a current monetary basis has been a commonplace procedure in such countries for some years."

"Adjustment of recorded dollars to a current basis in measuring net income is sometimes objected to on the ground that this represents a departure from 'actual cost.' This objection rests on a highly questionable conception of what is meant by cost. 'Cost' is not merely a number, a figure on a piece of paper. Cost is an economic force committed or expended. Accordingly, when there has been a substantial change in the value of the measuring unit recorded cost must be converted to *determine actual cost expressed in the new unit.*"

"Perhaps the most serious aspect of the overstatement of corporate earnings in recent years is the *compound error* that results when these figures are applied, without adjustment, to the amount of the stockholders' equity as shown in the accounts in computing earning rates."

"Speaking accurately, there is no such thing as 'profits before taxes'; 'profits before taxes' are a gross illusion. Actual profits emerge only after *all* expenses and other necessary charges have been deducted from receipts from customers, and it is clearly improper to attach a term generally used to describe the earnings accruing on capital invested to figures that include taxes, a major deduction in determining these earnings."

HOW HAVE STOCKHOLDERS BEEN FARING? *Michigan Business Review,* IV (May, 1952), 8-13. [300]

This article is, in part, an adaptation of the author's statement before the Steel Panel of the Wage Stabilization Board on February 14, 1952. (See § 299.)

A careful analysis of corporate earnings over the past years will show that the suppliers of risk capital, the stockholders, have not been faring too well. A large majority of the stockholders are persons of modest means and expect a return on their savings.

Converting the Dow-Jones stock averages for 1940 and 1951 into common dollars shows that on the average the actual dollar value in purchasing power of stock investments has declined. This is the reason for the decrease in the flow of funds into the new securities market.

When changes in the price level are taken into consideration, the return on an investment in steel stocks in 1940 shows an average yield of about 5½ percent on cost. This yield is less than the return on investment in the public utility field where the risk factor is not as high as in the industrial field.

It is impossible to keep prices from rising while at the same time continuing to increase taxes and wage levels.

SHOULD THE SEC CONTINUE TO "STUDY" UTILITY SYSTEM OPERATIONS? *Public Utilities Fortnightly,* L (October 9, 1952), 473, 480. [301]

Here published is a friendly, but critical, open letter to Chairman Donald C. Cook of the SEC.

Privately owned, state regulated utilities should not be brought under the control of the FPC, since such an event would eventually lead to socialization of the industry. While individuals have the right to believe in socialism, socialism will not, contrary to their beliefs, bring about greater freedom and happiness for most individuals.

Competent management is needed in operating a utility since there are many serious financial and business risks involved. The rights and potentialities attending risk capital must not be removed or such capital will disappear and funds provided through the government will be substituted.

Regulators must realize, when they take the cost basis as an approach to the rate base, that 1939 and 1952 dollars are not the same and that privately owned utilities must be allowed to measure depreciation in terms of plant capacity consumed expressed in current dollars.

Reduction in the degree of interference with the utilities will result in greater amounts of risk capital being provided, more efficient management, greater efficiency of operation, better integration of available facilities and more benefits to the public.

COMMON SENSE — THE CURB TO PUBLIC SPENDING, *Tax Digest,* XXXI (March, 1953), 81-83, 96-100. [302]

Basically the problem of taxation rests upon governmental spending. Cutting off the flow of tax revenues without reducing expenditures results in indirect taxation via inflation.

Citizens today have the attitude "that all good and perfect things flow from government . . . ," and this attitude of dependency and reliance upon government must be attacked and changed before government spending will be reduced.

We must remember that we live in a risk environment and that no amount of legislation can produce a specific volume of goods and services. Reallocation of the total wealth of the economy will not increase the amount of wealth — *"all of us cannot prop up all of us."*

Any system of pensions must be on an overall pay-as-you-go basis, and funds accumulated must be invested in productive resources and not in government bonds. Sixty to seventy percent of the items comprising the basic standard of living consists of goods and services which cannot be stored. The only way for an individual to improve his lot is to increase his stock of technical facilities. This means that attention must be given to the protection of venture capital.

With Howard C. Greer, UTILITY RATES MUST RECOGNIZE DOLLAR DEPRECIATION, *Public Utilities Fortnightly,* LI (March 12, 1953), 333-56. [303]

By holding that six percent is a fair return on investment without taking into consideration the depreciation of the purchasing power of the dollar, governmental regulation is causing public utilities to go out of business.

The general public, aided by politicians, has been erroneously led to believe that regulation of utilities will lead to more and better service at a lower price. However, owners of public utilities will not provide the new investment necessary to secure more and better service unless there is a prospect, not too dim, of earning a capital-attracting level of return on investment.

Five basic propositions are: (1) the primary concern of consumers is in an unhampered flow of goods and services, (2) consumer and producer interests are both hurt in the utility field by the regulatory practice of pricing below natural levels, (3) the regulatory practices in this field are out of tune with the economy of today, (4) the use of accounting formulas to determine a "fair return" is inappropriate in inflationary periods, and (5) a new approach to utility regulation is needed to insure survival of the industry and to allow it to benefit from dynamic management and investment.

Rate regulation theory differs from practice because of the decline in the purchasing power of the dollar. Communication and power companies are heading for the same fate as that suffered by the railroads and traction companies — loss of risk capital due to a lack of return on investment and maintenance of invested purchasing power.

Tax law discriminates against utilities by allowing manufacturers to use the *Lifo* inventory method and by special provisions relative to persons buying and selling homes.

Unless the decline in the purchasing power of the dollar is recognized with respect to plant and equipment depreciation, power and communication utilities will eventually be owned by the government and subsidized by taxes, will not have the benefit of private management, and, in the end, will cause the public to pay more for utility services.

PREMATURE REVENUE RECOGNITION, *Journal of Accountancy*, XCVI (October, 1953), 432-37. [304]

In a number of situations adherence to current accounting practices results in premature recognition of revenue that is neither earned nor realized. Current accounting practice credits the entire proceeds of the sale of a product, coupled with a guarantee to maintain and inspect, to current revenues. Current operating expenses are charged with estimated costs of such maintenance and inspection, and a liability account is created which is charged in later periods when the service is rendered. This improper accounting pads the revenues and expenses for the year of sale, and implies that the service department does not contribute to the earning of the firm's revenue.

Proper accounting would call for deferring a portion of the proceeds — an amount equal to the sales price (not cost) of the expected service to be rendered. Then in later periods as the service is rendered the revenue is earned and should be so recognized. Costs of rendering the service will be recognized as incurred and the department will then show a profit or loss.

Similar premature recognition of revenue can be found in the recording of used automobiles, received as trade-ins on new car sales, at the "allowance" price. Valuation of such used cars at net sales price (selling price less reconditioning and selling costs) does not correct the error. The used car department is deprived of an opportunity to earn net revenue on such sales.

Further examples of improper accounting with respect to revenue and cost recognition can be found in the treatment accorded shopworn merchandise relegated to the bargain basement in a department store, the "farm-price" method of accounting for unsold farm products, and the accounting for the cost and sale of lots in the subdivision of property — especially when costs are to be incurred after the sale of the lots.

THE DEPRECIATION DEDUCTION — A NEGLECTED ASPECT, *Michigan Business Review*, V (November, 1953), 23-26. [305]

This statement was presented before the Ways and Means Committee of the House of Representatives, July 22, 1953.

Capital is being confiscated through income taxation in that owners of depreciable assets are not permitted to deduct in their tax returns the *actual cost* of facilities used in serving their customers. "This condition results from failure to convert the varying dollars of plant cost to the common denominator of the current dollar in determining depreciation." Cost is economic sacrifice — purchasing power, not a figure on a piece of paper.

Lifo grants a form of tax relief to companies with heavy inventory commitments but there is no similar procedure available to the firm with heavy investments in plant assets.

The step taken in the 1951 amendment to the Internal Revenue Code was in the right direction, when it provided that no taxable gain was to be recognized from the sale of a home if the proceeds were invested in another home. However, this provision favors the party investing in a home as contrasted to one who invests in business property.

Congress should amend the present Internal Revenue Code to allow adjustment of depreciation charges for tax purposes by means of some appropriate price index.

LETTER OF PROF. WILLIAM A. PATON ON NONAPPLICATION OF "INCREMENTAL COST" PRINCIPLE TO POSTAL COST ACCOUNTING, DATED JANUARY 22, 1954. *Financial Policy for The Post Office Department*, 1954, pp. 221-25. [306]

Incremental cost means inescapable cost, or that cost "so closely tied to a particular department or function that it cannot be avoided if such department or function is undertaken and will be eliminated if the department or function is relinquished."

The incremental cost concept is useful in attempting to resolve a decision "with respect to the undertaking or the abandoning of particular functions, services, or products, especially those of a temporary, minor fringe, or ancillary character."

However, incremental costs have little, if any, value to anyone in accounting for the continuing activities of a business or other economic activity. The significant cost in continuing activities is actual total cost, including a reasonable allocation of common costs. No business firm could remain in operation for any considerable period of time if the prices it received covered only the incremental costs, department by department, rather than total cost.

Thus, the concept of incremental cost has little significance in postal operations, except, perhaps, in the area of minor functions where a decision may be required as to whether these functions are to be continued. To the extent that the costs of rendering the service have a bearing upon the rates charged, the costs to be considered are the estimated total costs, including a reasonable allocation of common costs.

SIGNIFICANCE OF DEPRECIATION ACCOUNTING WITH SPECIAL REFERENCE TO PLANT REPLACEMENT, *Federal Tax Policy for Economic Growth and Stability*, Joint Committee on the Economic Report (Washington: Government Printing Office, 1955), pp. 528-38. [307]

"Depreciation is simply plant cost (or value) in the absorbed or expired stage." For example, depreciation of a boiler is an actual explicit, out-of-pocket cost and is as real and valid a cost as is, for example, coal consumed. Furthermore, all costs are homogeneous as deductions from revenue.

Depreciation does not, as is commonly assumed, provide funds for replacement, but depreciation must be recognized even if an asset is never replaced. However, replacement cost, when properly defined "as the cost of replacing the capacity to serve represented in existing plant facilities, . . . is of outstanding significance to management."

Adjustment of depreciation by means of index numbers is preferred to basing depreciation on replacement cost, although the results may be somewhat similar. Conversion of unlike measuring units is commonplace in measuring changes in real wages, farm prices, exports and imports, gross national product, etc. The only place where conversion is consistently avoided is in business accounting. If items of plant assets, acquired at different times, are to be stated correctly at *actual cost* some conversion process must be employed.

Lifo introduced inequity into the tax structure by placing owners of depreciable properties, such as the various utility companies, at a serious disadvantage as compared to an investor in material and merchandise. A practical remedy might be to grant owners of long-lived properties a procedure akin to *Lifo*.

Correct measurement of cost will in no way guarantee sufficient revenues for "successful operation" of a business.

DEPRECIATION — CONCEPT AND MEASUREMENT, *Journal of Accountancy*, CVIII (October, 1959), 38-43. [308]

Understatement and complete omission of depreciation differ only in degree. Both will almost surely result in liberalization of the dividend policy and possible distribution of capital in the guise of earnings.

Revenues should be charged each year with the current cost of plant capacity consumed during the year, as this is "actual cost." Many accountants who support *Lifo* completely disregard the far more serious problem of the impact of inflation on plant assets.

Public utilities are hardest hit by inflation and by the tax laws regarding depreciation due to the regulation of their rates. In a few instances managements are considering the employment of economic analysts to convert the "heterogeneous data of conventional accounting reports" for price level adjustments. Accountants should be preparing such reports as it is well within the scope of the management services offered by CPAs. Accountants should also insist on presenting comparative converted-dollar statements covering long periods of time.

Tax structure changes to recognize converted-dollar depreciation would encourage plant modernization and expansion, "the crucial area of capital formation."

INDEX

NOTE. Numerals refer to digest numbers. As an aid to finding the views of a particular author the digests are consecutively numbered as follows:

1 - 42: Eric L. Kohler
43 - 119: A. C. Littleton
120 - 225: George O. May
226 - 308: William A. Paton